Dear
RAYMOND

Dear RAYMOND

THE STORY OF SPIRITUALITY AND
THE FIRST WORLD WAR

SOPHIE JACKSON

FONTHILL

Fonthill Media Limited
www.fonthillmedia.com
office@fonthillmedia.com

First published in the United Kingdom 2014

British Library Cataloguing in Publication Data:
A catalogue record for this book is available from the British Library

ISBN 978-1-78155-219-3

Typeset in 10pt on 13pt Sabon LT Std
Printed and bound by CPI Group (UK) Ltd, Croydon, CR0 4YY

Contents

Introduction

It is hard to believe that the start of the First World War occurred one hundred years ago. It seems so much closer, but perhaps that is simply because of the sheer horror and tragedy that stemmed from the war. Up until a few years ago I had relatives who could remember that tragedy, even though they are now gone the Great War still seems tangible, almost reachable – not a century old.

Yet it is precisely that distance that makes us remember how different life was in the early twentieth century. Though those who suffered the First World War were living in a 'modern' era they were still very much Victorian in their attitudes and ideas. For many science and technology were still inexplicable and misunderstood. Television was unknown, commercial radio would not properly appear until the 1920s. Silent films were perceived with uncertainty, the tricks of the movie trade far from the understanding of most of the audience. There seemed more than a small dose of magic flickering on that large screen.

This was a world where rural residents remained behind the times – in some places a firm belief in witchcraft would pervade until the Second World War. News could only be distributed by word of mouth or newspapers which were too expensive for a labourer to buy every day. So information disseminated slowly and often inaccurately.

When we realise all this it is hardly surprising that residents of the early twentieth century could be hoodwinked by spirit photography, haunting hoaxes and tales of fairies in Yorkshire. Old and new beliefs were fighting for room and in the background of it all, sparking many of these changes, was the upheaval of the class system.

Education and industrialisation was making many wonder why they continued to plod along working for an often cruel and mean master. Just before the war there was discontent, even stirrings of trouble and change, but it was trench warfare that truly became a catalyst for revolution. The Great War showed up the ridiculous class system in a way never before possible. The wealthy became officers because they had money, not because they had a clue what they were doing. They huddled in dugouts and ordered mass slaughters of other men, while remaining safe in the knowledge that officers had a far higher chance of survival than the Poor Bloody Infantry. It was those PBIs who populated the trenches; they vastly outnumbered the officers and were drawn from the working classes. They had the unhappy fate of being cannon fodder, often considered expendable by those same wealthy officers and sent to their deaths in vast numbers for the sake of a few yards of ground.

Crammed into the same few feet of mud, the PBIs now saw their superiors for what they were. They realised that they were no different from them except that they had money, and the PBIs resented that privilege. Death can bring a lot of things into perspective and it made the ordinary man realise that in the eyes of his officers he was deemed worthless, except as another body to go over the top.

Post-war there was no doubt this would have to change. The army itself would never be the same – no longer would a man become an officer simply because he had the right amount of money, instead he earned that privilege. So the army that strode out during the Second World War was a very different creature from that in the First. But the changes went even deeper as the Church of England was considered to be rooted in the worlds of the wealthy. The common man wondered where he stood in a religion that favoured privilege over spirituality. Couple that with a loss of faith the wartime slaughter had induced and there was bound to be turmoil in religious feelings. From the ruins of traditional religion new faiths emerged, some rising like phoenixes, others gasping at the air briefly before disappearing into the annals of history.

Nothing was the same post-war. Everyone was unsettled and uneasy, the young danced and drank because they wanted to feel alive and there was no knowing how soon another war might sweep them away. Older folk clung to the past dreaming about a time when the world was simpler and nicer; when change happened slowly and people were attuned to nature. Some craved that world so much they were prepared to accept any evidence that it still existed.

The story of spirituality post-war is under-explored, yet it paved the way for the modern age of religious freedom. The war threw up ghosts, cults, sects and fantasies. It also tested the traditional church and forced it to reassess how it served the country. It took religion out of politics and yet it also unsettled and upset many. Some felt there was no longer a safe haven in Christianity, while others believed the world was degenerating under a plague of black magic and devil worshipping cults. All in all it was a frightening and exciting time. In those brief two decades before the Second World War British culture changed forever. The story of how that happened is complicated and full of blind turns and dead-ends, but it is nonetheless important and a vital part of our cultural heritage. This is the story of how the First World War changed British spirituality forever.

CHAPTER ONE

A Death Among Millions

The telegram was cream-coloured with a black crown printed at the top between the words *Post Office*. Stuck onto the body of the telegram were narrow strips of white paper direct from the telegraph machine. They were torn along one side where the strip had been hastily divided to fit the paper and had been glued down at a sloping angle, so the words almost ran off the page. Words that so many had read and that so many dreaded.

Deeply regret to inform you that Second Lieut. R. Lodge. Second South Lancs, was wounded 14th Sept. and has since died. Lord Kitchener expresses his sympathy.

It was 17 September 1915 and Sir Oliver Lodge had just received the most devastating news of his entire life. News that would cause him to explore spiritualism, to study it scientifically and, eventually, to begin advising others to contact war dead through mediums and séances. His journey came close to ruining his reputation, but despite this he published several works on the subject including his most famous, simply entitled *Raymond*, the story of how he found his dead son through séances. His story was not unique, nor even unusual. Many families were grieving over horrendous losses and were looking for solace in spiritualism. Where Lodge differed is that he chose to promote his views and use his status, as a Victorian gentleman of science, to promote what he believed was the best news of the century – that an afterlife *did* exist.

His work came at a time when Britain's spiritual culture was tilting and changing forever; when the church finally lost much of its hold over the governing of the country, when other religions and forms of spirituality began to emerge. When the public became suddenly prepared to believe in fairies, talking mongooses, spirit photography and poltergeist activity. When even witchcraft, outlawed and persecuted for centuries, took a new hold over the general public. Between the First and Second World Wars Britain's belief system not only changed, but took on bizarre and intriguing forms. The only question is why?

The obvious catalyst was the huge sacrifice of young men during the Great War. This in itself was enough to spark resentment towards the Church of England which was influential at the start of the conflict in recruiting soldiers and bolstering the push for aggressive action. What followed was a pattern of disillusionment towards traditional religion, yet with people still seeking some form of hope in an afterlife, so previously niche religions took a new hold.

What makes this change so phenomenal is that for the first time in history dissenters were not heavily persecuted by church authorities. As peculiar and ludicrous as some of the new forms of faith were the church, struggling in its own way to save face and restore its reputation, did not go on the attack. Freedom of religion had begun. Even in the Victorian period choosing to follow a different faith or no faith at all had been enough to prevent people from joining certain societies and circles, even the Houses of Parliament. Now the trend was so great it was impossible to keep track of every one of the dissenters. Theosophists, Spiritualists, Southcottians, psychic investigators and even devil worshippers were no longer hidden away, but speaking aloud.

This change was so immense that it seems remarkable that it is often ignored in the history books. The way the years 1914-1918 demolished traditional views on faith and the church has to be one of the most important aspects of twentieth century history. Yet so many questions remain unanswered. Was the war merely a catalyst for something already brewing? How did the church so mismanage its own image during the war that it lost its grip on Britain? Why were the post-war public so ready to believe in ghosts, fairies and Satanism? And why did so many respected men of the age happily give their support to the most bizarre faiths and beliefs when it could cost them everything?

What really happened in those brief four years that changed Britain culturally forever?

In the Beginning

Every story has a beginning and there is no better beginning for an examination of the First World War's influence on spirituality than the life and death of Raymond Lodge, the youngest son of the famous physicist Sir Oliver Lodge. Born into a large family of twelve he was a middle child, with five brothers, one older sister, and five younger sisters.

Oliver Lodge had married Mary Fanny Alexander Marshal at Newcastle in the autumn of 1877, two years later Oliver William was born, followed by Francis Brodie (commonly called just Brodie), Alexander Marshal (Alec, the brother Raymond was closest to), Noel and then Violet. Raymond was born in 1889 a full ten years after his eldest brother. Soon to follow were Honor, Lorna, Nora, Rosalynd and Barbara. The large family moved to Birmingham at the turn of the century, where Oliver had taken the prestigious position of principal of Birmingham University. His name had been made by his experiments in physics. Lodge had made pioneering work on wireless telegraphy and on the ignition spark plug. His older sons later founded a business around the Lodge spark plug, which would go on to be used in the Sopwith Camel during the war.

When Raymond was born his family could be considered part of the burgeoning wealthy middle-classes. With several siblings considerably older than himself, he was naturally doted on by his elder sister and educated by teenage brothers. His father was enjoying the latter part of his career, when he no longer had to work late into the night, driving himself into intense headaches and fatigue. His older children had known little of their father growing up because he was so busy with his work, but with his youngest son he was able to take a positive part in his childhood. Lodge was distinctly making up with Raymond for his failure to be a part of his older children's lives.

Oliver Lodge had begun his career as an engineer and most of his children had inherited some of his creative talent for tinkering. Raymond was no exception; he loved inventing things from special tents for the family holidays, to sand yachts with huge sails to carry a person across a beach in seconds. He loved cars, he loved mechanics, he was his father's son and in the glory days of the Edwardian period, he thrived in a loving family.

Oliver saw much of himself in his youngest son. A picture of Raymond aged two shows a somewhat sullen looking child, with long brown hair curling about his ears. He looks at the camera anxiously, without the smiles of other children his age and very reminiscent of his father as a child. The similarities did not end in appearance; father and son shared the same personality and even curious traits. Raymond struggled to say the hard letters G and K, exactly as his father had done as a boy. Oliver had been schooled through the problem by a kindly aunt and used this knowledge to help young Raymond.

Father and son also shared a dislike of social gatherings. Oliver had never been comfortable at parties, even as a child. So he understood when at one Christmas party round a friend's house it was suddenly noticed little Raymond was gone. His father found him heading for the front door, determined to go home, sick and tired of the silly party. Oliver sympathised with him, having felt the same in his childhood and took Raymond home before returning to the party himself.

They were both rather serious and sensitive souls. Oliver felt hurts deeply and it seemed his son was no different. The horrors Oliver remembered from his school days encouraged him to send his children to a progressive school where they might not experience the hardships and bullying abuse he had endured. Raymond spent five or six years at Bedales School, which was unusual for its age as it was a mixed school teaching boys and girls, though admittedly the school roster showed the pupil intake was 97 per cent male.

When Raymond returned home he attended Birmingham University studying engineering and also spent time in Edinburgh. One thing he had not gained from his father was a love for physics, but he made up for this by his excellence in mechanics and Oliver looked forward to seeing his son turn into a first-rate engineer.

The outbreak of war ruined everything. Sir Oliver Lodge was in Australia on one of his frequent lecture tours when news arrived that war had been declared. He was not at first unduly troubled. There was an atmosphere of complacency about the Empire over the announcement. The British would knock the Germans off their perch quickly and show them what a real army could do. Lodge saw no reason to cancel the rest of his tour, and finished his lecture dates before he sailed back to England.

There was nothing to prepare him for the shock he faced when he arrived back at home. It had not crossed his mind that Raymond would consider joining the army, nothing could seem more anathema to the son he knew. But he neglected to recall one fact; Raymond had a strong sense of duty and honour, a need to help others wherever he could and a desire for adventure. It should not have been entirely unexpected to find him in the hallway of their home, Mariemont, dressed in the uniform of an officer.

'I've signed up for a commission.'

Raymond had not hesitated when the government had asked for volunteers. He was now a member of the BEF, the British Expeditionary Force. He was excited, in fact eager to be off. To march to a waiting ship with family and strangers waving him off and wishing him well, calling him and the other soldiers heroes and champions. Few were yet aware what horrors would await the brave young men who marched off in those early months of the war.

His father was more wary. He naturally feared for his son's wellbeing, but then so would countless others when their sons marched to war. His only hope was that the war would wrap up quickly and Raymond would not have a chance to see action.

Indeed, during those last months of 1914 Raymond stayed firmly in England, going through various training camps, lapping up the exercises like he was a boy scout play-acting at being a soldier. He was not so different from the other young men around him who were excited at the prospect of seeing a new continent, of being away from home for the first time, to act out the stories they had read as boys in books and magazines. None really realised the danger and misery they were headed for.

Christmas came and went along with promises of an early conclusion to the conflict. With each passing week it seemed more and more likely Raymond would be summoned to the fight. Then in March 1915 Raymond received his orders. He was to head out with the Second South Lancashires on the fifteenth. His family watched him go with heavy hearts. War casualties were mounting and the early confidence of the British Empire was dented. Lodge had to endure watching his youngest son, the boy who reminded him so much of himself, stride off to his possible death. He vowed to do all he could to keep him safe, even if he was trapped in England.

For King and Country

Raymond was a good correspondent and wrote home as soon as he arrived in France. Communication between the Front and England was regular and speedy, the military being aware how essential this was for boosting morale both in the trenches and at home. Raymond could write a letter and know that it would be with his family within a day or two; they were constantly kept abreast of his movements almost as they were happening.

Wednesday 24 March 1915, 11.30am
My servant has been invaluable en route [officers were always waited upon by a servant, a strange reminder of the class system still prevalent in Britain and the army]... He hunted round at the goods station at Rouen (whence we started) and found a large circular tin. He pierced this all over to form a brazier and attached a wire handle. As soon as we got going he lit this, having filled it with coal purloined from somewhere, and when we stopped by the wayside about 10 or 11pm he supplied my compartment (four officers) with fine hot tea. He had previously purchased some condensed milk. He also saw to it that a large share of the rations, provided by the authorities before we left, fell to our share, and looked after us and our baggage in the most splendid way.

Raymond's journey had begun in the style of a holiday. Looked after by servants with a magical touch for finding exactly what was needed in the most unlikely of situations and in companionable company, Raymond was hardly prepared for the horrors destined to face him. In fact no one was; the training camps in England had failed to even begin to equip men with an idea of the situation in France.

Friday 26 March 1915
I arrived here yesterday about 5pm and found the Battalion resting from the trenches. We all return there on Sunday evening. I got a splendid reception

from my friends here, and they have managed to get me into an excellent Company, all the officers of which are my friends. This place is very muddy, but better than it was, I understand. We are in tents.

For Raymond it was just like his school days. His friends had picked him for 'their team' and he didn't have to worry because they were all chums together. Raymond's naïvety was hardly unusual, what is startling is the army put such inexperienced men into positions of trust and responsibility, but this was a new war being fought in an old-fashioned way, where class mattered over experience.

Saturday 27 March 1915, 4.30pm
I am now permanently attached to C Company and am devoutly thankful. Captain T[aylor], is in command and the subalterns are Laws, Fletcher, and Thomas, all old friends of mine. F. was the man whose room I shared at Edinburgh... We went on a 'fatigue' job today – just our Company – and were wrongly directed and so went too far and got right in view of the enemy's big guns. However, we cleared out very quickly when we discovered our error, and had got back on to the main road again when a couple of shells burst apparently fairly near where we had been. There were a couple of hostile aeroplanes about too...

Raymond concluded by giving away his location in a cryptic clue. He was at Ypres, Belgium, one of the worst places to be during the First World War. This clear breach of security slipped by the censors because officers' letters were rarely checked. They were expected to stand on their honour not to include any vital information.

Saturday 3 April 1915, 7pm
I am having quite a nice time in the trenches. I am writing this in my dugout by candlelight; this afternoon I had a welcome shave. Shaving and washing is usually dispensed with during our spell of duty (even by the Colonel), but if I left it six days I should burst my razor I think. I have got my little 'Primus' with me and it is very useful indeed as a standby, although we do all our main cooking on a charcoal brazier... I will look out for the great sunrise tomorrow morning and am wishing you all a jolly good Easter: I shan't have at all a bad one. It is very like Robinson Crusoe – we treasure up our water supply most carefully (it is brought up in stone jars), and we have excellent meals off limited and simple rations, by the exercise of a little native cunning on the part of our servants, especially mine.

Raymond's life was in stark contrast to that of the ordinary infantry solider around him. Dugouts were for officers only and were not usually big enough to house the rest of the Company. In desperate times, such as a gas attack, men might try and scramble inside but for the most part they were expected to live outdoors, with limited shelter, in all weathers. Dugouts could become quite luxurious in the older trenches. Some were lined with wood panelling or wallpaper, decorated with pictures and furnished with chairs, tables and beds scavenged from local abandoned properties. The Germans excelled at this, turning the holes they had dug into the earthen sides of their trenches into underground palaces, with mirrors, ornaments, paintings, fine furnishings and tableware. Raymond could not aspire to such grandeur, but compared to the average soldier he was living a very comfortable life. An infantryman could expect to sleep, eat and even defecate in the trench he entered on his first day. There were toilets set away from the main trenches, but they were often impossible to get to safely, so men found a convenient corner and hoped not to be caught by an officer. No one wanted to be hit by a shell while using one of the latrines.

Soldiers scraped out shelters for themselves as best they could in the sides of the trench. They would be lucky to have a shelf of soil to cover their heads. They wrapped themselves in blankets and their rubber ground sheet and tried to ignore the elements that descended on them. The cold was just about bearable, it was when the rain fell in gushing downpours that drenched men and flooded trenches, that life became a misery. Even snow could not quite compare to the Ypres rain.

Thursday 8 April 1915
My platoon (No.11) has been very fortunate; we have had no casualties at all in the last six days. The nearest thing to one was yesterday when we were in the firing trench, and a man got a bullet through his cap quite close to his head. He was peeping over the top, a thing they are all told not to do in the daytime. The trenches at our point are about a hundred yards apart, and it is really safe to look over if you don't do it too often, but it is unnecessary, as we had a periscope and a few loopholes...

Billets, Tuesday 13 April 1915
We are all right here except for the shells. When I arrived I found everyone suffering from nerves and unwilling to talk about shells at all. And now I understand why. The other day a shrapnel [shell] burst near our billet and a piece of the case caught one of our servants (Mr Law's) on the leg and hand. He lost the fingers of his right hand, and I have been trying to forget the mess it made of his right leg ever since. He will have had it amputated by now. They make you feel awfully shaky, and when one comes over it is surprising the pace at which everyone gets down into any ditch or hole near. I wonder if you can get hold of some morphia tablets [for wounded men]. I

think injection is too complicated, but I understand there are tablets that can merely be placed in the mouth to relieve pain. They might prove very useful in the trenches, because if a man is hit in the morning he will usually have to wait till dark to be removed...

Sunday 18 April 1915

We always travel in single file, because there are so many obstacles to negotiate – plank bridges and 'Johnson' holes [large artillery shell craters] being the chief. Picture us then shuffling our way across the fields behind the trenches at about one mile an hour – with frequent stops while those in front negotiate some obstacle (during these stops we crouch down to try and miss most of the bullets!). Every few minutes a 'Very' (sic) light [a flare fired by a rocket or special pistol to illuminate the battlefield] will go up and then the whole line 'freezes' and remains absolutely stationary in its tracks till the light is over. We did get here [rest trenches] in the end, and had no casualties, though we had had one just before leaving the trench. A man called Raymond (in my platoon) got shot through the left forearm. He was firing over the parapet and had been sniping snipers (firing at their flashes). Rather a nasty wound through an artery. They applied a tourniquet and managed to stop the bleeding, but he was so weak from loss of blood he had to be carried back on a stretcher.

Raymond was starting to understand the reality of trench life, but with casualty numbers so low it was still possible for a young man to feel a certain thrill and excitement about the experience. There is a lot of debate concerning the remarks made by some surviving soldiers who claimed to have 'enjoyed' trench life. Other soldiers describe it as an episode of unremitting terror and horror. Which was the truth?

In fact it was both and it very much depended on the position of a man serving in the trenches, his outlook on life (and death), his rank and the exact time he was fighting. For instance, an officer might find it easier to be excited by the conflict because for much of the time he was safely ensconced in a dugout. Thus he only experienced the dangers of bullets and shells for short periods, making them thrilling – as Raymond describes. An infantryman stuck in a trench all day and night had a different perspective; he was constantly exposed to danger and it wore on his nerves. He had no retreat and lived most of his life under the very real threat of being killed. His perception was defined by this constant nightmare and the knowledge that the basic soldier was far more likely to die than any officer. It was hard to become excited.

Raymond was also writing at the start of the war, a time when hopes still ran high that it would be over soon and the huge sacrifices of young men had not yet taken its toll on the mental outlook of the soldiers. It was still possible to view it as an adventure. Raymond's platoon was also lucky in April 1915 to be away from the main action, so were not experiencing the massacres of other platoons. Raymond's attitude and optimism would change eventually in the short time he was at the front. He would not be spared the tragedy of loss forever.

Late April Raymond received a gift from home; a specially made periscope with spare mirrors that his father had commissioned. Oliver Lodge had a clear idea how he could keep his son safe, if he provided him with the latest in technological gear, as well as a few home-brewed contraptions, he would prevent Raymond from having to expose himself to unnecessary danger. At least to Lodge it felt as though he was doing something and gave him hope. The periscope was just one idea and it was a very useful one, it meant Raymond could look over the side of the trenches without exposing his head. Eventually the periscope became a common part of army kit for officers and lookouts in the trenches.

Raymond was also using his engineering talents, inherited from his father, to great effect.

Friday 30 April 1915 4.10pm
In the trenches one is not always doing nothing. These last three days in I have been up all night. I had a working party in two shifts working all night and all three nights, digging communication trenches. I used to go to bed about 4.30am and sleep till lunchtime, and perhaps lie down again for a bit in the afternoon. That is why my letters have not been so frequent. It is extraordinary that what is wanted at the moment is not so much a soldier as a civil engineer. There are trenches to be laid out and dug, and the drainage of them to be thought out and carried through. Often the sides have to be 'riveted' or staked, and a flooring of boards put in, supported on small piles. Then there is the water supply, where one exists. I have had great fun arranging a 'source' in my trench (the support trench that I have been in these last three days and that I have been in often before). A little stream, quite clear and drinkable after boiling, runs out at one place (at about 1 pint a minute!) and makes a muddy mess of the trenches near. By damming it up and putting a water bottle with the bottom knocked in on top of the dam, the water runs in a little stream from the mouth of the bottle. It falls into a hole large enough to receive a stone water-jar, and then runs away down a deep trough cut beside the trench. Farther down it is again dammed up to form a small basin which the men use for washing; and it finally escapes into a kind of marshy pond in rear of the trenches.

May saw events turning nastier for Raymond; the fighting was heavier and casualties were being taken even among his own ranks. One of his friends,

Laws, had been commanding platoon no.9, but shellshock had forced him back to England on sick leave. Fletcher had taken over his platoon.

On the night of 7 May Oliver Lodge had a peculiar dream. He dreamt Raymond was in the thick of heavy fighting, but that no matter the danger he seemed to be taken care of by spiritual forces. Oliver Lodge believed in the power of dreams as a tool for messages from the other side and wrote to Raymond describing this episode. Raymond was curious, on the 7 May he *had* been in great danger when his Company was ordered forward to the firing line.

Wednesday 12 May 1915

We had not gone far before the gunners saw us, and an aeroplane was flying alone and above with us. They sent over some 'Johnsons' but these all went too far; we were screened by a reservoir embankment. However, we had to pass through a ruined village and they knew it, so they put shrapnel over it. Still we were unaffected. But when we came out into the open on the far side, we caught it properly. Shell after shell came over and burst above us, and when I and about three men behind me had just turned a corner one burst above, in exactly the spot I should have wished it to if I had been the enemy. I looked up and saw the air full of flying pieces, some large and some small. These spattered down all round us. I was untouched, but my servant, who was immediately behind me, was hit on the knee, but only wounded slightly. He was rather scared. I led him back round the corner again and put him in a ditch. The rest of the platoon got in too, while I was doing this. I thought that was the best thing they could do until the shelling ceased, but Fletcher shouted that we must get on, whatever happened.

So I called the men out again, and, leaving a man with the wounded, we set off. I don't believe it was right, but we just walked along. It felt rather awful. I felt very much protected. It was really a miracle that we weren't nearly all 'wiped out'. The shrapnel seemed very poor stuff. As it was, we had one man killed and about five or six injured, all more or less slightly.

Raymond was becoming disillusioned, but his father's dream gave him some security. Lodge believed his dream had been recounting events as they happened to his son with a message of comfort and this gave Raymond confidence in his own odds for survival. We can argue that his dream was a logical one for any parent to have when fearful for their child, especially one with such strong spiritualist leanings. But we can't deny the dream gave both Oliver and Raymond a new hope.

Raymond's experience as an engineer proved essential to the army, who were constructing vast networks of trenches as the war continued at a stalemate. Raymond was a good trench builder and his battalion was temporarily selected as a 'Pioneer Battalion', meaning they were excused normal trench duties and just went out as a working party at night. They would dig trenches at night, under enemy fire and then sleep all day. In particular Raymond's battalion was sent to work on Hill 60, a man-made ridge that has become famous in the annals of the First World War.

Hill 60 was no more than a low rise on the southern flank of the Ypres salient. It was the result of earth waste from the nearby railway cutting. The nature of Ypres and the constant fighting, which had flattened the landscape, meant even the smallest rise could be advantageous to whoever held it. Just a month before Raymond went to Hill 60, the British army had executed one of the most cunning and risky operations of the war. The hill had been mined, literally long underground tunnels were dug by engineers and former miners, shored up with wooden struts and packed with high explosives. Six mines were completed, while several others were left unfinished for a variety of reasons. The work was painstaking and slow; the Germans were aware of the operation and had attempted to produce counter-mines. Both sets of miners would listen out for the enemy scraping away underground and try to judge where they were, on occasion there was real risk of the mines intersecting one another. But the major problem was who would get their explosives down the mines first?

On 10 April 1915 the British exploded 10,000 lbs of explosive underground, shooting debris 300 feet into the air and scattering it over 300 yards in every direction. Within the short span of 10 seconds Hill 60's heart was ripped out and hundreds of Germans perished, either in the first explosion or in the subsequent falls of debris and demolition of trenches. The event should have been a triumph, but the Germans counter-attacked and Hill 60 fell to them.

The British retook the hill in a bloodbath of a battle on 17 April and the 1st Bedfordshires were left to hold it. Defending the hill came at a heavy toll, the Germans were determined to take it and launched several assaults. Near the end of the month the Bedfordshires had lost around 700 men and had to be reinforced with another division, who suffered equally high casualty figures. It was around this time Raymond went to the hill to help dig in the defenders, 'the bulk of our work was deepening the trenches and improving the parapets'. It was to have little effect. Between the 1 and 5 May the Germans began gas attacks on the British defenders. The result was devastating; the unprepared front line troops were either killed by the gas or overrun by the German troops and were virtually annihilated. The Devonshire Regiment lost over 300 men to the first gas cloud alone, only two officers and seventy men scrambled out alive. The 1st Bedfordshires had recently taken on new drafts because of their earlier losses and most of these men were new to the trenches; they were massacred. A desperate defence ensued to prevent the

Germans from completely breaking through the front line, the hill was lost, but the Germans could not be allowed to get any further. The remnants of the Devonshires and Bedfordshires joined with the Duke of Wellington's Regiment to hold off the assault, the latter alone lost 100 officers and 3,000 men from its 5th Division.

Fortunately Raymond was not present for the battle and in his letter dated 16 May when he talks about working at Hill 60, he makes no mention of the catastrophic attack or the huge loss of life. That was natural enough, there was a general attitude of hiding the worst news from loved ones back home and putting a brave face on things. Raymond remarked, 'Don't think I am having a rotten time – I am not.' How much he really meant that sentiment we will never know. The toll of warfare was rapidly showing in others. Raymond's old friend Fletcher had to go away for a rest cure on 18 May, his nerves were shredded.

Lieutenant Eric Graham Fletcher had been in Belgium since January 1915. He was a year older than Raymond and had come to know him while he was training as an architect in Edinburgh. Just prior to the war he had been working as an architect's clerk. Raymond was sorry to see him go. 'He is my greatest friend in the Battalion, so I miss him very much and hope he won't be long away. He will probably go back to England, however, as his nerves are all wrong. He is going the same way as Laws did...'

Raymond's moods swung between optimism and despair, he could no longer mask it in his letters and had to apologise for grumbling and moping. If only the end of the war was in sight, he plaintively sighed, it would make things so much easier. With Fletcher gone he turned for company to his last remaining friend from the pre-war days, Thomas. They spent most of their time together when they weren't parading or digging trenches. Thomas was able to cheer Raymond with simple acts of kindness and comradeship. Raymond's morale rose again and for a while things did not seem so bad. Then the 16 June 1915 dawned.

> ...I am very sorry to say we have lost Thomas. He was hit on the head by shrapnel... and died about an hour later, having never recovered consciousness. It was a most fatal night – the whole battalion was ordered out digging to consolidate the captured positions. We got half-way out, and then we got stuck – the road being blocked by parties of wounded. We waited on a path alongside a hedge for over an hour, and though we could not be seen we had a good deal of shrapnel sent over us. To make matters worse, they put some gas shells near, and we had to wear our helmets though the gas was not very strong. It was exceedingly unpleasant, and we could hardly see at all. It was while we were waiting like this that Thomas got knocked out.

Lieutenant Charles Humphrey Rittson Thomas was not yet twenty-three when he died. In civilian life he had been an apprentice engineer, but had joined up in August 1914. He was originally from Cardiff, Wales where his father was a stocks and shares broker. Despite his quiet origins he proved himself a responsible officer, and kept a brave face no matter what, including when shells were bursting nearby. He never let his own fears reflect onto his men. He had been awarded the 1914-15 Star Campaign Medal of the British Empire, not that that was huge consolation for his mother Henrietta, who had lost her favourite son.

By this point Oliver Lodge and his family were becoming desperate for Raymond's safety. They could hardly miss the news reports of the big battles occurring, or fail to take note of the long casualty lists. Raymond's brother Alec applied to the War Office to have him sent home, presumably implying that Raymond would be more use in the Lodge Spark Plug business than at the front. Raymond doubted he would succeed and could not justify leaving the trenches when so many had to stay and fight. He had managed to stay out of the main action for the time being and had not even killed anyone. As much as he wanted to go home, he could not shake the guilt of abandoning his men.

Raymond was trained to be a machine gun officer in July 1915. The brief break at the training school and then home on leave was welcome, but it was short lived and soon Raymond was to find himself in the full horrors of the war. Ypres was hotting up and Raymond was right in the middle of it all.

Saturday 7 August 1915, 7.30pm

…just before we handed over these trenches to one of Kitchener's Battalions, the Germans went and knocked down a lot of our parapet, and also sent over some appalling things that we call 'sausages', or 'aerial torpedoes', though they are not the latter, they are great shell-shaped affairs about 3 feet along and 9 inches in diameter, I should think. They are visible during the whole of their flight. They are thrown up about 100 yards into the air and fall down as they go up, broadside on – not point first. A few seconds after they fall there is the most appalling explosion I have ever heard. From a distance of 100 yards the rush of air is so strong that it feels as if the thing had gone off close at hand. Luckily there is a slight explosion when they are sent up, and, as I said, they are visible all the time in the air. The result is our men have time to dodge them, provided they are not mesmerised as one man was. He got stuck with his mouth open, pointing at one! A Corporal gave him a push which sent him 10 yards, and the 'sausage' landed not far from where he had been. Although they have sent more than twenty of these things over altogether we have only had one casualty, and that a scratch. Their effect is to terrify everyone and keep them on tenterhooks…

I was in my dugout... when a shell blew the parados of the trench down, not far from our door, and the next wrecked the dugout next door to mine... We judged it was time to clear... and got away as best we could...

The trouble is, we have a number of mine shafts under the ground between our trenches and theirs, and they are fearfully 'windy' about them. They keep trying to stop us mining them, and their shelling is with the object of blowing down our sap-heads...

Late in August Raymond was in trenches near Hooge, another infamous site of the First World War. Hooge was a Belgium village hotly fought over by the Germans and British, at various times they both held the area. Not quite a month before Raymond went to Hooge the Germans had attacked using their newest weapon – the flamethrower. The British had counter-attacked and quickly retaken the site, but it would prove a bloody tug-of-war between the two sides for domination of Hooge. Raymond refers to the Hooge crater, which had been created in a similar attack to Hill 60 some weeks before. He was stationed nearby. There was heavy fighting in this area, after five months in France and Belgium Raymond was finally getting a taste of true warfare. However he still spent most of his time digging trenches.

In September Captain Taylor fell from his horse and sprained his ankle. Abruptly Raymond found himself in charge of the men, only a temporary situation, but one that was about to change his fortunes for good. On 12 September he did not have much time to write. 'You will understand that I still have the Company to look after and we are going into the frontline trenches this evening at 5pm...'

On 14 September Raymond was at Hooge. Inbetween digging trenches around the old stables and ruins of the Hooge château (once headquarters for the British) he was commanding the machine gun unit in the firing line. The trenches were churned into the usual quagmire and the constant shooting of the Germans raked on the nerves. Raymond was concentrating on his gunners when the commander of the artillery found him and suggested he move back from the firing trench as the British were about to start shelling the German line. The close proximity of the German and British trenches made it inadvisable for Raymond's Company to stay where they were. Raymond ordered C Company to withdraw to a nearby communication trench.

Machine gun Company Lieutenant Roscoe later wrote that he believed this manoeuvre had been seen by the Germans. Whether this was true, or whether it was just bad luck, as Raymond, his servant and another Lieutenant were bringing up the rear and entering the communication trench a shell crashed nearby and shrapnel flew everywhere. Raymond's servant Gray was hit in the head and would die soon after. Raymond hurried to find the Sergeant-Major and see about help for Gray, and was just talking to his superior when another shell came whizzing down. The Lieutenant who had been helping bring up the rear was struck and killed. Raymond was thrown forward as shrapnel hit him in the back.

Still conscious he was carried in agony to a dugout and tended by a servant. The wound was mortal, though exact details are missing. The shrapnel had probably stabbed Raymond's intestines and other vital organs. Bleeding alone would have been immense. Twenty minutes after his injury was sustained Raymond was able to talk to another officer and ask a few questions. A short time later Roscoe paid him a visit and found him unconscious and breathing with difficulty. 'I could see it was all over with him. He was still just alive when I went away.' Raymond only lived for around half an hour after he was caught by shrapnel.

Like so many, Raymond's death had been unexpected and cruel. His last minutes of life were agonising and distressing as his body weakened and failed. Raymond could have been under no illusion that he would survive long enough for stretcher-bearers to come for him, let alone to make it to a military hospital. All the hopes of a young man were gone within the seconds it took for the shell to fall and the shrapnel to pierce his flesh.

Those that remained alive packed up Raymond's belongings and wrote difficult letters to his mother and father including the usual platitudes – 'I'm sure he did not suffer long' – always wondering if the next such letter would be about them.

Eric Fletcher wrote from Liverpool where he was recovering from shellshock. 'Raymond was the best pal I've ever had… nobody could ever have a better friend than he was to me. I always thought he would come through all right, and I know he thought so himself, as, the last time I saw him, we made great plans for spending some time together when we got back, and it seems so difficult to realise that he has gone.'

Tragically Fletcher too would perish in the war. Having recuperated to a degree, and with officers desperately needed at the front, he was sent back to Belgium only to be killed on 3 July 1916.

Among the belongings returned to the Lodge family were Raymond's blood-soaked diary and a small pocket Bible which had obviously been read and annotated by Raymond. This came as a surprise to Oliver Lodge who had not known his son to have any particularly strong religious feelings, though he had once mentioned in a letter the service performed by an army chaplain which he had enjoyed. Raymond had clearly spent a great deal of time reading the Bible over and over. He had underlined passages that were significant to him and even wrote an index on the flyleaf for easy reference to them. Some of the Bible passages that meant so much to Raymond are shown below and give one of the clearest insights into his mental state while at the front, particularly his fear of dying. For the full list see Appendix 1.

I told you all this so that you will have peace of heart and mind. Here on earth you will have many trials and sorrows; but take courage, I have overcome the world. John, xvi, 33

Come to me and I will give you rest – all of you who work so hard beneath a heavy yoke. Matthew, xi, 28

The eternal God is your refuge, and underneath are the everlasting arms. He thrusts out your enemies before you; it is he who cries, 'Destroy them!' Deuteronomy xxxiii, 27

Rejoice, you nations, with his people, for he will avenge the blood of his servants; he will take vengeance on his enemies and make atonement for his land and people. Deuteronomy, xxxii, 43

See, God has come to save me! I will trust and not be afraid, for the Lord is my strength and song; he is my salvation. Isaiah, xii, 2

But they that wait upon the Lord shall renew their strength. They shall mount up with wings like eagles; they shall run and not be weary; they shall walk and not faint. Isaiah, xl, 31

He will wipe away all tears from their eyes, and there shall be no more death, or sorrow, or crying, or pain. All of that has gone for ever. Revelations, xxi, 4

Better than his carefully worded letters home these passages reveal the true Raymond and his attitude to the war, his genuine fear of death and the comfort God's words brought him, reassuring him there was a place waiting for him in the next life. Yet they also reveal his despair, his fear of his own sins – what had Raymond done that could be termed sinful? Perhaps, like many of us he reflected on mistakes he had made, errors of judgement, things said that should have gone unsaid, all the little bumps in life that we later regret. Raymond was doing a lot of soul-searching in the trenches when faced with his own mortality and was clearly finding God in a way he had not done before, in a way that even surprised the people who knew him best.

Robert Graves commented bluntly in his book *Goodbye To All That*, that there was no religion in the trenches, that no one believed or cared about God. His words are often repeated by historians as an accurate description of men's spiritual state at the front, but he was wrong. There were men who stuck to or found their faith, just as there were men who lost all hope in God. To make a blanket statement about religious feeling among soldiers is dangerous, as each man was an individual walking his own path. What is apparent from Raymond is that God was still to be found in the trenches and that Christianity had not been cast aside as some contemporary writers would have it.

Spirituality, in fact, could provide a much needed respite and place of retreat in a world gone utterly insane. Yet there were cracks forming in the old façade of traditional religion. Raymond was placing his hopes in his father's dreams and scouring the Bible by himself for comfort, rather than seeking out a chaplain or regularly attending services. Raymond still believed in God, but did he and his comrades still believe in the Church?

Raymond's short time at the front not only gives us a first-hand account of an officer's life, but also gives an insight into belief among soldiers. Remarkably his death would prove to be highly influential. Because of Raymond's untimely demise, his father started a journey into proving spiritualism, a hunt for the hereafter and proof that his son lived on. He was not alone in this adventure nor in promoting his journey to the general public adding to the growing confusion over religious beliefs. If Raymond had survived the war would Oliver Lodge have shown to the British population the power of spiritualism? If the many who perished along with Raymond had not died would the Church have gone through the same upheaval and ordeal as it did when people lost their faith through the tragedies of war? It's a good question, worth examining in context.

Victorian Conflicts

The Great War was a catalyst for the re-evaluation of beliefs on a large scale among the population, but it did not come out of nowhere nor emerge with an explosion into a religious society, rather it pulled together various strands of thoughts and ideas that had been circulating for some time.

In all centuries there have been agnostics and atheists and those drawn to alternate religions, but for much of human history these individuals have been persecuted as heretics and through necessity have isolated themselves and kept their views and activities hidden. The eighteenth century – the age of rationalism – started to change views and allowed alternative ideas to be spoken about more publically, but even this had limited impact on the majority of people who carried on their routines of prayers at night and church on Sundays. It would take the huge upheavals of the Victorian period, namely in science, to shake the foundations of this comfortable and homely belief.

Late Victorians would bemoan the revelations and changes the centuries had brought them. Scientific revolutions had upset ancient truths gained from the Bible. Darwin's theory of evolution countered the traditional ecclesiastical view of God creating every animal, including man. New discoveries about the Earth's age, including the dinosaurs, again called into doubt the Bible which gave the planet an age far younger than what it really was. More and more the hard facts people had once found in the Bible now looked preposterous, even contradictory. It seemed the faithful had been lied to.

All this caused immense confusion; some believers ignored the new discoveries, others began to view the Bible as allegorical rather than a straight history book. In either case these individuals were able to ride the tide of science versus religion. Yet others found themselves in a huge turmoil, uncertain what to believe or what to think. Everything had been so much simpler for their parents and grandparents; belief had not been questioned or undermined. There were those who wanted to believe, but simply couldn't with so many unanswered questions in their minds; and there were those that had come to the conclusion God did not exist and science had proved it.

Among all this turmoil the great institution of the Church of England looked insecure and old-fashioned. It carried on as ever, but it snapped at freethinkers and scientists and entered debates it could not win by trying to prove the Bible was an accurate history book. The Church wobbled and floundered, never in real danger of collapsing, but all the time losing believers who drifted away to other ideas.

It is hardly surprising that the Victorian period saw a surge in religious cults and ideology. Spiritualism remains the one cult everyone remembers and understands. In fact it caught public imagination because it seemed to offer definite proof of an afterlife. For many Christians this was a heavenly reassurance when Darwin and dinosaurs had cast doubts in their mind about the existence of God. Here was real evidence, or so it seemed, and spiritualism brought great comfort to many.

Other 'cults' were variations on the Church of England, most aiming to improve on the teachings of the traditional church, or to cut away the corruption or simply the doggerel that had evolved around the clergy. The Methodists, Quakers, Baptists and Salvation Army all brought their own ideas to the table and attracted Christians. In some cases they were denounced as heathen muckrakers; the Salvation Army in particular had a bad press because they sang loudly and marched about. In one instance a woman was declared insane partly because she had joined the Salvation Army. Other religions remained small and controversial; the Plymouth Brethren was founded in the 1820s in Dublin and did not hold with having an official clergy. Started informally it developed into an exclusive group, those who were 'in' were children of God, those who were 'out'... well they simply weren't going to heaven, and that included traditional Christians. The Brethren split early in its history into the highly conservative and the moderate, the parties warred and the highly conservative did not deem the other faction true Brethren at all. For one thing they shared meals with non-Brethren members, a huge taboo in the conservative league.

The most famous member of the Plymouth Brethren was Aleister Crowley, whose father was one of the highly conservative members and decried less strict Brethren. Crowley grew up in a very cloistered environment where everything was censored so as not to offend Brethren ideas. That Crowley ended up calling himself the Devil incarnate, dabbled in drugs and enjoyed sex with various men and women, would have shocked the sensibilities of his father who fortunately died before Crowley took the path to infamy.

For those disillusioned with religion but still desirous of some form of spirituality, there was plenty of scope in the beliefs of the past. The Victorians were masters of transforming history into chocolate-box idealism or an age of innocence. Many people hankered consciously for this variation of the past, when times were simpler, or at least, when they believed they were simpler. Scholars began doggedly collecting old legends and superstitions, pointing them out as the 'old ways' from a better time when science had not driven belief into a corner.

The curious fascination with these pagan beliefs and ancient magic resulted in the birth of the folklorist – a person who collected and analysed the old ways of England. One example of this is the book *The Golden Bough* by Sir James George Frazer, designed as a scientific and dispassionate study comparing mythology and religion it was very typical of its age, including that some of the legends and stories it contains are complete Victorian inventions. In fact a quick trawl of the Oxford Dictionary of Superstitions reveals vast numbers of 'ancient superstitions' whose origins cannot be traced back beyond the 1850s. The Victorians were not just curious about the ways of the past; they were prepared to make them up.

Paganism itself arose in the Victorian era with the ancient Celtic druids proving a popular icon of this new movement. The oldest English druid association was founded in 1781 and termed itself rather misleadingly the Ancient Order of Druids. During the Victorian period a fascination with old rituals performed by druids attracted certain groups to Stonehenge and other ancient sites to perform allegedly ancient rites. The groups were exclusively male and, dressed in white robes with false beards, they performed made-up rituals around the Neolithic stones. It might have been silly, but it struck a chord with many. This was harking back to the old ways, a time when the modern Church did not exist, and if the modern Church was in doubt because of science then perhaps the only way to move forward was to echo the distant past?

Around the same time a new interest in the Greek god Pan emerged. Pan is the god of the wild, of shepherds and mountains, of hunting and rustic music. In Victorian minds he was associated with sexuality and the untamed. Pan was half man, half goat, with horns, a tail and hooves, and was often depicted with an enormous phallus. In Greek mythology Pan actually dies, a rare event among the gods, and for many centuries he was a forgotten figure until the 1780s when he was revived among liberal scholars.

Pan was not an easy god to get past Victorian sensibilities; on the one hand he represented nature and the rustic old ways, but on the other he was blatantly a sexual figure. Despite this the town of Painswick in Gloucestershire started a parade in his honour, carrying a model of the deity through the streets. The practice died out in the 1830s, only to be revived by a vicar in 1885 who mistakenly believed it was an ancient custom!

Pan made his way into literature and art, becoming a popular icon of the spirit of the woods and of a world that was rapidly being lost with the surge of the Industrial Age. His most famous appearance is arguably in *The Wind in the Willows* where he appears anonymously to help Mole and Rat find Otter's lost son. However Pan had already been acquired by story-tellers centuries before to become the iconic image of the Devil. Cloven-hoofed, with horns and a mischievous persona, not to mention an obvious sexuality, Pan was difficult to unravel from the old ideas of Satan. Interestingly it has been argued that even this image of the Devil is a Victorian invention, feeding into the neopaganism movement. In any case Pan became mixed up with witchcraft and black magic and fell from favour with the more conservative minded.

If all this turmoil was not enough there was yet another aspect of the complex world of Victorian religion that would have its own influence on the way the Great War changed belief. Religion in the Victorian period often proved to be the reserve of the middle and upper classes. The working classes were almost lost to religion. Uneducated, struggling with poverty, working endless hours to survive and often excluded from churches where you had to buy a pew to enter, God had little meaning to them other than a vague idea.

For many of the poorest in Victorian society church was a luxury they could neither afford nor one which gained them anything in practical terms. When every moment was a struggle for money there was little time for leisure, or to attend a three-hour church service. The Church failed to help itself by striking hardest at the lower classes when it came to stamping out sin in English society. Drunkenness and prostitution were an intrinsic part of life for many of the poorest, along with incest and infanticide. For many women prostitution was the only means for them to earn a living, and girls as young as ten were encouraged into the trade to earn a little money. They were soon in a dead-end cycle and to numb the despair they turned to drink. Men were equally hard-pushed, working long hours for little pay and keeping out the cold, hunger and misery with gin. The Victorian moralists saw the symptoms of poverty, but failed to see the causes and so the lower classes were not helped but condemned. Why would any of these unfortunates wish to step into a church and hear themselves being spat at as sinners on a sure path to Hell, when they knew they had no option in the matter and would return to their pathetic lives as soon as Sunday was over?

Even legitimate workers found church hard to fit into their lives. Factory workers spent long hours making all sorts of luxury goods they could never afford with few hours to sleep and one day off a week; Sunday. When Sunday came around all they wished to do was to lie in bed and recuperate for the next long spell in the factory. In an age when workers did not have holidays, this endless, unremitting toil made the thought of dragging themselves out of bed and heading to church on Sunday completely unappealing.

This was the forgotten side of Victorian religion. While it is often imagined the Victorians were a highly God-fearing society, for vast tracts of the population God simply had no relevance in their lives. They had no time for him and were indifferent to religion and as each generation passed, so knowledge of God among the poorest was gradually forgotten.

When war broke out chaplains in the trenches were horrified to discover how few men from the working classes knew anything about God. Some had no idea who Jesus Christ was, others had never sung a hymn or heard a Bible story. This had not happened overnight, it was a culmination of factors developing during the Victorian period, but it took the war to wake up the Church to this crisis. The war was the catalyst that exploded atheism into public attention, along with alternate religions and beliefs, but it had begun with the Victorians. Now the modern Church had to deal with the situation during the worst disaster of the twentieth century and at the same time try and keep hold of as many believers as was humanly possible, when the bloodshed and tragedy was straining every man to the limit.

For Those Left Behind

Religious turmoil among those at the front is widely recorded and quite natural in the situation men faced of unrelenting horror. The question of belief among those left at home is harder to quantify and understand. On the one hand you have men such as Oliver Lodge seeking out new answers, yet firmly grounded in the teachings of the Anglican Church (Lodge would in fact end his long life as a churchwarden). On the other you had those same families who had sent sons to war with little or no concept of the state religion, trying to come to terms with agonising grief while the Church preached on about sacrifice and saintliness.

The problem was no easier for contemporaries to understand than later generations. It is often stated that congregations at first expanded with the start of war, with many praying for loved ones to come home safely and soon, and then contracted as the conflict and deaths dragged on. Yet even here there are exceptions to the statement with some parishes seeing increases in congregations throughout the war.

In the East End of London the churches became a focal point for people to come together for comfort and protection. On many occasions services were held while bombs were falling all about, the church at St Martin's in the Fields turned its crypt into an air raid shelter and was open day and night. Londoners found consolation in going to the church and being surrounded by their neighbours and contemporaries, all in the same position as themselves. There was a camaraderie among them when they gathered together and worshipped that could not be felt elsewhere. For them the church was a vital lifeline, not just spiritually but as a very real safe haven from the nightly zeppelin raids.

Further east, along the perilously exposed coast, pastors found an increasing need for their services as the terrified populations were nightly attacked by off-shore bombardments and Zeppelin raids. First-hand memories recording the role of the Church in this period are rare. In the post-war years churchmen wrote of their time in the war, but their memories were naturally distorted by the knowledge of the destruction it caused.

One rare account that gives an on-the-spot understanding of how war affected the church at home comes from a priest serving an east coast parish during the dangerous war years. His name was Canon Reginald Augustus Bignold. Born in 1860 during the glory years of the Victorian era; he was typical of his time, growing up with a staunch patriotism for his country and a firm belief in the power of the Almighty. He became rector to the parish of Carlton Colville, Suffolk in 1898 when he was two years off his fortieth birthday. To those who remembered him, he always seemed an old man, but he was sprightly and kind, deeply concerned with the affairs of his parish and the wellbeing, both physical and spiritual, of its inhabitants. He was popular and attracted large congregations even during the dark years of 1917 and 1918, including soldiers on leave. He also managed to maintain a Lads' Bible Class, though it was painful to him to know so many of the youths he was then teaching would shortly be going to the front. Bignold developed, like so many, a despairing and desperate attitude towards the war as it continued and so many died, but it did not begin that way.

When war broke out in 1914 there was a great deal of patriotism and pride among those first to enlist and the families who wished them off. Hindsight makes us wary of the horrors these men were to endure, but that autumn, coming just after a long, hot and glorious summer, there seemed very little to fear. There had been no such thing as a 'world war' and the hearty anticipation was that the British would march out, see off the upstart Germans and Austrians and be home for Christmas, or at least early 1915. Why should 1914 be any different to the previous campaigns the British had fought in the Boer Wars or the Crimean? No one could foresee the death toll up ahead, or the whole-scale recruitment which would eventually turn to conscription. The atmosphere in September 1914 was upbeat and positive. Bignold was among those keen to see the Empire flex its muscles against the enemy, unafraid of the future. On the 1 September he convened a meeting with the men of the parish to encourage them to enlist and forty-three joined the army there and then. Bignold himself had thoughts of being useful at the front, but at fifty-four his age was against him. By the 3 September he had been appointed an Honorary Recruiting Officer by the War Office for local parishes and was delighted to state on 1 November that 155 men from Carlton Colville had enlisted in the Army or Navy. He would later come to bitterly hate his role in enlisting men, but at the time the war seemed no more than a glorious adventure for the Empire.

Bignold kept track of the events of the war by writing a diary in the flyleaves of the parish registers. He had begun the diary in 1900 to record notable events, the years 1914–1918 gave him a wealth of material, (often bitter and sad) to jot into the papers. In tight, fine handwriting he tracked the course of the war, from its early optimism to its grim reality four years on, though he never lost his unflinching Victorian patriotism or his conviction that the Allies would be triumphant.

Bignold's account is a unique insight into a parish priest's view of the war and God's role within it, not that Bignold ever gave the impression that, like so many of his superiors, he was convinced God was fighting the war personally. God and the war almost became separated in Bignold's writings, as though the Almighty was like himself, standing back helplessly watching the carnage the world had unleashed upon itself.

In early 1915 Bignold could record that 250 Carlton Colville men had joined the forces. He knew many families who had all their sons in the war. Then there were the fishermen who were encouraged by the government to keep at their trade rather than enlist. Some had their ships converted to minesweepers or armed for hunting submarines. Staying at their fishing by no means guaranteed the lives of the fishermen. Their occupation was as perilous as that of the soldier, on some occasions more so – for an injured fisherman lost at sea had no hope of rescue while a soldier on the front just might be found by his comrades.

1915 also brought the first bombs dropped by airship. This shook the residents of Carlton Colville. It was the first time that civilians had been embroiled in a foreign war and the idea that no one was safe, even at home, terrified many. The first blackouts were introduced and Bignold recorded he had to cancel the evening services. Throughout the war he would note down the many Zeppelin raids, sea bombardments and the deaths they brought. He also kept track of the men charged with manning the anti-airship guns and their movements around the various parishes.

By June of that same year he was recording that 345 men from the parish, which had a total population in the 1911 census of 3,112, had signed up. That did not include the men who were still manning the fishing boats and acting as armed civilian shipping. By October he was recording the first casualties – nine lads had perished – but Bignold's verve for recruitment was not diminished. He had been appointed to supervise and organise a committee responsible for approaching 'unstarred' men between the ages of nineteen and forty-one to discover why they had yet to enlist. Lists had been compiled of men of suitable age – any who were in a reserved occupation and could not be asked to enlist had a star drawn next to their name, therefore 'unstarred' names belonged to men who apparently had no reason to resist volunteering. The process was done under the Derby Scheme and Bignold was just one of the representatives who tried to persuade eligible men to enlist. It was now winter in the parish and over 400 men were already serving in some military capacity.

From 1916 onwards Bignold became more and more concerned with the spiritual and mental toll the war was taking on his parishioners. Bombardments from the sea and bombing raids by Zeppelins had become regular occurrences. It is often forgotten that although casualty numbers were not as high as in the Second World War, the British public in certain areas of the country were in constant danger from German attack. The raids were entirely new and terrifying. Bignold recorded that hundreds of people would leave the neighbouring town of Lowestoft every night and camp in empty barns and sheds at Carlton Colville for fear of the Zeppelins.

Lowestoft was a prime target because of its harbour and connections with the Navy, but there was no doubt the Germans were aiming mainly at civilians. Bignold recorded on 25 April 1916:

> Lowestoft has been heavily bombarded by a German fleet. The people poured out of Lowestoft. On the Long Road, between here and Kirkley, they were so thick I had to get off my bicycle and walk. It was a very piteous sight – men, women and children all rushing along... It was most merciful that none of them was killed, as shells fell on both sides of the road.

However, there were deaths when cottages were struck. That same day forty houses were demolished and four people killed. Bignold's curate had a narrow escape when a fragment from a bomb struck the ground 10ft from him, and the rectory had a near-miss as a shell whizzed through the garden. The rectory frequently found itself the centre of unwelcome attention from the Germans.

These attacks on civilians were unprecedented and while they were frightening, they also galvanised the people's spirit of resistance. Three of Bignold's former curates joined up, two as army chaplains and one as a private.

Bignold's enthusiasm for recruiting waned at this period. On the 9 July there was a Church Parade of the RAMC which included many men wounded at the front. But the incident that really brought everything home to Bignold was the death of Stanley Wood. On 5 June 1914 Stanley was part of a scout brigade that went out on a boat on Whit-Monday. The boat capsized and six boys were drowned. Stanley was one of the boys who was saved. Bignold had presided over the funeral service of the drowned boys. The tragedy had had a huge impact on the parish, coming almost as a forewarning of the terrible losses of boys they were soon due to suffer. When Stanley Wood died at the front in July 1916, Bignold wrote: 'He was a bright, clever boy, respected and popular with everybody. I told him God had reserved him for greater things – and surely it was true.'

Yet bitterness was seeping into Bignold, as it was to seep into almost everyone. He soon stopped talking proudly about enlistment figures and instead started recording the horrific death toll being experienced by his parish – eight more Carlton Colville men had perished by October.

There was something that surprised Bignold enough to prompt him to record it in his diaries – the number of soldiers regularly attending his services. Though Bignold never goes into detail about his impressions from the soldiers he met of their religious feelings, he obviously found it significant enough that soldiers would freely give up their precious time to attend church to make it worth noting.

18 October About 120 soldiers were present at Church.

29 October Church very full – a large number of soldiers.

26 November A detachment of the R.A.M.C. went last week to the Western Front but there were as many as usual in Church.

We must not make assumptions about these high turn outs that Bignold witnessed throughout the war. Though it is tempting to imply that feelings of faith and comfort found in the Church were not entirely lost.

During 1917 and 1918 Bignold began to keep closer track on the lives and deaths of the men and boys he knew personally now serving at the front. Regular asides in his diary discuss someone with severe wounds he is praying for, or a son or husband missing in action, or a sad, short eulogy for someone lost too young. The war now felt very close to the residents of Suffolk. It was often possible to hear the loud, terrible explosions from across the Channel as a great battle was commenced. Bignold could stand in his rectory garden and hear the horrors happening in another country. It filled him with dread. On the 3 June 1917 the entire parish was able to hear the thundering explosions of the British bombardment before the Battle of Messines. Bignold had received a letter from one of his former Bible Class lads at the same time asking him, 'to pray for him today so that he might "do his duty and be protected", as his regiment had been warned that they would be engaged in very severe fighting for several days, beginning today. May God protect him. It does seem extraordinary that Sunday is almost always the day chosen for these terrible battles and bombardments.'

It is likely Bignold was the only one the poor lad felt he could write to about his fears and horrors. Many young men were terrified they would fail in their duty and be unable to go 'over the top' when the time came. Letters to family were always buoyant and optimistic to avoid unduly worrying those left at home. Bignold, in his priestly profession, was probably the only one the boy felt he could confess his fears to. But Bignold had always been a friend and comforter to the people in his parish and many of his 'old lads' visited or wrote to him. Bignold was also a vital link between the men at the front and their families. It was often deemed better that news of being wounded or of a death be delivered by Bignold than to arrive in an official letter. Bignold fails to record his feelings at this awful duty, though he was always quick to add that the women he broke bad news to were stoical and brave.

Bignold followed particularly closely the saga of Charlie Jacob, a former choirboy and journeyman butcher, who was wounded at the front and was eventually sent home. Charlie visited Bignold for dinner on 12 October 1917 and told him about religious feeling in the trenches;

> One remark [Charlie] made – and the truth of it has been confirmed by what many other lads have both said and written to me – was that if any man jeered at religion the others would immediately shut him up. They wouldn't have it, he said, but out there he had never heard anyone scoff at religion.

This might seem a sop to soothe the worries of Bignold from someone who cared about him and knew talk of godlessness would upset the old rector, but the usually anti-religious Robert Graves records a very similar anecdote in his book *Goodbye to all That*,

> James Cuthbert, the acting C.O., a Special Reserve major, felt the strain badly and took a lot of whisky. Dr Dunn pronounced him too sick to be in the trenches; so he came to Frises, where he shared a dugout with Yates and myself. Sitting in my arm-chair, reading the Bible, I stumbled on the text: 'The bed is too narrow to lie down therein and the coverlet too small to wrap myself therewith.' 'Listen James,' I said, 'here's something pretty appropriate for this dugout.' I read it out.

He raised himself on an elbow, genuinely furious. 'Look here, von Ruincke,' he shouted, 'I am not a religious man. I've cracked a good many of the commandments since I've been in France; but while I'm in command here I refuse to hear you, or anyone bloody else, blaspheme the Bible!'

Other letters revealed religious practice carrying on under grim circumstances. Ted Balls, a prisoner of war in Germany, wrote to Bignold in early February 1918 that, 'We have a service now and again in our room... so God is not forgotten in a P. of W. Camp.'

As the war drew into its final year Bignold's musings became darker and he kept greater track of the military manoeuvres happening across the Channel. On 25 March he recorded a most bleak entry.

> The battle is swaying to and fro and the Angel of Death is claiming hecatombs of victims. The enemy has pushed us back at various places, but only at a frightful cost to themselves. I have no fear of the eventual result – none of us have – but it is awful to contemplate this crucifixion of humanity.

The news was due to get bleaker. Everyone was anxious, the 'Great Battle' (as Bignold termed the the military actions of 1918) had left the entire community out of touch with loved ones at the front and the fear that the worst had happened was prevalent. The wave of tension and anxiety washing over Britain in 1918 was at its height as Bignold reported on the Manpower Bill and its suggestion that;

> All men, including the Clergy and Ministers of all Denominations, up to fifty years of age are to be called to the Colours...

The Bill was unsuccessful when it came to conscripting the clergy. Bignold gruffly remarked, 'owing probably to the fear of trouble from the Roman Catholic Clergy of Ireland – certainly not to the Clergy of the Church of England, 1,300 of whom are already chaplains while many others have enlisted.' On this Bignold was misguided, many Catholic priests were already at the front and the Anglican authorities were equally against the enforced call-up of clergymen.

There was a sickening feeling circulating in 1918 that the mass sacrifice of men Britain had endured for the past four years might be in vain. The last great push looked close to an act of desperation, was this to be the moment Britain won or lost the war? Bignold noted rather grimly that there was not a soldier nor man eligible for service left in his parish as the year crept on.

Summer and autumn 1918 were harrowing for those left at home. The death toll slowly increased, Carlton Colville ultimately lost seventy-four men

from the armed services and thirty-five fishermen killed by mines. Hardship
was pronounced, coal, matches and meat were all rationed and people were
sickening under the strain. As November loomed the first cases of influenza
appeared in the parish – the disease would go on to kill more people than the
war, but at that moment it seem an inconsequential matter.

Then came 11 November; 'Thanks be to God the terrible shedding of
English blood will now cease. Everybody, however, is taking it very quietly
– with vacant chairs in every home and with the crash of empires across the
water no one feels equal to wild rejoicings.'

The war had ended. Bignold held a Thanksgiving Service, the Church bells
rang for the first time in five years. Yet celebrations were muted; too many
were dead or unaccounted for and people felt too hollow to rejoice greatly.
Almost immediately Bignold found himself chronicling a new disaster; the
influenza epidemic had begun and the first parish casualty was Peggy Gabriel,
aged twenty, who died in London while helping with the war effort. 'This
influenza on top of the War losses – it seems so sad – but we can only see
through a glass darkly.'

It would take time for life to return to normal, except the post-war 'normal'
could hardly equate to what had been before. Bignold had kept his faith and
had held his parish together during the hard times, using his church as a hub for
war effort, consolation, comfort and of course spiritual salvation and praise.
But in many other places the community had drifted apart, and the Church
had been forgotten or had failed to reach the people. Bignold succeeded, but
in great tracts of Britain others did not.

For the churchmen left at home it was difficult to understand the religious
issues occurring at the front. With no first-hand experience they bumbled on,
some angered that British soldiers should be so fickle towards God, others
perplexed as to how faith had somehow become forgotten. Misunderstandings
were commonplace and when the two worlds of the home front and front line
finally came back together, the tumultuous collision of views and opinions
was bound to leave disharmony, not least within the Church.

CHAPTER TWO

The Soldiers' War

Why was there such division over religion after the war? There were several reasons, one being that no one at home could truly appreciate or understand the horrors endured at the front. Resentment was easy and many soldiers wrote of feeling anger towards the civilian population for its lack of appreciation for the sacrifices suffered. The Church, in particular, seemed too nonchalant about the losses. Some even felt it had condoned the bloodshed, and they weren't entirely wrong.

The First World War was the last war where religious authorities took an active stance and preached the righteousness of the British defence and that God was on the Allies' side. In the past this had been a typical response to conflict. For centuries the Church had told soldiers going to war that God was with *them*, that they were fighting for Him and doing His will. In most cases this had been in conflicts where the opponents worshipped a different God or followed an alternative faith. Thus soldiers believed they were following the true religion, while the enemy was not, and they would naturally win.

The First World War was different for a number of reasons, not least because Germany was also a Christian nation. Prior to the war Germany had been known as a country of advanced theological thinking, a nation that was both more religious than the British and more fundamental. Their Church was also preaching that God was on their soldiers' side. For the average Briton, conscripted from civilian life with only a limited knowledge of religion, this became a mind-twisting conundrum. God could hardly be on both sides, could he? But if he was on the British side because they were devoted Christians (as the clergy was stating) why had he forsaken the Germans who were said to be even more devout? Someone had to be lying.

W. H. A. Groom who was in the infantry during the First World War put the problem succinctly:

In 1914 all the belligerents believed they were fighting in a just cause, in defence of their country – they were being attacked – their freedom was at stake, and all the various Christian churches in the various Christian countries prayed to their national God for victory. What a dilemma for God!

When war broke out in 1914 Britain was still dominated by the Church of England, not just on religious grounds, but in politics too. The Church played a huge role in most people's lives, not necessarily because they attended services or even believed wholeheartedly, but because all aspects of English life were tied up with the Church. Bishops and priests were as ready to voice an opinion on political policies, civil reforms or ordinary life as they were on religious subjects. In comparison other religions fell into the fringes of society, the Catholic Church, just creeping up from years of persecution was a private and introverted body within England, keeping its opinions to itself rather than risk further lashes from the now dominant protestant faith. Between 1914 and 1918, when public debates about the war raged, the Catholic Church preferred to keep a low profile, unlike the Anglicans who paraded their ideas, however controversial they might be. Noticeably post-war there was a revival among ex-soldiers in pro-Catholic feelings, partly because the Catholic leaders had refrained from becoming involved in secular debates.

Other religious orders tried to remain neutral. The Quakers had been around for centuries and were noted for their belief-based objections to fighting, then there were Methodists and Baptists and various smaller groups that fell under the title of the Free Church. Interestingly there were proportionately more conscientious objectors among the Free Church followers than among the Anglicans.

Foreign religions were even less known and hardly thought of in Britain except as a novelty. Islam was something of an enigma, referred to briefly by travellers who had visited the Arab nations. Some of the upper classes became 'Mohammedans', though in a very token way and there was a general fascination for Eastern religion, often in a confused form, but it was still very minor in British society. The Church truly dominated, but it failed to realise both the responsibilities and risks this brought at the start of the war.

Even within the Church there was disagreement as to the role of clergy in modern warfare. Some believed that it was the Church's religious duty to promote peace, even appeasement, but far more believed the Church should stand firmly behind the government in its mobilisation of troops. The Church drafted official war prayers which including praying for the defeat of the Kaiser and a quick victory for the allies. They quickly drew internal criticism for being too war-mongering and vicious for a Christian nation. If the Church could not agree on a prayer what hope was there for united support for the government's war plans?

By 1915 the war was dragging on and more troops were desperately needed. The Derby Scheme was introduced to recruit further men and the national papers heavily promoted it. Church leaders also began to preach to their congregations about signing up and defending the country. At this point in the war it was still thought conscription could be avoided. British leaders were proud that their country did not require such an arbitrary and tyrannical approach to fill its military ranks. They felt confident enough men could be raised by voluntary means and patriotic calls to duty.

The Church led the way; the Archbishop of Canterbury told the nation that no one was exempt from helping the war effort in some way, though he was quick to defend the non-combatant status of the clergy. The Archbishop of York declared; 'the country calls for the service of its sons. I envy the man who is able to meet the call; I pity the man who at such a time makes the great refusal.' The bishops of London and Birmingham followed suit, as did the Archbishop of Armagh.

The Anglican Church was not alone in promoting recruitment. Roman Catholic Cardinal Bourne called for Catholics to join the fight, while Reverend F. B. Meyer was a recruiting spokesman for the Free Churches. General Booth called for volunteers among the Salvation Army and Chief Rabbi Arthur Henderson talked to the Jewish community. In secular society too there were famous voices calling for volunteers, among them the Poet Laureate Robert Bridges and writers Thomas Hardy and H. G. Wells. None of these men could have been aware of the great toll on human life they were calling for. It was foolhardy for the Churches to be so vocal, but natural too. No one had ever seen a war like this and no one could imagine the cost to come.

Taking God to War

The role for the clergy in the war was far from clear. The Archbishop of Canterbury had declared that the clergy were immune from fighting and this included the most humble of clergyman or even those still in training. For many ordinary men about to risk their lives it seemed incongruous that the young and fit local curate would not do the same. The Church worked throughout the war to ensure that clergymen could not be forced to fight, but for many it seemed unfair, especially as it was the churchmen who were so vocal about the conflict.

Private soldier Frank Richards remarked, '[They were] a funny crowd: they prayed for victory and thundered from the pulpits for the enemy to be smitten hip and thigh, but did not believe in doing any of the smiting themselves.'

In fact many of the clergy did choose to relinquish their safe roles and join up as soldiers, while others became army chaplains, trying to give comfort and peace at the front.

The problem surrounding fighting for many clergymen was theological. The idea of a churchman shooting or bayonetting the enemy was incompatible with the teachings of the Church. If a clergyman truly believed in his calling then becoming a soldier was not only impossible, but would constitute hypocrisy. Christ preached forgiveness and loving the enemy; that was inconsistent with killing him. There were chaplains in the front line trenches who would do all they could to aid the soldiers, but who refused to handle a gun because it was against God's will.

For many this seemed a hollow excuse; it still sounds it today. But, in fact, it was fundamental to Christian teachings and though the Bishops were calling for blood, many lower clergymen felt they should be calling for peace. The Quakers followed a very similar belief and many were conscientious objectors, but they never suffered the same backlash and anger that Anglicans did when they refused to fight, probably because the Quakers did not appear to be playing both sides and baying for German blood. Also there were far fewer of them, should the Anglican Church suddenly start promoting peace and non-combatant roles, the whole country would be in jeopardy.

The Church's apparent hypocrisy left the general public cold and angry. They were sacrificing their menfolk because the Church told them to, but the clergy would not do the same. In September 1916 one man asked, 'Why should these men who are so fond of talking about heaven be so afraid to go through its gates?' In other areas parish priests of fighting age were taunted by small boys who pointed fingers at them as in the famous Kitchener poster and shout 'Kitchener wants *you*.'

Church leaders were slow to realise the danger facing them. More and more people were growing antagonistic towards the Church and not just among the working classes; politicians and influential figures were agitating for the clergy to do more than just preach. Action was called for, but it was slow coming.

In 1916 small numbers of the clergy went to work in armaments factories, by 1917 Neville Chamberlain was working with the Archbishop of York to create a Clergy National Service Committee. The Committee announced in May of that year that 4,000 clergymen had volunteered for special service, and another 2,000 were offering general service. They were working in factories and mines, serving on ships as stokers, acting as car mechanics, engineers, postmen and even tax collectors. In Birmingham sixty-five clergymen were acting as special constables and others had joined local defence units. The clergy was not against helping its country in time of war, but the question of actual fighting still raised doubts.

Bishop Talbot knew that for many, holding to their principals was a terrible ordeal as they faced stigma, isolation, bullying and criticism. He also realised that it was necessary. 'Those that minister about holy things and hold their

Lord's commission must not have blood upon their hands, however justly shed.'

Bishop Moule was more pragmatic. While he believed a man of God should not be called to fight except in extreme necessity, by 1918 he felt the time had come for able-bodied clergy to take their place at the front. He wrote to all his eligible clergy to encourage them to enlist.

The dilemma was horrendous for ordinary clergymen. On the one hand they were being called traitors and cowards, on the other if they went to war they would be turning against God who they had sworn themselves to, perhaps even endangering their immortal soul. It was a situation only someone who believed could understand yet for many soldiers and civilians the war had left them atheistic in their views.

Conscription, however, remained off the cards for British clergymen. In contrast the French clergy was as liable to be called up as an ordinary man. Under pressure from the government the French Church had relinquished its right to exemption and 32,699 French clergy were mobilised, out of these 4,618 were killed. Seeing the clergy fight alongside them helped stem the tide of anti-church feeling among the French troops, however it did not prevent post-war alienation from the church in France, which only became apparent during the Second World War.

Possibly the British clergy could have done nothing to change the similar trends occurring in England. Whether they fought or not, the world of faith and religion was changing.

The confusion felt by clergy who joined as soldiers had to be resolved internally with no outside help. Fr Hubert Northcott of the Mirfield Fathers joined up as a private and later remarked, 'The Christian soldier has to be a Christian under almost impossible conditions: at least he has to revise his whole moral outlook...' Few fighting clergymen ever entirely resolved the incongruities of their two lifestyles – they were killing men they should consider Christian brothers, spilling blood while preaching forgiveness.

However, ordinary Christians were being commanded to sacrifice themselves and among Anglicans it was noticeable that conscientious objection was particularly low, around 7 per cent according to a Quaker source, this was less than the number of atheists who objected, which was calculated at 12 per cent. This is not necessarily surprising. The Anglican Church was almost unanimously against pacifism among its people, many of the bishops and church leaders were keen patriots. When an unnamed vicar declared himself a pacifist in 1918 Bishop Moule responded that he felt 'deep regret over a view which I can by no means share.'

Army Religion

For many churchmen service at the front meant becoming army chaplains. Unfortunately British army commanding officers had little time or use for chaplains in the trenches, though they did have a firm conviction that their men should retain some form of religious understanding throughout the war. Promoting religion was done in a bullish, blunt style. If the men were expected to attend church when they could then why not combine it with a good parade? Church parades were widely criticised, both for their dogmatic nature (thrusting religion on the common soldier) and for their pointlessness. They were firmly tied up with patriotism and military pride, though many failed to see how they could help religious feeling in the trenches. Company Commander James Jack wrote in his diary for October 1915, 'Today I attended church parade – as an example to those whose Faith is still intact. Besides, the practice helps to screw up one's sense of duty.'

Charles Carrington recalled; '[the] church parade conducted most seriously before the whole brigade in Hollow Square, and the communion administered after the service to a devout group in the corner of a field.'

The church parade failed to respond to the realities of life in war. For men on a brief rest period they were a nuisance, forcing them to polish brass and spent hours standing or marching, when all they wanted to do was catch up on their sleep. Some even preferred a return to the front trenches to leave behind the church parades! A few officers made church parades voluntary, leaving it up to the chaplain to draw a crowd, yet even this drew complaints with devout soldiers moaning that without compulsory church parades no religious provision was being made for the faithful. For the poor chaplain caught in this turmoil he was almost doomed before he started to speak. Whatever he chose to deliver his sermon on, someone would complain. If he followed the scriptures he was seen as 'out-of-touch' with the war, if he tried to talk on some theological subject well removed from thoughts of conflict, it was complained that he didn't talk of the 'usual' topics. Like so many things, the success of the church parade came down to the speaker, and many chaplains found themselves unable to adapt to the needs of fighting men.

The Army was determined to keep up the men's religious morale. More than 40 million Bibles, hymn-books and prayer books were distributed by religious organisations in the first two years of the war alone. SPCK, the Salvation Army, the YMCA and the Church Army all came to the front to spread the word and support the men. The Church Army alone created around 2,000 canteens and recreation centres and organised a fleet of fifty ambulances, driven by the clergy. They took their role as practical as much as spiritual and proved popular with the troops.

For chaplains in the trenches there was a great irony in the fact that on a quiet Sunday evening English and German soldiers would sing hymns to one another. Though this was mainly in the early years of the war it was still remarkable (and greatly disliked by the army chiefs). On one Sunday in 1915 when British and German trenches were only 40 yards from one another, the soldiers of the 5th Oxford and Bucks Light Infantry sang an old college evening hymn. When they sang 'Amen', a voice rose from the German trenches crying, 'encore!'

After this the Germans regularly called over for the British to sing the evening hymn, which it turned out was an old German one they were familiar with. Soon the British were calling for 'Fritz' to sing and the German who presumably had first called 'encore' appeared on the enemy parapet and sang arias from German operas. He ended by calling out '*Guten Abend Englisch*'.

Such comradeship could not continue – commanding officers feared it would induce friendliness towards the enemy and hamper military manoeuvres. As the war continued, in any case, it became far too dangerous to stand on a parapet and sing, resentment had set in and snipers were always ready to take out an easy target. Still, there is something very tragic and humble in such moments when two enemies came together in peace, only to be forced to step away and fire on each other the next day.

Stories such as this quickly spread to Britain and were widely reported. A false image began to form in the British public's mind that the war was having a positive effect on religious feeling. They anticipated a religious revival after the conflict. Others, who understood the realities of trench life, were quick to disillusion them. The Fabian, F. H. Keeling, who had little warmth towards religion anyway, compared any seeming revival at the front to whisky being drunk by so many to keep up their courage under the terrors of battle. There is no doubt in some cases he was correct. Flung into the horrors of the trenches men would reach out to religion to provide some comfort and sanity, yet their enthusiasm would soon dim once they became accustomed to the situation. There was to be no Christian religious revival post-war, quite the opposite.

A Hardening of Unbelief

There was already a sense among the church and the secular realms that faith was faltering and questions were being asked of bishops as to 'why the Church of England was not more effective as a spiritual and moral force?'

In Manchester Bishop Knox addressed a day conference of nearly 1,000 priests where he asked them if the war was to be a 'day of hardening in unbelief, or the beginning of a new life?' It was a difficult question for the priests, one they were unable to answer. The war was turning the whole world upside down and there was little knowing if religion would survive the calamitous situation facing them. Some among them had already suffered from doubts and even a potential loss of faith and were struggling to deal with their own spiritual crisis, let alone that of men on the front lines.

More to the point, many young men in the Victorian period had chosen the clergy as a career path and not as a calling. It was a ladder up in society for those who might not be able to find positions for themselves elsewhere. For the son of a well-to-do family who could not pursue most careers because they were 'trade', the clergy was an opportunity to spread their wings and do respectable work. Though there were many who felt a strong desire to serve God, there were equally those who chose the church because they had little else they could do. They suffered from a very lack-lustre conviction to their faith. In times of peace that was rarely a problem, but in times of strife these half-hearted priests found their faith tested and faltered accordingly. They were of little use to men equally torn apart by doubts.

It took time for this realisation to filter through to the higher levels of the various church organisations. It also took time to realise that traditional forms of service were failing to reach the men in the trenches. It was a tough topic; on the one hand if a priest preached a subject completely removed from the war, some men would find it welcome escape from the horrors around them while others would complain they would rather the priest discuss the salvation of souls for men soon destined to die. If a chaplain preached 'love thy neighbour' he was seen as a hypocrite. If he preached on forgiveness the men grew angry that *they* needed to be forgiven for defending *their* country. Many men found more comfort in the Catholic services which promised men that they would instantly be admitted to heaven if killed and enjoy immediate salvation despite the torments they had inflicted on the enemy. Others found such talk foolish and wrong, and felt the priest was saying it as a sop to ensure they went over the top when the time came.

The situation was not helped by the publication *John Bull* produced by Horatio Bottomley and known as the Tommy's Bible. Bottomley was scathing of the efforts of the Church and ridiculed chaplains regularly for calling soldiers to repent when, in his opinion, they should be calling them saints and heroes. Geoffrey Studdert Kennedy was a young Anglican chaplain serving at the front who was offended by the insults levelled at his calling by *John Bull*. He was well liked by the men who had nicknamed him 'Woodbine Willie' for his habit of giving a Woodbine cigarette along with spiritual aid to the injured and dying. He was also known to be brave, dashing out into No Man's Land to rescue wounded men, which won him the Military Cross after the horrendous bloodbath that was the attack on the Messines Ridge.

Kennedy preached to audiences three times a day, his congregations numbering anything from 500–1,500. He decided to attack *John Bull's* insults head-on during his services.

> I see *John Bull* says you're all saints; well, all I can say is 'eyes right' and look at your neighbour.

Some were offended by such statements, believing that their fighting gave them an elevated spiritual status. For others it was hard to feel a saint when you had just run a bayonet through a screaming man and watched him die.

Kennedy was also an amateur poet and was encouraged to write a poem for the men. In 'A Sermon in a Billet' Kennedy wrote;

> Our Padre says I'm a sinner, and John Bull says I'm a saint,
> And both of 'em's sure to be liars, for I'm neither of 'em, I ain't…

This was the first of his dialect poems, little ditties, very often amusing, which were written in a style that the ordinary soldier would appreciate and which sounded like something a Tommy in the trenches would say.

But in the wider world the Church was facing constant criticism. Church attendance in many areas was down, though this was not universal as seen by the writings of Canon Bignold of Carlton Colville. There had been hope that the war would bring people together on a spiritual level, this was not happening. If anything people were drifting apart. In 1914 Lord Parmoor, Vicar-General to the Archbishop of Canterbury wrote; 'Each day the weakening influence of Christianity becomes clearer.'

Part of the problem was the Church failed to be unanimous on its stance concerning the war. There were those who felt it should shout loudly about the conflict, that it was being too pacifist, while others claimed it wasn't pacifist enough. Others felt the Church had lost its grip on society because it had failed to address social issues before the war, such as poverty, thus alienating the vast number of working classes. Whatever the Church did it was criticised. It was impossible to please everyone and with the opinions and thoughts of the population at home and at the front being gradually divided and polarised, the position became even more impossible.

A report on the reasons the Church was failing at this vital time, compiled by various churchmen and bishops, included the following complaints;

i) The Christian message as was being taught and delivered by the Church was out of touch with the ideas and thoughts of the time.

ii) 70 per cent of the Army described themselves as Church of England, but very few really knew about the Christian faith or used the sacraments.

iii) The Church lacked brotherhood and fellowship.

iv) The clergy were out of touch with the ordinary people.

The failings were stark and bleak, perhaps not entirely fair on all the clergy, some of whom tried very hard to be in touch with the people in their care. While the complaints were listed very clearly, little in the way of solutions or alternatives was offered.

There was no denying the need for reform. The Victorian ways of preaching and running the Church had caused it to stagnate, and many people felt separated from the man in the pulpit. Suggestions were made that from now on the laity should be encouraged to take a more active part in services. For instance, parish orchestras playing at church services should be encouraged, many having been abandoned for standard organ music. The prayer book should be revised and made more accessible and the Communion should once again form the central part of a service. All of these changes are still observed today.

In various ways the church of the two centuries up to the war had become elitist and isolated. There was too much emphasis on power and prestige. Churches in the Victorian period were often subscription based – a person paid for a pew in the church so they might attend services. This instantly made the working classes and the poor outcasts from the House of God. They could not afford a place in church so they simply did not attend. By the middle of the Victorian period it was realised what an awful state the country's religion was in, that many people had no idea at all about the Bible simply because they were prevented from attending church. The problem was so great a Bill was passed that enabled the government to supplement the building of new churches which would have a percentage of 'free seats' within them for the poorer classes. When the news that one such church would be built in Margate there was rejoicing in the streets.

Yet many churches were still the domain of the wealthy and the poorest members felt awkward or ashamed to enter. By the time World War I broke out the problem had far from diminished and the chaplains in the trenches quickly discovered a shocking lack of knowledge of God among men who supposedly came from a Christian country.

The chaplains were facing an uphill struggle not only to help men keep their faith but to develop it in those who had never known God. They were not helped by the terrible contradictions of the front. The trenches were often only yards from one another and the men regularly heard their German neighbours talking. They also could hear their church services. It seemed impossible that two Christian nations, who believed in the same God, should be fighting each other and each be claiming God was on their side. In *Under Fire* (published in France as *Le Feu*) French novelist Henri Barbusse summed up the contradiction when a badly burned pilot tries to describe the strange experience he has while flying low over No Man's Land. He is confused to see two identical crowds of soldiers either side of the line when he is unaware of any battle due and then it dawns on him:

Then I understood. It was Sunday, and there were two religious services being held under my eyes – the altar, the padre, and all the crowd of chaps. The more I went down the more I could see that the two things were alike – so exactly alike that it looked silly. One of the services – whichever you like – was a reflection of the other... I went down lower... then I could hear. I heard one murmur, one only, I could only gather a single prayer that came up to me *en bloc*, the sound of a single chant that passed by me on its way to heaven... 'Gott mit uns!' and, 'God is with us!'... What must the good God think about it all?

CHAPTER THREE

God's Work under Fire

If there was such a sway towards unbelief, what hope was there for the poor chaplain trying to save souls under fire? Persecuted, criticised, it must have seemed a thankless task trying to spread God's message among the mud and blood of the trenches.

The Anglican chaplain is regularly laid open to abuse in both the history books, memoirs from the period and fictionalised accounts. He is often portrayed as cowardly, keen to save his own skin and always trying to avoid the front lines. In contrast the Catholic chaplain is portrayed as heroic and eager to serve his flock even in the height of peril.

This notion, unfair to many Anglican chaplains who risked their lives (and sometimes lost them) at the front, has been helped along by the inaccurate myth that the Church forbade its chaplains to go into the frontline trenches throughout the war. Even history books have made this error, reiterating a belief that is only half true but which appears in works by such individuals as Robert Graves. Their word on the matter has been taken (excuse the pun) as gospel.

When chaplains first arrived in France and Belgium it is true they were banned from heading to the trenches not only by the Church authorities, but also by the Army commanders who could see no point in having a chaplain in the frontlines. Fortunately many chaplains proved a determined bunch and simply ignored the regulation, heading out to where they were needed the most – the frontline trenches. Unable to stop them and finally recognising the vital role they could play for morale both the army and the Church withdrew the ban and from then on Anglican chaplains were as free to roam the trenches as their Catholic comrades.

So if the story of Anglican chaplains never appearing in the front line trenches is a myth, why is there an enduring image that the clergy was absent from the frontline? Poor organisation has to be blamed along with a simple lack of numbers. Chaplains roamed as best they could, but were always outside the army system and never certain where the troops would be next. The constant fluctuations of the frontline trenches meant from one day to the next it was almost impossible to know where exactly a unit would be. Added to this was the pitiful number of chaplains serving in comparison to the number of men who needed them. Not to mention the inexperience of many. It would be dishonest to state that all chaplains served the troops well and that none of them had a strong sense of self-preservation and stayed clear of the fighting trenches. There were those who, for whatever reason, let down their calling and stuck in the minds of soldiers as the incompetent and cowardly chaplain.

The Church had blundered, it had rushed into war without thinking and the calamity this caused would have lasting repercussions, not least for the poor clergyman who stepped into a warzone with no clue as to what to do, who to seek out or even how he would live and survive.

A prime example of this is F. R. Barry who was commissioned in 1915 having only been a priest for a matter of months. He was twenty-five, inexperienced at even ordinary church work, and found himself aboard a ship sailing for Egypt. He was scared stiff and completely out of his depth, but made the best of a bad situation and eventually established a canteen. Many similar young men simply floundered in their new role and were useless to the troops in their care. It wasn't until 1916 that an initiation course was established for chaplains to help them cope with life at the front.

If rushing young chaplains into action wasn't bad enough, the army chiefs had very little idea what to do with them once they arrived. In the mobilisation plans no one had made any provision for transporting, accommodating, paying or even feeding the unfortunate chaplains. Simply put, they had been forgotten. Army officers had no use for men of religion in their ranks during those early days and were bewildered about what to do with the priests. Barry later wrote:

> When the padres first went out... the army had little idea what to do with them. In battle, they were left behind at the base and were not allowed to go up to the fighting front. What on earth, it was asked, could they do up there? A colonel would say, 'No work for you today, padre', meaning by that, no corpses for burial. The chaplains' job was to take church parades, on such rare occasions as they were practicable, to run entertainments, to help in censoring letters, and in general to act as welfare officers, thereby helping keep up morale. But was that what they had been ordained to do?

The Unfortunate Chaplain

This disorganisation at the very foundation of the army chaplain system led to confusion, inconsistency and for many secular critics gave the impression of inadequacy within the church. Robert Graves' book, as mentioned above, has been fundamental in spreading this view, and there is no doubt many agreed with him. He wrote

> Anglican chaplains were remarkably out of touch with their troops. The Second Battalion chaplain, just before the Loos fighting, had preached a violent sermon of the Battle against Sin, at which one old solder behind me grumbled: 'Christ, if one bloody push wasn't enough to worry about at a time!' A Roman Catholic padre, on the other hand, had given his men his blessing and told them that if they died fighting for the good cause they would go straight to heaven or, at any rate, be excused a great many years in Purgatory. When I told this story to the mess, someone else said that on the eve of the battle in Mesopotamia the Anglican chaplain of his battalion had preached a sermon on the commutation of tithes. Much more sensible than that Battle against Sin. Quite up in the air, and took the men's minds off the fighting.

Graves had once been deeply religious but various experiences, both before and during the war, had turned ardent Christianity into ardent atheism. He was slightly resentful, therefore, of the chaplains, having a hankering for the consolation belief could bring, but no longer able to justify it. With the typical zeal of a convert he slandered the church as often as he could and, writing many years after the war when his life had taking a dramatic, and almost disastrous turn, he was not immune from the disaffection towards the church others had felt during the twenties and thirties. He was writing at a time when the Church was a prime target for attack, yet this is rarely taken into account when his work is repeated and oft quoted in the history books.

He was not alone in this attitude. Guy Chapman, later Professor of Modern History at Leeds, wrote *A Passionate Prodigality* in 1933 having served in the First World War. In it he remarked

> These Catholic priests impressed one. Leeson never dropped a word of religion in my hearing, but one felt a serenity and certitude streaming from him such as was not possessed by our bluff Anglicans. Already there was a growing dislike of these latter. They had nothing to offer but the consolation the next man could give you, and a less fortifying one. The Church of Rome sent a man into action mentally and spiritually cleaned. The Church of England could only offer you a cigarette.

Siegfried Sassoon was equally disillusioned. Before the war he had been religious and fond of Christianity, but the experiences of the trenches eroded away these earlier memories. It is debatable whether he actually lost his belief,

but he certainly struggled to align God and the Church with the chaos of
bloody warfare.

> The Brigade chaplain did not exhort us to love our enemies. He was content
> to lead off with the hymn 'How sweet the name of Jesus sounds'! I mention
> this wartime dilemma of the Churches because my own mind was in rather
> a muddle at that time.

Sassoon was torn. He was uncomfortable with the Church ignoring its usual
lines of guidance because of the war, and was one of the ones who missed
the consistency. Others would have praised his chaplain for not being a
hypocrite.

However not all major writers who emerged from the confusion of war were
so critical or so self-confident as to not notice the conflict within themselves.
Wilfrid Owen complained the Church was not recognising the grim realities
of war or facing up to the toughest parts of the Christian ideal in a time of
conflict, yet he also was aware that he was exactly the same. He believed in
Christianity, loving thy enemy and turning the other cheek, yet he could not
bring himself to become a pacifist. He was grappling between his patriotism
and his faith and had realised that the two ideals of the Empire (patriotism
and Christianity) were not perfect bedfellows. Still Owen struggled on.

> I am more and more Christian as I walk the unchristian ways of Christendom.
> Already I had comprehended a light which never will filter into the dogma
> of any national church; namely that one of Christ's essential commands was:
> Passivity at any price! Suffer dishonour and disgrace; but never resort to
> arms… It can only be ignored: and I think pulpit professionals are ignoring
> it very skilfully and successfully.
> [Letter to his mother, May 1917]

This leads to another point in the matter of faith at the front, the difference
between belief in the Church and belief in God. Many felt the latter while
finding the motives, dogma and sermons of the former incomprehensible. The
Church was faltering for a number of reasons and it was not just because
of bloodshed. It was because the Church had made the error of becoming
indelibly linked with politics. While the bishops back home were calling for
more recruitment and bigger pushes at the front, the men in the trenches were
the ones suffering and wondering how supposed men of God could be asking
for greater and greater slaughter?

The upheaval of the class system was an even more dangerous threat facing
the Church. The Victorian class system was tough and static; people rarely
changed classes, you were born into your place in society and that was where

you remained. Even if a man became successful in business and found himself
wealthy he could not consider himself one of the 'Upper Class'. He might have a
bigger disposable income than some of the toffs at the top, but he would never
be one of them – ever. The class system could be loosely divided into the working
class, the middle class and the upper class, within each band there were various
grades (so you might have an upper middle class man, for instance), but while
the odd working class man might just pull himself into the middle class, no one
could be promoted to the upper class. That came through birth and birth alone.

In a modern, almost classless society, the strictness of these hierarchies
seems unimaginable, but it was extremely strong and often detrimental
to those at the lower end of the scale. And it was from this lower end, the
working class, that most of the infantry came. The footsloggers, the PBIs
(Poor Bloody Infantry), the men who walked in their thousands across No
Man's Land and were slaughtered. Those who had to live in open trenches,
no matter the weather, while the officers and their staff huddled in the relative
comfort of a dugout. There was no greater indicator of the class divide than
this. The infantry suffered and died, while all the officers did was complain
about laziness, Trench Foot (seen as self-inflicted) and the lack of effort the
men were putting into the combat. Resentment thrived, especially as officers
were far more likely to survive the war than an infantryman.

Regularly enduring long, arduous days of work laying wire, digging
trenches or repairing damage, then going onto sentry duty with virtually no
rest, the men were pushed to breaking point – and many broke. Men found
sleeping at their posts due to exhaustion were often shot for dereliction of
duty. Suddenly there was more than just one war. There was an internal fight
between the infantry and the officers – between *them* and *us*. And the symbol
of this serious class divide was the polite, sermonising Anglican chaplain.

Before the war the Church had become an establishment for the middle and
upper classes. The lower classes were railed against for their slovenly moral
standards and constant poverty – surely if they just tried a little harder they
would not be so poor? There were huge campaigns against vice among the
lower orders, from the Temperance movement to family planning, and it was
often resented by those it targeted. The working classes, especially those at
the bottom, felt persecuted by both politicians and the Church, who were so
keen to improve Britain's moral standards. Now in the trenches, not only were
the chaplains realising that many of the men around them had absolutely no
concept of God or the bible, but that the class system was fracturing.

This leads to another, curious insight – the difference between officer and
infantry views on religion. Sassoon, Graves, Chapman and other writers who
condemned God and the chaplains were almost exclusively from the officer
class. Their views came from a different mind-set to the men below them and
cannot be taken as the typical view of the Tommy.

No book can make this clearer than *Poor Bloody Infantry* by W. H. A. Groom, first published in 1976. Groom was an ordinary soldier and he became irate over the years at the lofty and superficial works his superiors had written about the war. In particular he hated the constant reference to the worst thing in the trenches being boredom, or that men died gaily and happily, pleased to have given their lives for their country. For Groom, life in the trenches was one of constant terror and horror.

> A man without fear is inhuman – a robot – because fear is a creative human emotion. It is part of the divine spark and only so long as it is part of our make up shall we have humility, love, and normal human attributes.

Groom comes across as a gentle soul in his writing, horrified as much by the slaughter around him as the detachment of his superiors who were constantly ordering it. He also maintained a simple faith during the war and after. He might have found the sermons of the Church contradictory, but he never lost the comfort belief in God could bring. Groom also provides another side to the chaplain debate.

> Our padre was High Church, tall, handsome, completely fearless and he often went over with the troops in an attack. He had already been awarded the Military Cross. He used to hold communion services in full regalia in the reserve trenches before an attack. He was an admirable type and yet one could never get very near him as there was always a certain detachment, possibly a barrier he could not help. His sermons on the compulsory church parades were full of the usual platitudes. How could it be otherwise? I think the position of the padre was almost impossible – it was compromise, compromise, compromise.

Groom showed a rare understanding of the problems faced by a chaplain. He did, briefly, undergo a religious revival and take part in running services. For a time this gave him the strength to continue fighting.

He was not alone. Church learning among the men brought them closer together as they had something in common. Though many had little concept of the bible, they knew certain hymns from school or in churches where the poor could attend. Using this universal knowledge they adapted the words of certain hymns to make new tunes. To the tune of *The Church's One Foundation*, they sang;

> We are Fred Karno's army the famous infantry,
> We cannot shoot, we cannot fight, what bloody use are we,
> And when we get to Berlin the Kaiser he will say
> Hoch Hoch mein Gott what a bloody fine lot are the boys of the L.R.B

It might not have been quite how the bishops had imagined men coming together, but it was one form of sharing Christian learning.

Groom's views on the Church were made on the battlefield of Passchendaele. Having gone over the top and seen comrades brutally slain, Groom found himself alone and lost in No Man's Land. It was a bitter survival, for so many friends had perished within the last few hours and he had no idea if he would ever make it back to the trenches, let alone back home. Trapped in a shell hole as German artillery thundered overhead he found himself thinking quite seriously about God, between the moments of terror and panic that otherwise engulfed him.

> Where, oh where, was God in this earth-covered ossuary – this mud swamp receptacle for the bones of the dead? It was I suppose for me the moment of truth. I thought of the patriotic national churches all praying for victory. How could God choose? We Christian killers killing Christians. Could there be a personal God who would listen to me if I regularly confessed to be 'a miserable sinner with no health in me'. I felt miserable enough but more sinned against than sinning.
>
> I had had doubts before but I now saw clearly, I think for the first time, that the Church's teaching of personal salvation with all the emphasis on sin, forgiveness, confession, absolution was a selfish creed. If I survived I should have to find a more selfless religion than that of the Church – if I survived. As I have said before I have always been interested in, and a keen student of religion and now on this day, with this traumatic experience, my belief in a Church which condoned killing faded away. I would not again voluntarily attend or take part in the communion or other Church services, and rightly or wrongly, that was that. Deep thinking on this day in this place of useless sacrifice, but would there ever be a more appropriate time and place?

There is perhaps no better quote to sum up the deep conflict the war created between faith in God and faith in the Church.

Some Good Souls

The Anglican chaplains tend to become cardboard cutouts in discussions about the First World War. They are mostly anonymous, voiceless and easy to misinterpret. Yet so many were far from that. They were as terrified as the men around them, and as determined to survive. Generalising about them can only lead to unfair assumptions and to neglect the many diverse characters who served within their ranks.

Geoffrey Studdert Kennedy is one prime example, affectionately known as 'Woodbine Willie', on his death in 1929 he had a poem he had written about his nickname laid on his coffin;

> For the men to whom I owned God's Peace
> I put off with a cigarette.

Kennedy felt, even at his last, that he had failed in his role as a chaplain and messenger for God, yet he had tried so hard. Kennedy was thirty-one when war broke out and he had no hesitation in joining up immediately as a chaplain, even though his asthma made warfare slightly difficult. Kennedy was patriotic to the last and though he regularly encountered and criticised the strange paradoxes of war he never lost his fervour nor his belief that Britain had to keep fighting no matter the cost.

> You ask me what we are fighting for – I give it you in three words: Freedom, Honour and Peace. You ask me what we are fighting for, and I give it in one word: Christ.

Kennedy was a true fighting chaplain; he toured with the bayonet and physical training school accompanied by a boxer, two wrestlers and an NCO who had killed eighteen Germans with a bayonet. Kennedy had no fear of encouraging the men into battle, however incongruous it might be to his beliefs, and he had no qualms about going with them to rescue the wounded. Still, he was well aware the horrors of his environment. On being asked to give a sermon before the King he began with, 'I have come from the bloody slime of the trenches…'

Kennedy's first thoughts were always of the men under his charge, and not just officers, but the real soldiers of the infantry. When a big push was due he would spend night after night at Rouen entertaining the departing troops by playing the piano in a coffee shop and leading them in song. At quieter moments he would write home for them or pray with them – were these the same men Graves described as having no faith in God? When they finally filed into a train for the front he passed out copies of the New Testament and cigarettes, his pain almost palpable as he sent them off probably to their deaths. After many nights of this he would return to the camp canteen utterly exhausted.

His real concern was building a bridge over the class divide that invisibly separated many of the men from the chaplains. Kennedy had no qualms at playing the fool among the men, as can be seen from his dialect poems. He was criticised by other clergymen as acting like a clown, but he insisted he did it for Christ's sake. After all it worked; he earned an affectionate nickname from his pals in the trenches and brought a little comfort in times of great despair.

Yet it was not without its cost. At a lecture he gave for the School of Chaplains he said; 'You know, this business has made me less cocksure of much which I was cocksure before. On two points I am certain: Christ and His Sacrament; apart from those I am not sure I am certain of anything…' It was not what his superiors wanted to hear.

Kennedy's faith was shaken the most when he came upon men who he had recently spoken or prayed with who had died in some awful manner. He found it hard to juggle the concepts of religion he had been traditionally taught with his natural feelings of anger and heartbreak. Kennedy spent much time on the battlefield (another stab to the myth Anglican chaplains never went to the front) often burying the dead. At Messines he won the Military Cross for his bravery in rescuing the wounded, but more often he was called upon to bury men where they lay, sprawled flat on his stomach to say the service to avoid being shot.

He was also deeply understanding of the moral difficulties the men faced, particularly where it concerned sexual temptation. This gentle understanding, forgiveness, compassion and a resolve to not preach at the men, drew many to him and none who had been given a cigarette as they lay wounded by the scrawny, panting padre would ever forget their dear 'Woodbine Willie'.

Charles Raven was another brave soul who saw it his duty as a chaplain to be a companion and friend to the men. He had actually tried to enlist as combatant but was rejected three times on medical grounds, so became a chaplain in 1917. Though he hated fighting (and later became an influential pacifist) he considered the trenches of the First World War a spiritual experience. He certainly placed himself in the thick of the action.

On one occasion he spent an hour nestling in a small hollow with an unknown private while howitzer shells exploded overhead. The private kept moving about and Raven was convinced he would be hit, so he pleaded with him to remain still. That was when he realised 'that at each explosion he had put his body in the mouth of the hollow between it and me, offering his life for mine many times under conditions that try the manhood of the bravest'. The experience deeply impressed upon him the bond of brotherhood between men. He never forgot the friendships he formed in the trenches or his experiences, nor was he ever so easy with his divine platitudes or talk of Godly omnipotence. He believed there was a need for a new form of liberal Christianity which did not rely on the authority of the Church or the bible. He believed future chaplains would need to refrain from trying to enforce acceptance of the Church authority on men, or trying to hammer into them the teaching of the bible which so few understood. Truly Raven was a modern Christian.

Fr John Groser was another who clung to his principals throughout the war, despite strong opposition. Trained in a tradition of Catholic socialism, his teachings were more sacramental than most army chaplains and did alienate some as seeming narrow and exclusive. Groser served in France between 1915 and 1918, following the men into the trenches. It was there that Groser came into conflict with one CO. A recent battle had resulted in heavy casualties and the CO asked Groser to take command of a group of soldiers, fearful the men would not hold their position without an officer in command. Groser flatly refused. He would not take part in any killing. The CO was exasperated and later said,

I reminded him that scores of men he knew had fallen that day after having done their utmost; and I was conveying to him – in what words I cannot remember my despair of a religion that could teach that such a patronising stand-offish attitude was the right one, when my words were drowned by a terrific outburst of fire from our own guns, who had spotted a counter-attack forming up. When the firing was over Groser told me that he would do what I wanted provided he didn't carry arms. To that I readily agreed.

As absurd to the commanding officer as Groser's refusal was, it was entirely logical from a religious perspective. Other chaplains faced the same dilemma; they were men of God and it would be hypocritical to slaughter others. But this gesture of defiance in the face of all-out war and violence was challenging and controversial, even the Church was not clear on the matter. By the time Groser came home injured in 1918 the continual bloodshed had destroyed his last shred of patriotism. He now believed the conflict was a crime against humanity.

John Michael Stanhope Walker faced a similar crisis as he saw the cost on humanity the war brought. Born in 1871 he went to the western front in 1915 as an Anglican chaplain and found himself trying to bring comfort to the dying at a casualty station. Within three months Stanhope Walker had buried around 900 men. In one twenty-four-hour period 1,300 casualties arrived at the station, another night 700 appeared after 11 p.m. The scene was horrific; the tents were over-crowded and stank of fetid wounds, putrefying flesh and bodily waste. The smell alone was nauseating; but the doctors and nurses worked around groaning men with terrible wounds. Bellies would be split open and spewing a man's guts, limbs were shattered, lost or stinking of gangrene. Gas victims gagged on their own blood, dying from the inside out and writhing in terrible agony. Victims of head injuries would lie with chunks of their faces lost, or holes in their skulls. The sight was traumatic and stupefying and in the midst of it all Stanhope Walker was trying to offer what little spiritual consolation he could, no wonder he remarked 'Tommy does not want religion. I don't persuade him.'

After the first day of the battle of the Somme the horrors were horrifically magnified.

> We have 1,500 in and still they come – 3–400 officers, it is a sight – chaps with fearful wounds lying in agony, many so patient, some make a noise, one goes to a stretcher, lays one's hand on the forehead, it is cold, strike a match, he is dead – here a Communion, there an absolution, there a drink, there a madman, there a hot water bottle and so on – one madman was swearing and kicking, I gave him a drink, he tried to bite my hand and squirted the water from his mouth into my face…

Under such circumstances it was remarkable anyone could maintain their sanity, let alone their faith. However Stanhope Walker not only did, but also remembered his duty to those men others forgot. When battle was raging and the casualties were being brought in every moment, injured German soldiers who had been rescued were often ignored because pressure was on to save English lives first. Again during the Somme, Stanhope Walker borrowed some morphine so he might ease the pain of two or three German patients who would have to wait some time before being attended by the doctors.

Stanhope Walker was desperate to try and create something good in the midst of madness. In a burnt out old car factory which had been set up as a hospital he created a small garden where beans, tomatoes and marrows grew. It was a little drop of life and colour among the carnage. Yet even he found himself pushed to the brink of a nervous breakdown by the constant horrors. One minute he would be trying to give the Eucharist to a man who had lost his entire lower jaw and another minute hearing the confession of a dying man who was desperate to be confirmed before he passed. It was harrowing and what made it even harder was the knowledge that while he was respected and liked as a man, few of his patients were interested in his work as a priest. 'They would come [to a service] as a favour to me if I pressed them, at least some would, but what is the use.' Stanhope Walker retreated to his country parish after the war feeling he had utterly failed the soldiers at the front and God during the past four years.

The chaplain Dick Sheppard was equally destroyed by the suffering and Godlessness he saw at the front. Going to France in August 1914 he threw himself into his work with a terrible earnestness and compassion, so deeply did he identify and sympathise with the men that within two months he was broken in spirit and body. He could not comprehend or justify the suffering he saw all around him and each fresh case cut into his soul. The worst strain was preparing a man to face a firing squad for desertion. There was an average of one such judicial murder a week and few chaplains could condone or understand the action. One wrote,

It has just fallen to my lot to prepare a deserter for his death. That meant breaking the news to him; helping him with his last letters; passing the night with him in the straw of his cell (a wayside barn) and trying to prepare his soul for meeting God; witnessing the execution and burying him immediately.

Yet there was one chaplain who was so unique and bold with his ideas that to this day his memory lives on in Belgium. He strove to bring emotional salvation to men, to give them freedom and peace. He looked forwards, towards the time when war was over and Britain had to rebuild herself. For him, preaching of bloodshed and sin was not the way, he was far more practical and down-to-earth. His name was Tubby Clayton and his activities at the front still remain the best known of any chaplain who served in the war.

A Haven in Hell

Phillip 'Tubby' Clayton, Army Chaplain, looked up at the neat three-storey house in the Belgium town of Poperinghe. Its façade was lined with tall windows, adorned with decorative lintels and the front door was ornate with curly ironwork. It looked a typical townhouse, a little worn about the edges from the shelling of the Germans, but aside from that it was pretty and pleasant, and about to become 'Talbot House'.

Inside the house the damage from shrapnel shells was visible, the back rooms had recently been hit and needed to be repaired. Upstairs, in the attic, the floor groaned under the weight of Tubby's feet, and various army engineers and officers would declare it rotten and unsafe for use. Tubby only saw a prospective home for a small chapel, tucked away in the eaves, a Haven in the Hell of frontline warfare.

The house had been found by Neville Talbot, another Church of England chaplain who was concerned for the mental, as well as the spiritual, wellbeing of the soldiers in the trenches. Even when on leave the men had no escape from the constant battering of the German guns and the risk of death. Sooner or later they would break. Talbot had the idea of setting up some form of retreat, a club where the men could come on leave and spend a few hours of peace, perhaps the last they would ever know.

Such clubs had been established for officers, but nothing had been done for the ordinary infantrymen, despite them heavily outnumbering the officers and being the in the worst positions and at most risk of death. Talbot wanted his club to cater for everyone, no one would be excluded because of rank, and this house, once the home of a wealthy brewer, was to be an oasis of calm and civility in a world that had gone crazy. Naturally the house would be named after the man who was trying so hard to bring some respite to the soldiers, and run by his unlikely friend Tubby Clayton.

Talbot House was founded on religion, but it was not a religious house. There was the chapel where services took place, many impromptu for there was no knowing when soldiers would arrive or have to leave. Then there was Tubby's Office which a nearby sign indicated with the phrase; 'Come upstairs and risk meeting the padre.' But it also contained a library, a games room, sitting rooms for peaceful reading or piano playing and sing-a-longs. Tubby also offered the radical idea of discussion groups in the conservatory, debating various war issues along with other political problems. It was a rare place where men could air their views and listen to those of others, something unheard of in the trenches.

Tubby and Talbot both understood the men they were catering for; they knew to give the house an overt Christian aura was to put off many, that was one reason they refused to name it 'Church House'. Tubby would not exclude anyone from his haven and though everyone knew a chaplain was running the place that was no reason for non-Christian soldiers to avoid it. Not when the chaplain kindly avoided preaching and offered a home from home for struggling soldiers.

The purpose of Talbot House was relaxation and fun. Tubby hung up a sign, 'Talbot House 1915-? Every-Man's Club', over the front door and he meant it. That he gave no finish date implied he would be there as long as the war lasted in fact. The news of Talbot House soon spread and it was given the affectionate name 'Toc H', Toc being the signallers code for 'T' and H, for the 'H' of house. Tubby littered his new home with amusing signs to remind people how to behave, a jovial way of teaching everyone the house rules. 'Abandon All Rank, Ye Who Enter', read one, while another stated 'To Pessimists, Way Out' with a hand, like those seen in railway stations and other public buildings back home, pointing towards the door.

Another sign read 'Genius is Constitutionally Untidy. But - !' Politely reminding members to tidy up after themselves. Nearby was 'If You are in the Habit of Spitting on the Carpet at Home, Please Spit Here'. While on the stairs there was, 'No Amy Robsart Stunts Down these Stairs'. Amy Robsart was the wife of Robert Dudley, Elizabeth I's favourite. She mysteriously fell down a staircase while alone in her house and there remains to this day suspicions of foul-play that Dudley might have done away with his wife to enable him to marry the queen. The story had been immortalised in a Walter Scott novel and Tubby knew many of his visitors would be aware of the legend and would hopefully smile at the sign.

In the entry hall he put up a noticeboard which was always over-flowing with news and created a friendship corner, a rudimentary form of messaging service. Friendship corner contained a board where men could pin cards containing details of friends or family members serving in the army they were trying to contact. They also might leave their own name in the hope someone they knew would come to Toc H and spot it. Some of the cards were light-hearted. Gunner A. J. Edwards of 29th Light Railway Operating Coy put up a message saying he would like to meet any old pals. Gunner A. W. Gasser and Corporal Rowson just posted their names and military numbers to let people know they had been through. More poignantly Bombardier F. R. Hayward was looking for his brother George, as was F. Gibson of R.F.A. Headquarters. Newcomers stopped at the board to take a look and place responses. Returning visitors would then read the board, dreading to see a card that indicated the person they were looking for was dead.

As for the chapel – despite its floor being condemned by anyone with the slightest knowledge of structural engineering that Tubby spoke to – it survived the war. Even with a rickety portable organ at one end and often an overflow of attendees, many of whom had to stand on the ladder that led up to the chapel as there was no room inside. Tubby did take the precaution of telling the congregation that when they knelt or stood to sing they should do so in a staggered procession to avoid unnecessary movement on the floor.

Tubby was not neglectful of the civilians around him, many of whom were children. There was a disarming air of misery among these innocents of war, constantly plagued by the risks of shelling, (the German line being at times only miles from them) and the real threat of being overrun by the enemy at any point. Tubby held an annual Christmas party to which the local children were invited and the soldiers on leave entertained them. They started inauspiciously. The first year a school party of Belgium children game along. Tubby asked a sad looking boy what games he liked to play. Miserably the little boy looked up and replied, 'Belgium children have forgotten their games.' A failed attempt at a game of 'hunt the slipper' quickly proved the boy right, but Tubby was undeterred. He smeared an apple in ration jam and tied it to a string suspended between two blindfolded contestants who had to try and take a bite from it. This proved the turning point of the party and suddenly it was as if a cloud had been lifted from the children.

Every year after that Tubby's Christmas party was an eagerly anticipated event among the depressed locals. Cheese, toffees and toys were given to the children, rare treats in the war years. English songs were sung, often to the bemusement of the children and in general the crowd left lighter-hearted than when it had arrived. There was only one year when the Germans interrupted the celebrations. That was in 1918 when a bombing raid began shortly before the end of the party. Fortunately no one was hurt, though the English papers reported the story as a massacre of Belgium children!

Despite illness (Tubby suffered repeated bouts of malaria) and the ominous threat of German invasion (at one point it looked like Toc H would have to be abandoned, so close had the enemy come), Tubby ran Talbot House throughout the war. Its success is marked by the fondness of its memory to so many servicemen. Some found God, others simply enjoyed a spell away from the cold, misery and fear of the trenches. It reminded them what they were fighting for, and the civilisation they had left behind in England was recalled in the modest lending library where novels sat beside history books. It was a place for men to talk and share their thoughts, and for a brief period to stop being soldiers. In that sense Toc H was one of the most significant places of the war, its only sadness being that it was not repeated elsewhere, and could only ever touch a fraction of the men it needed to.

Yet it proves something. It proves that there were chaplains fighting through the mud of Flanders and trying their hardest to bring comfort to their flocks. Toc H was a small miracle, a drop of hope in the bleakness of war. Between Tubby and the many chaplains in the trenches, a small portion of humanity was being salvaged. Unfortunately it was such a small drop in a vast ocean that it is easily overlooked; however for the men it reached it was invaluable. There were good and bad chaplains, just as there were good and bad officers. It is just a shame that too many wish to focus on the latter, and not on the kind souls who sacrificed everything to bring God into the trenches.

CHAPTER FOUR

Sir Oliver Lodge and his Heart's Desire

On 11 November 1918 a strange sound echoed across the damp, cold fields and towns of England. It was a sound people had almost forgotten, that some children could not remember having heard before. It was the peel of church bells announcing up and down the country that the war had ended.

There was rejoicing but it was half-hearted. Effigies of the Kaiser were burned and crowds flooded into churches to offer their thanks to God, but it was a stilted celebration. Too many young men would not be coming home, and too many returned maimed for life. Countless wives, mothers, and daughters had lost the entire male element of their family.

For some the situation was even stranger. The war, as horrific as it had been, had created a unique sensation of being truly alive, of living for the moment and ignoring the future. Almost everyone had been changed by it, there was no return to the life that had been before and some even found a sorrow that the comradeship of the trenches was now going to be lost.

The church was divided; returning chaplains recognised that there was a great need for change, while those who had remained on the Home Front, failed to grasp the realities and horrors of war in the trenches. When Westminster Abbey was filled to bursting point with crowds on 11 November 1918 and other churches were conducting services from 11.30 a.m. to midnight to accommodate all the worshippers, it seemed there was no rush to rethink how the Church reacted to the community. Surely this was the promised religious revival?

The war had completely uprooted British society and class boundaries. It had opened eyes and changed minds. It had stripped people of the old comforts they had known – faith, patriotism and the might of the Empire. Suddenly everything seemed very uncertain.

If older Church leaders had thought they could carry on as they always had, they were sorely mistaken. Chaplains returning from the front were eager to revise the Church of England and bring it back to the people. By the early 1920s several of the most vocal Church reformers were now Bishops and capable of instigating the changes they had talked about. This was the upshot of war, but there was also a downside.

In 1914 610 deacons were ordained into the Church or England, but in 1919 the figure had dropped to 161. Since then the number of clergy ordained in any one year has only exceeded the 1914 total once, in 1962-3. The trend was alarming. In 1911 there had been one clergyman for every 1,457 of the population, by 1951 this figure had dropped to one for every 2,111.

The sudden drop has to be taken in context. First there had been a significant population loss within the young male section of society, initially because of the war and then because of the dreadful influenza epidemic that hit Britain and the Continent, snatching the lives of many who had survived shells, bullets and bayonets. Naturally this left fewer men to enter the clergy. Sons, who would have considered a career path in the Church, instead went into their father's business or occupation because an elder brother or their parent had been slain. Men were needed elsewhere first, in essential industries.

Another reason for the significant drop was a change in attitudes. The war had shaken people's faith and opened the Church to criticism. For centuries the clergy had been viewed as a career path for younger sons of well-off families, who had a loose idea of their own faith, instilled in them by parents and school. Sometimes it was evangelical and often it failed to be substantial. Pre-war that didn't matter, but the tragedy of 1914-1918 had changed the situation considerably. Now not only was it less appealing to go into the Church, (with the way the population was constantly hammering religion for its failings), but those who had always held a token faith, enough to get by in peacetime, now suffered a complete loss of that certainty. Like Robert Graves who had considered the clergy as a career path before the war, they were thrust instead into a wistful form of atheism.

Only the true believer, who could cling to his faith in the face of insult and onslaught, would now choose to be ordained. In some regards this was not such a bad thing. It whittled out the token Christian clergyman, who never really understood his belief, and would therefore pass on his limited knowledge to his congregation.

Then there was one final reason, a reason that had nothing to do with loss of faith in God, but everything to do with a dislike for the current practices of the Church of England. There were clergymen and prospective clergymen who were so disillusioned with the traditional Church that they either left it or refused to be ordained into it. They went their own ways into offshoot religions.

To top it all potential clergy were now emerging not from the middle and upper class families (those who had been officer material), but from the lower classes. At last religion was becoming a choice because of belief and not because of career potential. But these new men worried the older clergy.

They were not the public schoolboys they were used to and were rougher, less sophisticated. The class structure had been turned on its head and it would take some getting used to.

The war had heightened feelings and brought them bubbling to the surface, but there had been lots of trends emerging before the war that had been spurred on by the conflict. Britain's religious outlook, in fact, expanded with the end of war. The Church of England failed to comfort some and they sought out other forms of faith. Post-war Britain gives the impression of being a land where the population was floundering for 'something'. Many nursed a desperate hope that there was more to life than the harsh realities of blood and death. Religious sects, cults, new movements, fairy tales, myths and ghost stories all emerged from the conflict as people groped around blindly for something to cling to. There were those who found the Church and considered it a lifeline, and there were those who found faith in the most bizarre of experiences, such as communication with the dead. Society had been turned topsy-turvy in a million ways and religious belief was just one of them.

Finding Raymond

Grief is a dreadful thing, littering the mind with doubt, guilt, unsaid words, regretted actions and always the thought of what might have been. Nothing is worse than the loss of a young person who has hardly begun their journey through life. Oliver Lodge knew that as well as the next person, possibly more so for he had spent much of his life investigating the world of psychic phenomena and as such had been faced with the grief of families who had lost children unexpectedly. During the nineteenth century Lodge's name was well known for two reasons; on the one hand there was his work as a scientist. On the other, within the intimate circles of psychical research, Lodge's name was as familiar and readily used as that of Sir Arthur Conan Doyle. Even in the 1940s writers on the subject would refer to 'Lodge' and know their readers would instantly think of the bald-headed physicist and paranormal investigator. In his lifetime Lodge's fame was extraordinary; he was caricatured in papers, with his slightly hunched shoulders and Darwinesque domed forehead. For fifty-odd years the name Lodge was instantly recognisable, if not entirely respected.

Lodge had spent more years than he cared to remember trying to prove the afterlife existed. Lodge was not interested in promoting any particular faith (he was Church of England with spiritualist leanings) and his religious views were quite silent in his paranormal work. What he wanted, especially after the war, was to bring comfort to those who had lost loved ones, to give them hope that this life was not the end. For many years he had done this quite quietly in the background. While believing in 'something' beyond this world he would also come across as a cynical scientist. Until the loss of Raymond, that is.

Lodge had led a rather fortunate life. He had twelve living children, having lost one daughter as a very young baby. It might be argued that if he had lost any other son aside from Raymond, Oliver would not have felt the same pain. Grief yes, misery yes, but the kinship he felt with Raymond was something else. They were like two people sharing the same soul and losing Raymond was like losing a part of Oliver Lodge.

Suddenly Oliver truly understood the grief he had witnessed time and time again at séances. He also knew that countless others were experiencing the same tragedy as he was. Not long after Oliver lost his son, he knew he was about to begin a new journey, not only to find and communicate with the spirit of Raymond, but to prove to others that such a thing was possible, that no one was truly gone. Blinded by his own grief he was determined, whatever damage it might do to his scientific reputation, to publish his views and experiments on speaking with the dearly departed.

For Oliver this adventure all began with a strange message from deceased psychic investigator Frederic William Henry Myers (1843-1901), founder of the Society for Psychical Research (SPR) of which Oliver was a member. The message came through an American medium, Mrs Leonora Piper, using automatic writing, who happened to have previously been investigated by Oliver Lodge and Myers. Another investigator, William James, had become convinced Leonora was genuine, until she started to receive messages from fellow SPR member, the late Richard Hodgson, which James found very suspect. Lodge was of a different opinion. He continued to believe in Leonora and when he received his 'Myers message', (communicated to Leonora by the same Richard Hodgson) he was deeply impressed. The message was cryptic: 'Myers says you take the part of the poet and he will act as Faunus'.

After consulting various classical scholars Lodge came to the conclusion that the message was a coded reference to the account by the poet Horace of a tree falling and nearly striking him; the tree was deflected by the timely intervention of the horned god Faunus. There was argument among classical scholars as to whether the tree actually hit Horace and Faunus merely lightened the blow or whether the tree missed him entirely.

Lodge read deep significance into the message which arrived in early September 1915, just days before the death of Raymond. He believed for the rest of his life that Myers had meant the message as a consolation and a promise that he would help the family recover from its grief. Initially Lodge could not make out how this would be achieved.

On 25 September, eight days after learning Raymond was dead, Mrs Lodge attended an anonymous sitting with a friend. The sitting was not for Mrs Lodge, though she was hopeful she might receive some message, it was for a French lady who was a friend of the family and had recently lost both sons in the war. Mrs Lodge and her friend went to visit a private medium, Mrs Kennedy, without revealing their names. During the sitting a message was directed at Mrs Lodge. TELL FATHER I HAVE MET SOME OF HIS FRIENDS. Mrs Lodge asked who the speaker meant, the reply was MYERS.

Lodge was startled when he heard what had happened and started to put two and two together. Myers had spoken of helping the family and now at an anonymous sitting Raymond had apparently come through and said he had met the very same Myers. Could it be Myers was helping Raymond to speak to his family? Lodge now began a new investigation in earnest. He paid a visit to another medium, Mrs Leonard, who was known for her spirit guide Feda, a Native American child.

Gladys Osborne Leonard was a British trance medium. This meant she would apparently slip into a state of semi-consciousness during a sitting and her spirit control – Feda – would take over. Feda was child-like, sometimes obstinate and silly. Sitters remarked she spoke in broken English and sometimes struggled with the language. Mrs Leonard would later work with the SPR and though she was tested regularly she was never publically declared a fraud even by sceptics. Today the remaining transcripts of her work appear to suggest she was very good at drawing information from people during séances to enable her to give accurate responses to questions.

Lodge first saw her on 27 September 1915. It was an anonymous sitting arranged through Mrs Kennedy, though as Lodge was a well-known Victorian figure it is possible he was recognised when he arrived. Much of what Feda said on the first visit was standard séance fodder, few facts were offered. Raymond, through Feda, said he was happy and had met a number of friends, including 'M', which Lodge assumed meant Myers. Feda also said she saw a dark cross falling onto Lodge, but just as it was going to strike it was knocked aside. Lodge took this as a direct allusion to the Faunus message.

Attending other mediums the same messages came through again and again, particularly that Myers and Raymond were going to help Lodge prove spiritualism to the world. This was quite a common refrain in spiritualist sittings, but Lodge took it in all earnestness. Unfortunately there was a lack of any real evidence which he could present to sceptics, until that is the episode of the photograph came up. The story began on the same day Lodge was visiting Mrs Leonard. His wife was having a separate sitting with another medium called Peters. During the sitting Peters said,

> You have several portraits of this boy. Before he went away you had got a good portrait of him – two – no, three. Two where he is alone, and one where he is in a group of other men. He is particular that I should tell you this. In one you see his walking stick.

For the moment Mrs Lodge was baffled. They had several portrait shots of Raymond in uniform on his own, taken before he left, but no group photographs. Mrs Lodge was sceptical and thought it was a guess by Peters, and one that had gone wide of the shot. Still the piece of conversation was recorded along with all the rest as Mrs Lodge knew the importance of note taking at séances.

Oliver Lodge was more intrigued by the strange episode. He thought it odd that Raymond was 'particular' about telling them of the photograph, but since there was no group photograph known to him it seemed a pointless thing. Two months passed and then a letter arrived on 29 November from a Mrs Cheves. Mrs Lodge did not know a Mrs Cheves, but was aware that Raymond had served with a Captain Cheves and discovered this was his mother. Mrs Cheves was writing because her son had just sent her a group photograph taken on the front in August, among the officers in the picture was Raymond Lodge. Would Mrs Lodge like a copy of the picture if she did not already have one? Mrs Lodge replied she would indeed like a copy, but as it happened nothing arrived at once and in the meantime Oliver Lodge had a sitting with Mrs Leonard. Speaking to Feda he asked about the photograph.

Lodge: Do you recollect the photograph at all?
Feda: He thinks there were several others taken with him, not one or two, but several.
Lodge: Were they friends of yours?
Feda: Some of them, he says. He didn't know them all, not very well. But he knew some; he heard of some; they were not all friends.
Lodge: Does he remember how he looked in the photograph?
Feda: No, he doesn't remember how he looked.
Lodge: No, no, I mean was he standing up?
Feda: No, he doesn't seem to think so. Some were raised up round; he was sitting down, and some were raised up at the back of him. Some were standing, and some were sitting, he thinks.
Lodge: Were they soldiers?
Feda: He says yes – a mixed lot. Somebody called C was on it with him; and somebody R – not his own name, but another R. K, K, K – he says something about K. he also mentions a man beginning with B.
Lodge: I am asking about the photograph because we haven't seen it yet. Somebody is going to send it to us. We have heard it exists, and that's all.
Feda: He has the impression of about a dozen on it. A dozen, he says, if not more. Feda thinks it must be a big photograph. No, he doesn't think so, he says they were grouped close together.
Lodge: Did he have a stick?

Feda: He doesn't remember that. He remembers that somebody wanted to lean on him, but he is not sure if he was taken with someone leaning on him. But somebody wanted to lean on him he remembers. The last what he gave you, what were a B, will be rather prominent in that photograph. It wasn't taken in a photographer's place.

Lodge: Was it out of doors?

Feda: Yes, practically. (Speaking as if to Raymond) What you mean, 'yes, practically'; must have been out of doors or not out of doors. You mean 'yes,' don't you? (To Lodge) Feda thinks he means 'yes,' because he says 'practically'.

Lodge: It may have been a shelter.

Feda: It might have been. Try to show Feda. At the back he shows me lines going down. It looks like a black background, with lines at the back of them. (Feda here kept drawing vertical lines in the air).

Lodge was naturally excited to see the photograph and impatiently awaited its arrival. Mrs Lodge went through Raymond's diary, an unpleasant task for it was soaked with her son's blood and she had not looked at it previously, but there on the day marked 24 August was a significant entry – 'Photograph taken'. The Lodge family had no knowledge of this photograph, it had been taken after Raymond had been home on leave and he had not mentioned it in any letter. If Mrs Cheves had not written to them they would never have known about it. So the question arose how did two separate mediums know of it and would Feda's observations prove accurate?

The photograph arrived on a wet afternoon in December. Raymond's younger sister Rosalynd received it and took off the wet outer packaging to show a 12 x 9 print, enlarged from a smaller 5 x 7 copy. The photograph showed twenty-one officers standing before an army hut. Raymond sat at the front, sporting a new thin moustache, he was smiling at the camera and while he did have his officer's stick, he was not holding it, merely resting it on his feet. Raymond looks awkward in the photograph, mainly because the man behind him, sitting on a bench, is leaning his arm on Raymond's shoulder forcing him to tilt slightly to the side. It's a very obvious part of the image because Raymond looks shoved to one side and the man behind quite clearly refuses to sit straight on like his colleagues, but has turned himself at an angle causing him to have to lean on Raymond.

Aside from this remarkable similarity to Feda's observations there were others that caught Lodge's eye. The hut had a pitched roof which was distinctly marked by vertical batons, and the background was very dark and in parts, due to open windows, it was black. However Lodge was still a scientist and he noted both Feda's and Peters' downfalls. Peters had talked of a stick and when doing so had made a motion as if to put it under his arm. Raymond's stick was resting on his feet. Feda had only mentioned vertical lines, but equally visible in the picture was the planking on the side of the hut which ran in horizontal lines.

Lodge began to analyse the other things purportedly communicated by Raymond. Raymond had called the group a 'mixed lot' and looking at the photograph this became apparent as the officers were from various companies (there were too many on the image to be from a single company) but were probably all from the same regiment, except one man who had a cap badge in the shape of a thistle rather than the three feathers of the Lancashires.

What about the prominent figure with the initial B? Lodge tested several friends, asking them to look at the picture and choose the person who seemed most prominent in it. A number of them indicated the man standing on the right, who was brightly lit and standing just aside from the group, defining him from everyone else. This happened to be Captain S. T. Boast. There were also officers in the group with names beginning with C and R who Raymond would have known. However, there was no one with a name beginning with K, only an individual whose surname began with a hard C.

Lodge decided to explore the story behind the photograph. The negative had been sent to England by none other than Captain Boast and had arrived on 15 October 1915, more than a fortnight after the first mention of it in sittings with mediums. The picture had been taken by a Belgium man who had been shelled out of his house, so had no means of processing the photograph. The officers bought the negatives off him and had them sent to England to be printed. It actually happened that more than one photograph of the group was taken. In another the intruding officer behind Raymond is leaning on him with his leg, while in the last he is not leaning on Raymond at all. Lodge found it remarkable that Raymond had correctly described the image Mrs Cheves intended to send, if she had sent any of the others it would have appeared that Feda and Peters were completely wrong. There was also another photograph that Lodge only learned of later. This was of a group, including Raymond, taken completely out of doors, with Raymond standing not sitting. Had this image arrived with Lodge before the other he would have completely disregarded the observations of Feda and Peters.

Lodge was convinced he had clear evidence of Raymond communicating with him. Even today it is hard to offer a logical explanation for the matter other than suggesting a fortunate coincidence was at work. Could it all have been a lucky guess? If so would Feda have said someone was leaning on Raymond? Surely better to be vague with guesses, than to be so specific they are likely to be proved wrong. What about the mention of 'B' for Boast?

Yet at the same time there were errors, the position of Raymond's stick, the mention of vertical but not horizontal lines, the name beginning with K.

The other alternative is to suggest some form of elaborate hoax was afoot. This seems highly unlikely considering the circumstances, requiring not only the coordination of two separate mediums (which could be feasible), but the assistance of the photography shop who developed the image, as well as both Mrs Cheves and Captain Boast, who was still out in France with more immediate concerns than fooling Sir Oliver Lodge. The negatives did not arrive in England until October. The first mention of the photograph was on 27 September. The case of Raymond's photograph has to remain something of a mystery – for Lodge it was conclusive proof that he had found his son in the hereafter.

Lodge continued his journey with new enthusiasm, keeping careful records of everything that occurred. Many of the conversations with mediums were standard séance fodder, reassurances that everything was fine and that Lodge should continue with his work. On one occasion the medium described Raymond as stood between two sisters, one living the other not. The 'other' was little Laura (who came across as Lily in séances). She had died a few minutes after being born and Raymond would barely have known her, if at all. At a table tilting session Lodge asked Raymond to tell him what his nickname with his brothers was. Table tilting involves, as its name suggests, the table tilting in a certain way to indicate yes or no, or the letters of the alphabet. Letters were counted out by table tilts, so for instance the letter F would be indicated by six tilts of the table. One tilt indicated no and three indicated yes, which could occasionally cause confusion with the letters A and C.

The problem with table tilting, as Lodge admitted, was that it could never be ruled out that expected answers were caused by unconscious (or conscious) movement of the living sitters. Only answers that meant nothing to the sitters could be taken as evidence and even then, only if they could later be found to make sense. Lodge knew Raymond's nickname when he asked for it. The table spelt out P, A, P, and shuddered as if it was aware this was incorrect. Lodge asked him to try again and again the table spelt out P, A, P, and then shuddered, followed by P, A, S. The first two letters were correct, but not the last which Raymond (or another) was struggling with. Lodge asked for this letter specifically. He got a T, which spelt Pat and was Raymond's correct nickname, but even Lodge found it hard to take this as evidence.

So he asked another question, what was his brother's name? Raymond could pick from five! The table spelt out N, O, apparently the beginnings of Noel, but then R, M, A. The last letter Lodge took as a 'no' since the table was spelling out Norman, and no one was called Norman. So he halted proceedings and suggested Raymond try again. This time the table spelt Noel. What Lodge did not know until later, when speaking with his sons, was that Raymond had a general nickname for his brothers which happened to be Norman.

There was one other aspect of the table tilting session that had a strangely morbid air. Lodge mentioned Lieutenant Case, who had been one of the last to see Raymond alive. The discussion began with how he was, and Raymond reported he was well. Then they moved on to whether he had a message for Case. The table seemed hesitant and then spelt out SO IM NOT (a pause) SO IM WUO, then confusion. Lodge had the troubling feeling that the words should read as SO IM WOUNDED and Raymond was referring to the last words he spoke to Case. He decided to get off that subject quickly.

As the sittings continued Lodge became more and more fascinated with what Raymond could tell him about heaven, and this proved to be the most controversial aspect of Lodge's work. While sceptics were prepared to tolerate his rambling conversations with a lost son over inconsequential family matters, when he started to talk about the afterlife and what it was like he landed himself in a whole heap of unpleasantness. People were not happy being told that in heaven it was possible to get a whisky – "they can make anything here", Raymond explained. Teetotallers in particular were unimpressed at the suggestion that heaven was just a mimicry of earthly life and a drunkard could continue his habits after death. Lodge explained that was not the case, early cravings were indulged to accustom people to their new life, but they rapidly cast aside such habits realising they were not important and no longer desirable. Still the controversy ran; Raymond said he appeared as a fully formed person, others argued that surely he should be as a spirit? And when he started talking about 'levels' within heaven which people progressed through depending on their qualities, he had most Christians up in arms. Heaven was starting to sound all too much like the mortal world!

Lodge published the reports of his sittings with Raymond, as well as his views on the afterlife, communication with the dead and other aspects of spirituality, in November 1916. By that point the casualties on the front seemed endless and almost every family had been touched by some loss. Lodge knew the abuse he would get from publishing his personal story. He knew the criticisms that would be aimed at him from old scientific friends, so why did he do it? Actually, for the simple reason that he hoped it would bring some comfort to a grief-stricken country. It was not about inspiring people into a new faith, just about giving them a promise of a life after death where their loved ones were safe. Lodge felt certain that even the worst souls who had died at the front would now be in heaven, and this went down very badly as it made it seem that heaven was an open club where anyone could go no matter how good or bad they had been. Lodge stuck to his guns, but it was far from easy. His quaint views of a peaceful hereafter were being over-shadowed by cynicism and extremism. Where did his view of heaven fit in with traditional religious views? Where did it fit in with the new cases of hauntings such as at Borley Rectory? More significantly, where did it fit in with another war looming? Lodge lived long enough to witness the horror of a new war which would take the lives of a new generation. He saw his wireless technology used as a tool of warfare and felt the bitterness of yet more families suffering grief without solace. He died in 1940, uncertain how strong an impact his book *Raymond* had had, but at least secure in the knowledge that he was going to a better place where the son he lost twenty-five years before would be waiting for him.

Remembering the Dead

Oliver Lodge was right about one thing; a grieving public needed something to focus on. If it was not an afterlife, then they at least needed a place to shed their tears, a site to go to mourn. Mothers, fathers, wives, sisters and brothers wanted a location they could visit, lay flowers and commune with their dearly departed. In usual circumstances this would be a grave, but the First World War had left many dead in the Flanders mud. Some were found and buried in purpose built graveyards, but many more were lost in the turmoil, their bodies disappearing into the ground or being incorporated into further trenches, their identities forgotten. Today there is still an on-going hunt for these lost men, unfortunately even when skeletons are found it is often impossible to identify them.

Many men were never coming home alive or dead. Their families had no place to mourn. The idea for war memorials was suggested as a means of helping grieving relatives. Memorials were first erected during the American Civil War when monuments were placed in every town and village listing the dead, but the concept had not initially spread, and memorials of this sort were not common in Britain prior to 1918.

Interest in this novel idea arose from the lack of graves for many of the fallen and in 1919 there was a special exhibition of designs at the Victoria and Albert Museum and the Royal Academy. Manufacturers quickly jumped on the trend, advertising stained glass window designs, plaques and stone monuments. Many were inspired by the crucifixes seen dotting the roads of France and Belgium. There was a popular trench myth that even in the heaviest shelling God would protect the crucifixes from harm and they would always remain standing. Crucifixes were not as popular a religious icon in Britain, but the sight of them in France, standing amid destruction, inspired a number of giant stone crosses as memorials in British towns, with the honoured dead listed reverently beneath the towering stone. Similarly memorials were created for civilians who were killed through bombardments or war work.

While memorials were in general considered a good idea, there were those who struggled with them. Bishop Moule was in favour of memorials but was concerned with the way they were being used to give out a false message. They were often decorated with swords and other war instruments and emphasised the sacrifice of the war. There were those churchmen who felt these demeaned the unique sacrifice Christ had made on the cross. Moule was troubled that the memorials were turning soldiers into saints, that their bloody deaths gave them instant passage to heaven. He was very torn in his feelings and when dedicating a war memorial he tried to emphasise that heaven was not a reward for suffering, while at the same time saying:

> I do not mean that God does not care for the brave sacrifice our sons have made. They who enter that world, because Jesus died, find the Father and the Son attentive to every tear.

Yet he wanted people to realise that this did not mean people should not strive for individual salvation through faith in Christ. Death in war was not an instant ticket to heaven, in other words. But the grieving masses were not inclined to heed this, especially as the Spiritualists were happily telling them that every lost soul had found its way to the 'Summerland' as Oliver Lodge's deceased son referred to it.

On 6 November 1919 George V sent a message out to the Empire announcing that he hoped all his people would come together on the eleventh hour of the eleventh day of the eleventh month and hold a two minute silence so that; 'in perfect stillness the thoughts of everyone may be concentrated on reverent remembrance of the Glorious Dead.' The practice was adopted readily, in St Paul's the hour bell tolled in the middle of a hymn.

> Men became as motionless as the marble figures which surrounded them. If women moved it was because they shook with emotion... In an interval of seconds, men must have revisited the torn and blasted fields of France, the ridges of Flanders, the beaches of Gallipoli, and many a cemetery where long rows of wooden crosses mark the resting place of those who fell.

There were those for whom this form of remembrance was abhorrent. For the mentally or physically scarred revisiting the fields of Flanders in memory was a painful and bitter experience, only made worse by the unemployment that faced so many of them post war.

Remembrance Services held a bitter feeling for some. When Robert Graves was asked to speak at one by the Rector of Islip, he chose to read war poems by Owen and Sassoon. The grimness and lack of patriotic fervour within them scandalised the congregation. Graves then launched into a rant that the men who had died were neither particularly wicked nor virtuous and survivors should thank God they were alive and do everything possible to avoid wars in the future. Though this upset a chunk of the congregation, the ex-servicemen among them felt a touch of pride when Graves' implied they were on equal footing with their fallen comrades.

It was this contrast that was one of the many difficulties the Remembrance Services and memorials faced. They seemed to glorify the dead, while the living survivors struggled on facing poverty, hunger and illness. On Armistice Day 1921 thousands of unemployed workers marched towards the Cenotaph waving pawn tickets instead of their medals. Other ex-servicemen felt the practice had become hollow, the words meaningless, even glib. It was as though all the horrors and turmoil they had faced could be brushed under the carpet by this once a year ritual. Many would rather put the war behind them than to keep revisiting over and over again a time of agony and suffering. And who could blame them? Once a year they had to relive the event that had ruined their lives, killed friends and family and left them scarred for life. No wonder some envied dead comrades who were now honoured as heroes while the poor survivors limped along trying to earn a penny or two. It seemed the treasured dead had completely overwhelmed the existence of the living.

The Magic of Conan Doyle

While controversy reigned over war memorials and remembrance services, another significant Victorian figure was about to spark his own scandal. Sir Arthur Conan Doyle could count Lodge as one of his comrades in the struggle to promote spiritualism as a genuine religion. He admired Lodge's frank account of finding Raymond and his bravery at making his discoveries public. Doyle now found himself contemplating risking his own reputation to bring hope of an afterlife to the masses.

The war had left few unscarred and Doyle was no exception; Sir Arthur's son Kingsley had died of pneumonia caught after being badly wounded at the Somme, his brother Innes had fallen sick in the 'flu epidemic that arose in late 1918 and died also of pneumonia in early 1919. His nephew, Oscar Hornung, had joined up in 1914 and was killed the following July. All these blows hit Doyle hard. He heard of his son's death as he was mounting a lecture platform to talk about spiritualism. He faltered for a moment, then took his place and continued with the lecture.

Like Lodge he knew the strain grief brought. Always prone to depression the loss of so many family members could easily have pushed him into a spiral of despair. His only salvation was his burgeoning faith in spiritualism.

Doyle had been raised as a Catholic, but lost his faith as a young man. He felt Catholicism left too many things unexplained. The death of his uncle Richard pushed him in a new direction. Richard had told his nephew of the premonition he had had of his own death; he had painted a strange watercolour of a hay cart loaded with dead bodies and another of an old man cutting long grass in a graveyard while children passed by and threw flowers on a grave. Richard had always been an inspiration to his nephew, a talented artist his work was often dotted with fairies and elves, for which he had a strong love. This would encourage Doyle to tentatively explore the world of spiritualism. Still confused over his own beliefs, but desperate to know that some form of afterlife existed, he turned to recent research done into spiritualism for answers.

It was another death that took Doyle further into the realm of séances. His father Charles died in 1893; the unhappy man had been an alcoholic for years, finally succumbing to fits which forced him from work and into an asylum. At the same time Doyle's wife, Louise, had been diagnosed with tuberculosis, effectively a death sentence. Doyle's interest in psychic matters took on a renewed urgency. He was close to falling into a bout of depression brought on by watching his wife die and distracted himself by joining the British Society for Psychical Research and focusing on realms beyond understanding. Places he could escape to and which might bring him hope. By 1894 Conan Doyle had also joined the Society for Psychical Research (SPR) and was actively pursuing his first ghost hunt.

The SPR had received a letter from a Colonel Elmore of Dorset, a veteran of the Afghan war with a scarred face. Living in a large house with his wife and only daughter (a sour-faced spinster of thirty-five according to Doyle), he had recently been troubled by unpleasant sounds in his property. Moaning, weeping and the dragging of chains had disturbed his sleep, sent servants running and caused his dogs to refuse to enter certain rooms. Uncomfortable with the matter and loathed to admit his house haunted, Elmore had written to the SPR in desperation, making it plain that whoever came to investigate should not reveal their intentions to his wife and daughter; rather they should pretend to be old army buddies recently returned from India.

Doyle arrived at the house with Frank Podmore and Dr Sydney Scott from the SPR in time for dinner. The trio played their roles perfectly, discussing the Afghan war and making no reference to ghosts. After the meal they sat down with the colonel for a hand of whist in the card room, while mother and daughter retired to the drawing room. They went to bed at 10 p.m. and slept untroubled the entire night. Undeterred they stayed the following night and this time Doyle lay half-awake in his bed waiting for something to happen. Suddenly he heard the heart-breaking sound of a woman uncontrollably weeping and moaning words softly. Seconds later he heard the dragging of chains. Dashing out of his room he found Podmore and Scott who had just witnessed a white-garbed figure moving by with blank, cold eyes.

Suspicious about the solid nature of the ghost, on the third night Doyle proposed that the three men should leave pillows in their beds to give the appearance of sleeping bodies and hide in the shadows awaiting the spectre. It was not long before they heard the weeping and the dragging of chains, but springing out of the shadows they found no one around. Elmore's daughter had been absent all the previous day, but when she appeared for breakfast the following morning she had distinctly puffy and red-rimmed eyes. Doyle suspected she was the ghost and quietly confronted her. Miss Elmore confessed her crime, driven to it probably by the despair and desperation of her situation. She promised to end the charade if the truth was not revealed to her father. The members of the SPR left Dorset having laid to rest the Elmore ghost.

Doyle, despite his leanings towards spiritualism, was rather dubious about mediums. He had an unfortunate experience with Frederick Foster Craddock, a medium working near London, which crystallised these suspicions. Craddock's spirit control, Rosetta, had been recently unmasked as the medium himself dressed in nightgown, wig and lipstick. Despite exposure of his drag act Craddock retained popularity and when Doyle went to visit with a colleague, Admiral Moore, there was a full audience for the performance. Craddock produced a series of spirits, of various sexes, ages and celebrity. At one point a cloaked individual approached a lady at the table and she declared to her husband, 'It's your father!' The husband answered back, 'No, it's your mother!'

Admiral Moore decided to resolve the debate by grabbing the figure which, with its moustache, did appear to be the lady's father. The surprisingly corporeal ghost struggled in his arms, the moustache flew away and for a moment no one was sure if they were witnessing a male or female figure. Then the spirit escaped the Admiral's arms and, robes swirling, raced to the fireplace and snatched up a coal shovel. For one awful moment it seemed set on attacking the unfortunate admiral and then an assistant switched on the lights and the audience gasped as Craddock was revealed before them wearing a hideous rubber mask, swaddled in a sheet and with a handkerchief wrapping his head like a turban. Disappointed by the fraud, Doyle nonetheless retained a sympathy for the spiritualist movement.

During the war Doyle's views of spiritualism slowly changed from hopeful sceptic to firm, even ardent, believer. There is no denying the loss of Kingsley, Innes and Oscar had all played their part in shaping his beliefs. The multitude of strange ghost stories emerging from the trenches also helped; the legendary Angels of Mons and the story of the reappearance of the late Kitchener, gave Doyle pause for thought no less than the story of William A. Speaight. Speaight stated he saw his dead best friend in a dugout on the Ypres salient pointing to a specific spot on the floorboards. When Speaight dug up that spot he found, three feet down, a narrow tunnel with a time delayed mine sitting in it. Had he not found it the mine would have blown up that portion of the trenches and killed many soldiers. Doyle found such stories convincing evidence of some form of survival after death.

At the same time a family friend, Lily Loder-Symonds, was staying with Doyle due to her fragile health and lack of income. She took care of the children from Doyle's second marriage (he had married again after the death of Louise). Lily had lost three brothers at Ypres and had sought comfort in the art of automatic writing. This had been in favour with certain mediums for some time. The idea was that an individual would take pencil and paper and allow a spirit to guide their hand rather than to write consciously. Though sceptics felt the practice was suspect and easily faked, many believed in the messages thus delivered. Lily had written a vague message on the day the *Lusitania* had been sunk and Doyle took it as a prediction of the entry of America into the war. Taken together these incidents made a great impression on Doyle and, for better or worse, he poured his heart into spiritualism. His enthusiasm would soon blind him, but his objectives were sincere. Like Lodge he wanted to bring comfort to the many who were grieving.

His change of heart was not without criticism, not least from his mother who had no time for spiritualism and from whom he kept his belief a secret for years. When his sister Ida wrote in 1917 criticising Oliver Lodge's book *Raymond*, Doyle wrote back,

Your views about the spirit land seem to me a little unreasonable. If Percy were called away, which God forbid, you would not complain that he was, 'hanging about clamouring to communicate with earth' merely because he wished to assure you that all was well with him. When people first pass over they have the desire, but after a little, and especially if they find no corresponding desire in those who are left behind, it soon passes...

I am sorry you don't like the prospect but what you or I may like has really nothing to do with the matter. We don't like some of the conditions down here. But if you try to define what would satisfy you you find it very difficult. ...we don't carry on our weaknesses we are not the same people & so it is practical extinction. I may be very limited but I can't imagine nothing more beautiful & satisfying than the life beyond as drawn by our art, literature, music, architecture, but all with a far wider sweep. Our bodies are at their best. We are free from physical pain. The place is beautiful. What is there so dreadfully depressing in all this?

The fact is that people read Raymond who have read little else of psychic matter, and so they have nothing by which to compare & modify it. It seems crude because they take it crudely, on some items like the whisky paragraph, as if forces which can make anything could not make whisky. It is said in half jest in R, but to read the comments one would think the life beyond is drinking whisky!

Cheer up, its not so very bad!

Doyle also wrote directly to Oliver Lodge, discussing his own experiences at séances and contacting his son Kingsley.

We had strong phenomena from the start, and the medium was always groaning, muttering, or talking, so that there was never a doubt where he was, suddenly I heard a voice.

'Jean, it is I.'

My wife cried, 'It is Kingsley.'

I said, 'Is that you boy?'

He said in a very intense whisper and a tone all his own, 'Father!' and then after a pause, 'Forgive me!'

I said, 'There was never anything to forgive. You were the best son a man ever had.' A strong hand descended on my head which was slowly pressed forward, and I felt a kiss just above my brow.

'Are you happy?' I cried.

There was a pause and then gently, 'I am so happy.

Doyle was now a convinced spiritualist, vocal in his views on the subject and lacking the critical eye he had once brought to séances. This cost him dearly at times; his old friend and fellow writer Jerome K. Jerome denounced Doyle in a stinging remark on mediumship. 'The darkened room, the ubiquitous tambourine, the futile messages, proved frequently to be 'concoctions', vague prophecies of the kind that we can read in any Old Moore's Almanac.'

In 1919 Doyle paid a visit to Belfast to meet the Goligher family, Irish cloth cutters who all claimed mediumistic powers. Critics had been flabbergasted that anyone could find the cheesecloth the family exuded during séances to be genuine phenomena. There was a popular rumour among psychic investigators that the Golighers were hiding extending poles about their person to move tables – the women were said to hide it in their vagina, the men in their rectums! In fact amateur investigator and engineer W. J. Crawford, who vehemently believed in the Golighers and conducted experiments with them for many years, regularly proved they were fraudsters. He, unfortunately, refused to believe the evidence and concocted some ludicrous theories to explain away his results. Doyle was fascinated by the family, though he did quietly distance himself after Crawford committed suicide in 1920. He did not, however, voice any concerns that they might be fakes. Doyle had effectively decided to sift the evidence presented to him of mediumship – frauds were quietly ignored and not denounced, anything genuine was hugely praised and magnified – resulting in a very biased outlook. Nothing was going to interfere with Doyle's quest to enlighten the world on spiritualism, not even the ugly truth.

Doyle's beliefs ran deeper than just ghosts and spirits. His uncle Richard had fascinated him with folklore and made him a firm believer in the fairy-world. During the Victorian period there had been a fascination for fairies, encouraged by the new hobbies of folklore study and antiquarianism. The 'old ways' had a cosy revival, even the term 'folklore' was coined in 1846 and a number of investigators, including academics, went about collecting oral stories about the little folk, as well as finding 'physical' evidence, in the form of misidentified historical objects. Far from being confined to the romantic or superstitious, even respectable individuals became involved; the Reverend Sabine Baring-Gould wrote extensively on the subject describing how he had witnessed goblins running beside horses at the age of four in 1838. Music, paintings and stories all emerged discussing fairies and the old ways, but this quaint little pastime, romantic and carefree, suffered a blow during the Great War. It was hard to believe in wee folk when sons, husbands and brothers were dying horribly in a foreign country.

Doyle was therefore ecstatic when he learned from a friend that fairies had been photographed in Yorkshire by two young girls. The case of the Cottingley fairies (explained fully in Chapter Eight) still provokes mixed responses, but for Doyle there was no argument – fairies were real and the Yorkshire photographs proved it. Doyle spent considerable time analysing the photographs and marvelling at the little fairies. He admired their delicate wings, their elegant movements and the musical instruments they played. They were identical to the Victorian ideal; all those paintings and illustrations of fairies had been correct! Doyle made the photographs the basis of his book *The Coming of the Fairies* in 1922 and was fortunate to be then going to Australia for a lecture tour as the backlash from the publication came fast and fierce. The newspapers had a field day pulling apart the pictures and Sir Arthur Conan Doyle. A damning critique was given by the *Westminster Gazette,* while the New York paper *World* published a letter which included the line, 'When Peter Pan called out to the audience in London at a recent performance the famous question about fairies, Conan Doyle was the first to give an affirmative.' Doyle had become a laughing stock. People had been prepared to accept his fervent spiritualism as a bit of eccentricity, but fairies?

Doyle was untouched by the matter, though he was rapidly alienating former friends by his dogmatic beliefs. In Australia he was introduced to the dubious Charles Bailey, a former boot-maker who specialised in apports – random objects suddenly appearing in a room. Bailey was somewhat of a celebrity in Australia despite having been repeatedly caught in the act of removing key apports from his boots or mouth to present to the sitters. In 1910 he had caused to a nest with two birds to appear, but unfortunately a local bird-seller recalled a gentleman matching Bailey's description buying these exact birds two days before. Critics speculated Bailey had hidden the birds in his rectum, which was almost as absurd as believing he really had caused them to magically appear.

Bailey gave séances for Doyle, and during one he was tied into a sack naked with only his head protruding. After much wriggling and muttering words that sitters thought were either Hindu or Welsh, Bailey produced a bird's nest and a speckled egg. Doyle asked where it had come from and Bailey's testy spirit guide crossly stated 'India' as if it was obvious. He declared it was a Jungle Sparrow egg. A dubious Doyle took the nest to the Museum of Natural History in Melbourne, who believed it was from an Australian bird, but definitely not a Jungle Sparrow.

Despite this scepticism Doyle continued with Bailey. At his next séance he produced an Assyrian tablet, but when it was analysed it proved to be a modern forgery. Doyle still defended Bailey, *obviously* it was easier for the spirits to nab the forgery than a real Assyrian tablet, since it had been recently handled by humans so was still surrounded by human magnetism. Even for Doyle this was a stretch. Doyle left Australia with mixed feelings; while acclaimed by some others had demonised him. At one lecture he had been called the Anti-Christ by anti-witchcraft groups and a woman had leapt up and shouted that he was Jack the Ripper. When he tried to talk about communicating with Kingsley someone in the audience cried, 'It must have been through the Devil!' This was not the reaction Doyle had anticipated and both he and Lodge, were learning how perilous it was to declare oneself a spiritualist.

Back home Doyle threw his support behind the notorious practice of spirit photography. The concept was simple enough. Suitable mediums would take a photograph of a living person and the spirit of someone departed would superimpose itself on the glass plate. When developed there would be an 'extra' on the image. Time and time again these spirit photographs were proved frauds, and were so uniform from medium to medium it was almost laughable. In some cases the same 'extra' appeared on several photographs of different sitters and was variously identified as a dozen unrelated people. Most suspicious of all was the way the extras sometimes appeared upside down, as if the glass plate had been put in the wrong way. However spirit photographers had several notable supporters, not least the Archdeacon of Colley who declared he had seen his deceased mother in one photograph and now firmly believed in the art form.

Aghast, the editor of the *Sunday Express* had a professional photographer mock-up his own versions of spirit photographs. He invited Doyle, among others, to attend the sitting and take part in the staged photographs. The plates to be used were all signed to prevent substitution and the photographer took three pictures, all including Conan Doyle. Doyle and the others followed the photographer into the darkroom, they searched him and satisfied themselves he was concealing nothing, before allowing him to continue developing the plates. Doyle was stunned when on one picture a woman with upturned eyes appeared next to him and, on another, a ring of spectral girls danced around him. The photographer explained he had previously taken pictures of the girls in the *Sunday Express* office and had superimposed them onto the new photographs in the darkroom. He demonstrated to his disheartened audience how he had slipped in the extra images during the process of developing, the semi-darkness of the room aided his trick. While some spiritualist papers reported the images as 'genuine' with the usual line that the photographer was an undiscovered medium, it was becoming harder to believe in spirit photographers.

Doyle still managed it using an array of mental gymnastics to convince himself the dead could appear in photographs. He retained his belief despite some of his favourite photographers being exposed. He shared an interest in the elderly photographer Mrs Deane with Oliver Lodge, who once invited her to stay at his home and when it was demonstrated she had used images of celebrities from magazines to create her 'extras', he defended such actions as being the result of pressure to produce results. No doubt all spirit photographers, argued Doyle, sometimes faked images to produce results when the spirits were being uncooperative.

In 1922 Doyle was distracted from fraudulent spirit photographers by a personal crisis. He had gone to America for a lecture tour about his experiences with spiritualism and while he anticipated some abuse during his tour he never expected to be blamed for a rash of suicides. In comparison the spirit 'extras' scandal seemed mundane.

In April 1922 Maude Fancher gave the disinfectant Lysol to her two-year-old baby Cecil to drink. Lysol was a popular suicide method and it did not take long to kill the unfortunate toddler. Maude went on to drink a dose herself but her death would take considerably longer. Maude was a recent convert to spiritualism and had a warped idea in her mind that if she was to die she would be able to return as a spirit guide to help her husband who was suffering from business failures and sickness. Maude was clearly a disturbed person. In 1916 her father had committed suicide and three years later she had attended séances with her husband to try and contact him. Somewhere along the line she developed the notion that she would be more useful in the afterlife to her beleaguered husband. It was said that the lectures Sir Arthur Conan Doyle had given on the life beyond had helped to confirm an idea in her mind that the hereafter was much nicer than the now. As a poor woman with a sick husband, little income, a child to raise and no hope for the future it is perhaps natural to see why she started to contemplate suicide.

Doyle was questioned on the matter and stated 'that a suicide sacrifice would be in vain because the spirits of those who took their own lives were sequestered for a period on the other side of the grave and were forbidden the consolation of conversation.' These comments were not mentioned to the distraught husband.

Fast on the heels of this tragedy came the story of Frank Alexei who stabbed his wife in the forehead with an ice pick because he saw an evil spirit in the shape of a raven fly in from Carnegie Hall and sit on his wife while she slept. Another young man killed himself and his roommate on the understanding there were no gas bills in the hereafter.

In yet another incident a troubled girl was found unconscious in a touring car garage with a bottle of bromides – a sleeping draught – nearby. First thoughts were that she had attempted suicide. The girl was deeply disturbed, claiming she was the maid of Harold Vanderbilt (he denied this) and that her name was Mildred Preston, though she sometimes gave the surname Passwick. Mildred explained that on the night she was found she was overcome with the urge to visit St. Michael's cemetery and try to contact her deceased mother. When she arrived at the cemetery the gates were locked, so she walked and walked until, exhausted, she came upon the garage. Mildred latterly claimed she was an artist with a studio in Greenwich Village, though an address found written on a card in her pocket was for Portsmouth, Ohio. She said that was her father's address and she had not lived with him for several months, having come to New York and gained employment with Mr Vanderbilt. Mildred and the other cases mentioned were clearly mentally unwell individuals, but that did not stop a hue and cry being raised against spiritualism and directed towards Doyle.

Doyle did his best to counter the accusations. He said they were caused by ignorance of the true meaning of spiritualism and were not a direct result of his lectures. Indeed none of the individuals had mentioned Doyle explicitly, but it had been later implied by the newspapers. What was obvious was the dangerous hold spiritualism could have over the naïve and poor. Even more apparent was the rising fear of evil and demons. Doyle had been accused of communing with the devil in Australia, and now a man in America had murdered his wife because an evil spirit had appeared to him. Back in Britain there was also a dark element emerging. Aleister Crowley was calling himself the Devil, Dennis Wheatley was writing hugely popular novels that explored satanic rituals and witchcraft, and even the Cottingly fairies represented the dark side to some. Psychic investigator Harry Price was examining aggressive poltergeists and a homicidal invisible mongoose (not without reservations, however). He would later dabble in his own satanic experiments in Germany, as a publicity stunt.

For Doyle and Lodge, two men who had tried to raise the profile of spiritualism to bring hope to the masses, this counter-productive trend was upsetting and difficult to understand. Papers claimed there was a witchcraft epidemic (in fact, wholly untrue outside of novels) and the general public seemed to be more confused about faith and religion than ever before. In some regards it was just as well Doyle passed over himself in 1930, before the height of black magic madness. Doyle was soon making guest appearances at séances after his death. At his memorial service in Albert Hall the medium Estelle Roberts said she saw him walk onstage in full evening dress and take his place on an empty seat strategically placed between his wife, Jean and son, Denis. Doyle was soon making guest appearances across the globe. While some thought it natural for the exponent of spiritualism, sceptics saw it as a good publicity stunt. Whatever the case, Doyle had left his mark on post-war spiritualism, for better or worse.

CHAPTER FIVE

What Makes a Medium?

It became quite fashionable between the wars for amateurs to investigate hauntings, test mediums and dabble in all things strange and wonderful. There were certainly enough mediums needing testing to go around. Just as one case of psychic talent was proved fraudulent, another 'completely genuine' case emerged. For a brief period it seemed every impoverished family in Britain was suddenly developing clairvoyant powers and attracting media attention.

So it was that W. J. Crawford, a mechanical engineer at the Belfast Polytechnic learned of a fascinating case of mediumship in 1916. Crawford was like Lodge in many ways, with his background of scientific knowledge and reasonable education. In fact most psychic detectives of the period came from the middle classes and showed a hunger for learning. Crawford's big chance came when he heard of the Goligher family.

The Golighers were a working-class family living in Belfast. Mr Goligher was a collar-cutter, a piecework occupation with little pay, and his daughter Kate was a blouse-cutter who was drawing attention for her mediumistic powers. The family had become known as the Goligher Circle and Crawford was drawn to investigate them even as war raged in Europe. Kate produced typical phenomena at séances – tables lifted and raps could be heard, even with the medium's feet tied to her chair legs and everyone in the circle supposedly holding hands. Though the sittings were conducted in darkness, if warning was given it was permitted to light a red lamp, or to use a card painted with phosphorescence, or even to take a photograph. In one image Crawford captured a hazy white light appearing to fountain up from Kate. Crawford believed this was the visual manifestation of the psychic force that lifted the table and that it had appeared specifically for his camera. Kate shuddered and convulsed for ten minutes after the photograph was taken, convincing Crawford further that an excess of energy had been used to create the object.

Crawford was hooked. Using his knowledge of mechanics he described Kate's psychic projections in terms of engineering rods that projected from the medium's body and moved the table. He spent time measuring and examining in complete darkness these objects and came to the conclusion they could vary dramatically in size, shape and even hardness. He said they had suckers on the ends which would stick to the base of the table. At times, he explained, he heard the suckers slipping over the wooden surface of the table. After almost a year of study he was finally allowed to hold one of the rods in his upturned hand. Crawford was astonished by its strangeness which seemed impossible to describe, at once it was hard and soft, solid but liquid, heavy yet light. On occasion he felt his hand pass completely through it, with a sensation of a sticky, cold breeze passing over his skin.

Crawford wanted tangible proof he could show to others and placed trays of clay under the table during séances to get an imprint of the rods. Instead he found marks resembling the texture of the stockings Kate wore. Others would have considered this proof Kate's feet had worked loose of their bonds, but Crawford was far more fanciful in his explanation. Clearly when the ectoplasm escaped from Kate it slipped down her leg and had to pour through her stockings before emerging, thus it would briefly retain the pattern of the stocking fabric which it imprinted onto the clay. He was equally unflappable when he found clay on Kate's shoe – it had obviously been deposited there by the ectoplasm as it returned to Kate! He was convinced he had seen the psychic substance wriggling across the floor and up the medium's leg. He also attributed the scuffling noises he heard around Kate's feet before the table lifted as being caused by the emergence of ectoplasm.

Crawford was clearly deluding himself, but he persisted nonetheless to be as thorough as he could so he might prove his case. He wanted to know where the ectoplasm came from precisely, and had Kate don white calico knickers sprinkled with powdered carmine, under the supervision of Mrs Crawford, to produce a trail. To his satisfaction this proved that the rods (or at least something) were emerging from between Kate's legs and returning there when done. Unlike some mediums Kate did not perform naked and when she started producing solid ectoplasm it appeared to be the infamous cheesecloth falling from under her skirt, where it had no doubt been hidden.

There was also a sexual element to all this. Kate shuddered and groaned before the ectoplasm emerged, her pulse rose rapidly and her body tensed. Crawford rested his hand on her thigh and felt her flesh soften, sink in on itself and then expand again. He felt her breasts and confirmed they had become full and firm. A lot of séances seemed to degenerate into strange men groping young women under the pretences of rational investigation.

The stage magician and famed debunker of mediums, Harry Houdini, met Crawford during his investigations and was shown the photographs. To his eyes the 'psychic manifestation' appeared like twisted cloth emerging from beneath Kate's skirt, but Crawford was adamant he had discovered genuine phenomena. When he had left, Houdini was asked what he made of the engineer. 'He seems mad to me.' He answered.

Mad or not, Crawford was suffering mental problems. He was in the process of completing his third manuscript on the Goligher experiments when he suffered a nervous breakdown and committed suicide. In a letter that could almost be deemed a public suicide note he wrote to the editor of *Light* assuring readers that the Goligher sittings had had nothing to do with his fall. He still believed, he said, and the work he had done prior to his breakdown would stand the test of time. He affirmed positively that the grave was not the end of existence, and perhaps his suicide can be viewed as one final experiment to prove this to himself.

Unfortunately for Crawford his work did not stand the test of time. Another investigator was asked to visit the Goligher Circle and confirm Crawford's work. Almost immediately he proved the ectoplasm was nothing more than muslin. The Golighers were adamant he was wrong. Crawford had worked four years before he was satisfied, surely his successor could give them the same attention? But Crawford had been blind. The Golighers were recorded as cunning (but far from subtle) frauds and quietly consigned to the annals of spiritualist history.

Scientific American and 'Margery'

Rationalists began to feel rather under-threat as the 1920s boomed. Spiritualism, tapping into the high emotions left over from the war, seemed to be gaining the upper hand in the popular imagination. Scientifically there was nothing conclusive about mediumistic powers other than those proved conclusively fraudulent, but that failed to deter scores of believers. It was starting to feel, with ghosts and séances becoming regular news headlines, that something practical needed to be done to even the balance. The US magazine *Scientific American* came up with a clever idea. In 1922 they announced they would give $2,500 to the first person who could produce a genuine psychic photograph, or other psychic phenomena, that would convince a panel of scientists and paranormal investigators. That sort of money was equivalent to over $33,000 today and a significant sum of money to people suffering the poverty of post-war life. It could hardly fail to bring the genuine forward.

Harry Houdini was invited onto the committee of experts who would test prospective mediums. Known for his cynicism towards psychic phenomena and his knack for revealing fraud, he was the ultimate test for any clairvoyant. The honest had nothing to fear, but the hoaxers out for a quick buck would be in serious trouble. The lure of all that money was, however, a hefty temptation and many mediums came forward. Only two were deemed worthy enough to be examined by the committee. The first of this pair was quickly exposed as a fraud when a device indicated he was out of his chair while spirit activity was happening in the darkened séance room. That left the medium 'Margery' as the sole contender for the prize.

Margery was in fact the wife of successful Boston surgeon L. R. G. Crandon, and was not motivated by financial gain to fake her powers. Her husband was wealthy enough as it was to make $2,500 seem a trifle. Margery had visited Paris, convincing investigators Geley and Richet of her talent, along with the SPR and BCPS in London, before coming forward for the *Scientific American* contest. Margery astounded her select audiences with moving furniture, apports of roses and pigeons, mysterious floating lights and speaking in the voice of her deceased brother Walter, who could be mischievous or just plain obnoxious.

Sitting before the committee, naked accept for a dressing gown, Margery produced her usual range of tricks. Several of the investigators were fascinated, but Houdini was outraged. He saw Margery as nothing more than a charlatan and was so frustrated when his colleagues continued to give her the benefit of the doubt that he angrily abandoned the committee.

Margery had the *Scientific American* panel divided and Eric Dingwall was asked to come to America from the SPR and give his opinion. By this point Margery was entertaining her predominantly male crowd with ectoplasmic phenomenon which could be recorded by photography. In an early photograph Margery is seen obscured by a cloud of luminous light said to be created by Walter, and the sitter on the left has a vague shape hovering almost beneath his hand, suggested to be a baby's hand clutching his little finger.

Ectoplasm did not just emerge as light from Margery. During a series of sittings with Dingwall in 1925 she began producing meat-like ectoplasm from her abdomen. Margery's séances now took on a strangely disturbing sexual element. Naked except for stockings and dressing gown, which was open to allow the 'ectoplasm' to escape, Margery emitted groans in the darkened room and permitted her (male) investigators to touch her naked skin and feel the strange forms emerging from her. In one sitting Dingwall heard a rustling in Margery's lap and ran his hand up her leg until he reached her thigh and felt an object he compared to uncooked liver. Even today it would seem salacious for strangers, under the guise of scientific research, to sit in a dark room, groping a naked woman who was producing fleshy objects from her feminine quarters.

Dingwall asked to take a photograph of the extrusions and this was permitted. The images illustrate exactly how lascivious the situation had become. In one Margery reclines in a chair, her dressing gown open from the waist down to show her lower body. For modesty someone has placed a handkerchief over her pubic region, though failing to entirely cover it, while an object that looks distinctly like raw liver sits on Mr Crandon's hand, just above his wife's genitals and apparently connected to her naval by a string of similar flesh. It should be noted that it was well known that female mediums would hide objects inside themselves to produce during séances and this had caused a good deal of fascination among investigators, who would often insist on given vaginal exams before a sitting.

In another photograph Margery is facing the camera (everyone has turned their heads away at the moment of the photograph because of the powerful flash used), her legs splayed wide and held on one side by Mr Crandon and on the other by Dingwall. A cloth has hastily been pressed between her legs to maintain her dignity, if that is how you can describe the scene, while another fleshy hand lurks on her abdomen. Dingwall took his photographs to various people including one of the *Scientific American* committee, William McDougall, professor of psychology, who gave it as his opinion that the substance on Margery's stomach was animal lung or trachea cut crudely into the shape of a hand. Dingwall then spoke to a gynaecologist who considered it entirely possible for the 'hand' to be hidden in the vagina and expelled when needed. Not long after this Margery suffered a uterine haemorrhage, which ended the ectoplasmic manifestations and Dingwall returned to Britain with mixed feelings. The ectoplasm was fraudulent, but other strange things had occurred during séances which he could not explain, so he retired with an open mind on the case. As for *Scientific American* they never did find a genuine medium to give their $2,500 to.

Harry Price – Dubious Detective

One of the harshest critics of mediums and spiritualists between the wars, and an enemy to Lodge, was the arrogant, cocky and self-confident Harry Price. Harry was tall, with a long, heavy face. He could not be termed dashing or handsome, but he had a charm to his features when he wasn't looking down on people. He usually reserved his charms for pretty girls. He made his living as a paper bag salesman, but preferred to promote himself as a psychic detective, a great debunker of ghosts and, above all, a master publicist for the supernatural.

Harry was a natural showman with a flair for self-publicity. He was also a liar. Readers of his 1942 autobiography were led to believe that he was born in the country surroundings of Shropshire to a genteel family when in fact he was born in a typical Victorian slum tenement at 37 Red Lion Square, Holborn, London. His mother, Emma Price had met Harry's father Edward when she was around thirteen or fourteen, she was pregnant soon after. Edward was a grocer in his forties and the scandal ruined his business, as many customers boycotted his shop. Edward was forced to move with Emma, who he married in 1876 when she was fifteen, and restart his life. Emma gave birth to Annie Price, Harry's older sister, but pregnancy at such a young age took a heavy toll on her and after Harry's birth in 1881 she was often ill or away in hospital. Harry masked this scandalous early life from his colleagues, friends and potential audience, presenting himself instead as a middle-class cockney gent. It was a complete fabrication.

Yet, whatever his origins and scruples regarding the truth, there is no denying Harry Price became one of the most influential figures in post-war supernatural circles. On the one hand mediums and spirit photographers were jumping up everywhere to play on people's grief and on the other there was Harry, who through his connections to various organisations (one being the SPR), spent many hours attacking mediums. It might have been a noble cause, but unfortunately Harry was in it for the money. He didn't particularly care if a medium was real or fake, just as long as investigating them brought him fame and income. Such a fickle character seems to be rather typical of the post-war era when so many were manipulating national grief to their own advantage. The only difference with Harry was that he was not selling the afterlife, but destroying it. Because of this alternative stance, and his tireless self-promotion, he is still remembered rightly or wrongly as a formidable figure in early psychic investigation, and for the assaults he launched at Sir Oliver Lodge and his complicated relationship with Sir Arthur Conan Doyle.

Harry was a poor academic, but had ambitions beyond his limited education. In 1899 he claimed to have made one of the first working portable wireless sets and wrote a piece for the *Westminster Gazette*, adding that he had been able to photograph a radio wave. Considering Oliver Lodge had only just invented the coherer to detect sparks from a transmitter and Hertz had only recently proved radio waves existed, it seems unlikely this failed student and poor engineer could achieve what greater men had been struggling for years to demonstrate. Besides, the supposed photograph was never forthcoming. Perhaps this is evidence of Harry's earliest fabrication to gain fame for himself, but it does suggest something else. Harry was always antagonistic towards Lodge, and mocked him openly for his beliefs (particularly after the publication of *Raymond*) and never ingratiated himself with him like he did with other spiritualists such as Sir Arthur Conan-Doyle. Could this in part have been due to jealousy?

Harry was thirty-three when the First World War broke out. When medically examined he was classified as 'C3', fit only for sedentary work on the Home Front. It is not apparent why this was the case. There was no evidence of bad health, though Harry was a heavy smoker and may not have been capable of extended exercise, such as long marches. He also later recorded problems with his heart, but it is not clear if these were genuine ailments or an excuse to avoid people. In any case Harry spent the war in England, and Harry being Harry, the drama, horror and devastation of the war drifted over him and failed to dent his busy self-absorption. He was working with the British College of Psychic Science (BCPS) on spirit photography in 1914 when he claimed to have captured a disembodied spirit hand in a photograph.

Despite this work Harry felt he had 'missed out' on the war, so he started to spread grandiose stories of how he helped the war effort. He told his loyal followers he had tried to interest the Royal Flying Corps in his skills as a photographer, going so far as claiming he had improved the photographic filters they were using for aerial reconnaissance. Naturally this was nonsense.

He subsequently alluded to the factory he owned and ran for making shells. In reality Harry was simply another munitions worker, probably at Allen-West, Brighton and while making shells was by no means a safe or pleasant occupation, it was a far cry from the experiences of soldiers at the front.

The war stirred up a lot of 'ghosts'. Sir Arthur Conan Doyle wrote,

> The deaths occurring in almost every family in the land brought a sudden and concentrated interest in the life after death. People not only asked the question, 'If a man die shall he live again?' but they eagerly sought to know if communication was possible with the dear ones they had lost. They sought for 'the touch of a vanished hand, and the sound of a voice that is still'.

Into this new world Harry presented himself as the great sceptic, as the hero of the rational thinkers and the defender of those who might be exploited by fake mediums. He would later change his persona and become the most ardent defender of certain mediums (when it suited him), but during the war and just after he was dead against it. He enjoyed exposing frauds and regularly criticised those who believed in mediumship. He quickly spotted a target in Sir Oliver Lodge.

Lodge's book about Raymond had won him appreciation and respect among spiritualists. *Raymond or Life and Death* was an almost instant bestseller and gave hope and comfort to many, but it only won antagonism from Harry. From a safe distance he belittled Lodge's work and remarked that the evidence for Raymond's 'return' was nowhere near 'the standard of evidence that Sir Oliver would have demanded from one of his own students who claimed an important discovery in the field of physics'. This was stern talk from a man who would later see no harm in faking paranormal activities himself when he needed 'proof'.

Lodge avoided taking Harry's criticism personally and maintained an apathetic disbelief in Harry's work. Their paths would cross continuously in the future, as the ghost hunting world was small.

Just before the war Harry had been introduced to another influential figure in the spiritualism debate – Harry Houdini. Houdini at this period found a confederate in Harry. Harry's personal views on spiritualism, hauntings or ghosts were never clear and it is probable he had no concrete convictions, other than that chasing ghosts was a good moneyspinner in post-war Britain. Harry linked himself with Houdini because it was good publicity and Houdini might prove an important sponsor. Throughout his life Harry recognised the need to have a 'big name' to make introductions for him and in the 1920s Houdini was the biggest in both ordinary and spiritual circles.

Houdini was a first-rate conjurer and escapologist. He toured his native America performing magic and demonstrating how mediums produced their most spectacular hoaxes. He could manufacture ghostly notes, free himself from bonds to show how a medium might release themselves to trick an audience, fake spirit manifestations and demonstrate how writing might mysteriously appear on blank slates or objects be thrown about the room. Mediums usually performed séances in darkened rooms, sometimes also with curtained cabinets, giving plenty of scope for impressive illusions. Houdini could achieve the same results on a well-lit stage, further exposing the fraudulent nature of séances.

However, Houdini was a conflicted man when it came to spiritualism. He had lost his beloved mother and throughout his life held out a candle of hope that there was some form of afterlife and that she might be contacted. Through all his experiments he hoped that one medium would prove to be the genuine article so he could obtain a final message from his mother. He failed in this, but while Houdini was struggling with his own emotions, the outside world only saw a first-class debunker. Lauded by the sceptical, feared by the spiritualists, Houdini was the ultimate meal ticket for any would-be paranormal investigator.

Harry ingratiated himself with Houdini and for a time was both friend and confidant to the magician – in this instance Houdini's usually wise judgement and sixth sense for fraudsters failed him. To confirm his status as a pseudo-scientist of the paranormal, Harry became the BCPS's leading investigator of mediums.

One of his earliest cases was that of Ada Deane, a spirit photographer from Islington and a person who had impressed Sir Oliver Lodge and had been invited to stay at his home (see Chapter Seven). Ada Deane was a peculiar character variously described as simple and honest, or cunning and disreputable. There is little doubt Ada was faking her photographs, often with very basic methods. That she was not caught out more often says more about the hopes and desperation of her clients than about any great skill on her part.

In 1921 the *Daily Sketch* published a story that had originally appeared in *Light*, the spiritualist weekly. The story told how a woman, Adeline Perryman, had gone to visit Ada and was certain photographs taken of her and her late father (who emerged spiritually on the plates according to Ada) were fakes. Adeline was planning on taking the plates and having them examine for fraud. She was certain this was why Ada had 'accidentally' allowed her cat to destroy them. Once the story was in the *Daily Sketch* it was out before the general public and before long the Occult Committee, a group of select magicians who aimed to expose fraud, had hired Harry to investigate Ada.

Harry quickly proved that Ada was using clippings of peoples' faces from popular magazines to create 'spirits' on her photographs. While the result failed to impact on Ada's trade (it would take an even more dramatic hoax on her part to do that) Harry had hopes his success would work wonders on his career within the paranormal investigation scene. So he was disappointed when his involvement in the case was virtually glossed over by the Occult Committee report.

However more work soon came his way via the Society for Psychical Research (SPR). The SPR had been tracking another spirit photographer, William Hope. Hope was a working class man from the poverty struck districts of Manchester. The *Illustrated London News* described him as 'a niggardly, coarse-mouthed man'. Despite his working class origins and rough appearance, Hope quickly attracted flocks of people after taking a photograph of a co-worker that included the image of the man's long-dead sister.

As with all spirit photographs we will never know if Hope's first image was a fluke or a fake. A stray burst of light or damage to the plate might have created the first anomaly, which was then wistfully transformed into the face of a loved one. Afterwards fraud was necessary to keep results coming. Or perhaps Hope saw an opportunity to make a comfortable career for himself and was faking his photographs from the start.

Hope developed his business in spirit photography and became part of the Crewe Circle, a group of nine friends led by a Mrs Buxton who had been praying for the gift of spirit photography. Hope to them was a god-send and they regularly posed for him. Just before the war Hope moved with Mrs Buxton to London and there they operated the Crewe Circle under the patronage of the BCPS.

Unlike Ada Deane, Hope did not appeal to Sir Oliver Lodge. Perhaps it was his coarse manner or low origins, but he failed to impress the scientist as the benign and elderly Ada had. Hope refused to give an interview to Lodge before the war and the SPR were highly sceptical of his talents. Yet try as hard as they might to prove Hope was nothing but a common trickster, the cunning photographer stayed one step ahead. He was well aware that his new career and his finances relied solely on preventing exposure. He stayed as far away from the SPR as possible.

The only option was to get a man on the inside and the likely recruit seemed to be Harry Price. Harry was not only a member of the BCPS, but he was friendly with James Hewat McKenzie and his wife, who had founded the college. As a trusted member he would have no problem getting access to Hope. Harry was sensible enough to realise his involvement with the SPR could cause a rift between him and the McKenzies, especially if he proved their new project was a fraud. So he distanced himself by introducing James Seymour, a member of the Magic Circle, as the person who would perform experiments on Hope's talents.

Price was invited to submit a package of photographic plates to Hope before the experiment. This was typical practice and was supposed to prove to a sceptical audience that the plates had not been tampered with – that is, if you believed the plates used at the photograph session were the ones you had previously supplied. Harry doubted it, so he decided to arrange a trap. In collaboration with the factory that supplied the photographic plates he had the originals exposed to x-rays and an image of a lion rampant marked on them invisibly. The four plates he intended to send had a quarter of the lion on each, so when placed together they became a set. Only when they were developed would the lion be seen.

When Harry attended the sitting he was convinced he had seen Hope switch plates, but the real proof came when the Crewe Circle, Hope's supporters, innocently asked James Seymour if he would like to develop the plates himself. He did in Hope's dark room and rapidly saw that the plates had no lion marked upon them.

The resulting exposure of the fraud sent Hope into hiding while his valiant supporters, among them Sir Arthur Conan Doyle, rallied round and accused the SPR of being the perpetrators of fraud! Conan Doyle was particularly vocal in suggesting the marked plates had been deliberately switched by the SPR so that Hope would be exposed no matter if his spirit photographs were genuine or not.

A few days after the scandal was announced Doyle received a mysterious parcel of a blank photographic plate. An anonymous note with it stated the plate was none other than the one marked with a lion that Hope had deliberately switched. Since the lion was not visible on the plate until after it was developed it seemed only an insider could know this was the correct one. That the note with it came on BCPS headed paper was also suspicious. Doyle sent the plate to the headquarters of *Light*, who developed the photograph and confirmed it was one of the four x-rayed plates. *Light* planned to publish the story in its Christmas edition, however Harry wanted some publicity for himself and, still smarting from being brushed over in the Occult Committee's report, he leaked the story to *Truth*, the main rival to *Light*.

This naturally went down badly, but Harry was determined to get as much as he could from the Hope case. He published a pamphlet on the story *Cold Light on Spiritualist Phenomena: An Experiment with the Crewe Circle*. It seems highly likely Harry was the person who anonymously sent Doyle the undeveloped plate. Only he and James Seymour could have known which one it was. The irony of this is Doyle believed firmly that Harry had been duped by the SPR and that if another experiment with Hope was done it would be obvious that he was genuine.

Harry was riding the wave of publicity the Hope case had provided. He planned to reprint the book, *The Revelations of a Spirit-Medium* (first published anonymously in 1891), along with Eric Dingwall, research officer of the SPR. The book was in essence a how-to guide for fraudulent mediums, describing how to trick a gullible public. Houdini wrote a gushing review of the book believing it educational in the exposure of frauds.

Dingwall and Harry had become friendly since the former had returned from American. It was Dingwall who had suggested Harry as the man for unmasking Hope. In 1922 they set out on a new case to investigate the medium Willi Schneider in Germany. Four years previously England and Germany had been at war, and now they were collaborating in the most bizarre of ways.

Schneider was in the charge of Dr Albert von Schrenk-Notzing who had already spent a great deal of time examining the medium's talents during séances at his mansion flat in Munich. In May 1922 he wrote to England asking that someone from the SPR come over and see this wondrous medium he had discovered. Schneider had won over many sceptics when, in a trance, he appeared to change personalities, becoming a girl named Lola Montez who in life had been the mistress of Ludwig I. Despite being firmly tied up, dressed in a one-piece robe and dotted with luminous pins that enabled sitters to see his outline in the dark, Schneider still managed to get an accordion to play a tune with a strangely nebulous hand-like shape fingering the keys. A handkerchief knotted itself, a tambourine rattled and ectoplasm dribbled from his mouth.

Though his tricks were far from new (tinkling tambourines and ectoplasm were common features of pre-war séances) it was the fact that no one had been able to catch him out that made him seem so remarkable.

Dingwall and Harry duly went to Germany and sat in on a séance with Schneider. Dingwall was entranced by the medium and came away convinced by his powers. Harry, always quick to see the way the wind was blowing, chose not to oppose his colleague and cast aside almost two decades of sceptical thinking when he whole-heartedly agreed Schneider was the real deal.

Harry's reversal in stance was characteristic of his opportunism. Going against Dingwall would be dangerous for his career, especially after the Hope scandal and rumours of fraudulence on the part of the investigators. However when Harry wrote an article on the matter he chose to hedge his bets with the result he was criticised by Dingwall for being 'flagrantly double-edged, pointless, unfocused and so far from the truth that few would recognise it.'

Dingwall was frustrated by Harry's lack of commitment to Schneider, but also angered that he had not been included or informed of the article before it was published. Harry found it was too late to care. He had already sold the exact same article to another magazine and when that was also published his friendship with Dingwall was effectively over, as was his association with the SPR.

The publicity Harry had received over the Hope and Schneider cases launched him as a writer and speaker on psychic matter. His name was immediately recognisable in the papers and he attracted an eager audience who believed in him completely. Unfortunately for them, Harry's convictions were less about proving or disproving the existence of spirits, and more about the glory and money he could make from psychic phenomena. Harry was no different from the mediums he debunked. He played his audience, gave them what they wanted and was not opposed to trickery to achieve results. Harry began to mimic Houdini in giving performances on how séance phenomena was faked, yet despite this Doyle remained firmly convinced that Harry was an ardent believer in spiritualism.

Harry was everything to everybody, but his duplicitous act would eventually catch him out. While he was cashing in on his links with Sir Arthur Conan Doyle – who could introduce him to the right circles – he was also mocking him. Yet Sir Oliver Lodge remained his prime target. One anecdote he liked to relate was a story about Lodge being shown a photograph of a Red Indian spirit guide that turned out to be identical to a picture of an Indian recently published on the cover of *My Magazine* in October 1920. Instead of denouncing the photograph, Lodge told a sceptical public that there was a danger in jumping to conclusions about fraud as, 'we do not know how the photograph had been obtained.' Harry found it highly amusing that the great scientist could be so gullible.

Harry was quickly cashing in on his new persona as the great debunker of spiritual fraud. In 1922, when *Scientific American* offered its prize of $2,500 to the first medium who could produce a genuine spirit photograph, the magazine editorial board felt they were on fairly safe ground as so far no one had produced a photograph that was not easy to prove a fake. Harry, always short on funds, saw the prize as a grand opportunity and set about finding a medium he could present to the *Scientific American* panel as genuine.

Stella Cranshaw almost fell into Harry's lap, and the pretty and tractable twenty-one-year-old auxiliary nurse rapidly became his favourite medium. Harry alleged later that he had met her on a train when she ran out of reading material and they exchanged magazines. More likely he was introduced to her via another spiritualist who had known the Cranshaw family for many years. In any case Stella was quick to convince Harry of her talents. In 1923 Harry published a pamphlet about her skills – *An Account of some Original Experiments in Psychical Research*.

1 Oliver Lodge was a man of science and religion, he staked his entire reputation on proving his son had survived death.

2 Raymond was always a serious child, some might say sullen, but he was kind-hearted and liked to help others. He was also a clever engineer like his father.

3 Raymond was fascinated by cars, which were an expensive hobby pre-war. He regularly drove with his older brothers and in one séance Raymond was reported to have described a motoring trip.

4 Another genius Raymond invention, the sand yacht, designed with his brothers, could race across the sands at a high speed. It appears a forerunner of the vehicles seen today using kites to glide along. Raymond never had a chance to pursue and improve his idea.

5 In this picture Archduke Franz Ferdinand's assassin is hauled away by police and military officers. The murder sparked a war, but it also contained an element of mystery because Ferdinand's old tutor allegedly dreamed of the assassination several hours before it happened.

6 One of the last photographs of Raymond, taken formally by a photographer for the family.

7 Raymond, like so many, had portrait photographs taken before he left his family in case he failed to return.

8 An early batch of soldiers about to leave with the BEF. Many would not return, but in the first days of war there was a sense of adventure about the trip. Raymond Lodge would have stood just like these men waiting to catch a train to the front, hardly expecting he would never come home.

9 This stark image is the sort of nightmarish scene Britons were regularly envisioning. Entitled 'The Grey Horde' the picture shows German troops marching across a Belgium field. The enemy was vilified to an extreme level during the war.

10 Trench life was particularly grim and demoralising for the soldiers. Officers, like Raymond, had the opportunity to live in the reasonable comfort of a dug-out, but ordinary soldiers slept in the open, as can be seen in this image.

11 It is the iconic image that summoned thousands of men to war and made Lord Kitchener the face of the conflict. Kitchener's influence, however, ran further than a mere poster.

12 Loved and despised in equal measure Lord Kitchener was viewed by some as having the power to win the war. His death was devastating and led to constant 'sightings' of the departed man.

13 General French was the bitter rival to Lord Kitchener. French thought Kitchener mad, but his rival had more clout than him and Kitchener was eventually able to have French replaced.

14 Raymond was posted to Ypres, which he mentioned to his family when writing home. Ypres was a devastated place as can be seen in this wartime image. Soldiers would flit through the ruins under bombardment, while the few remaining civilians with nowhere to go eked out a life until the destruction grew too bad.

15 Talbot House still stands and remains part of the Toc H movement. It was severely damaged in the war but 'Tubby' Clayton was determined to make it a 'Haven in Hell'. *With Permission of Cheilbuseyne*

16 The Toc H movement had been so successful that it was determined to keep it going after the war. It was hoped it might promote peace, though this was not the case it still exists to this day.

17 The Cenotaph was unveiled in 1920 and became a focal point for future Remembrance services. Throughout the twenties spirit photographer Ada Deane would attend the Armistice Day service in front of the Cenotaph and take photographs of 'spirits' in attendance.

18 The selection and burial of the Unknown Warrior was almost mystical in itself, and served as a focal point for all those families who had lost men and never had a chance to bury them. Like the Cenotaph it caused some debate as to its appropriateness.

19 The tragedy of the immediate post-war years was the terrible poverty many surviving servicemen faced. Here a group protest at not being able to find work. It was not unknown for unemployed servicemen to attend Armistice services wearing pawn tickets instead of medals.

20 This is the first image of Raymond (front row, second from right) the Lodge family received after a séance informing them of its existence. Oliver Lodge thought it clear proof of communication with the spirit world as the medium had claimed someone was 'leaning' on Raymond in a way he disliked. It is clear in this image that the man behind Raymond is leaning on him and causing Raymond to tilt awkwardly to the side.

21 This photograph was taken at the same time, but shows the sitters in slightly different positions. Raymond is no longer being leaned upon. Oliver Lodge remarked if he had seen this picture first, rather than the previous one, he would have assumed the medium had been making vague statements.

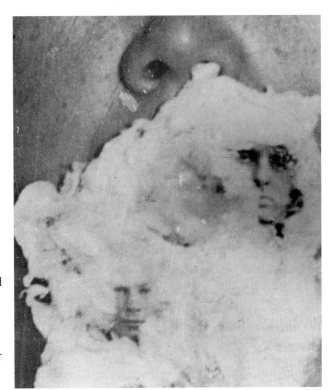

22 This strange image of an unknown medium appears to show a teleplasmic appearance of Raymond and one other person. It could also look like regurgitated cheesecloth with small photos interspersed. The one said to be Raymond seems very similar to his portrait, but it is not clear and could be someone else.

23 Sir Arthur Conan Doyle staked his reputation on proving Spiritualism, partly due to his wartime losses. He was a close colleague of Sir Oliver Lodge.

24 Harry Price was either the great sceptic, or the great believer depending on the mood he was in and what publicity he could achieve. Here he sits for notorious spirit photographer William Hope, who he went on to expose as a fraud. *With Permission of PerfectBlue97*

25 Borley was a typical late Victorian rectory. Its reputation was based on a series of stories made up by Harry Price and others, but it remains known as one of the most haunted houses in England. *With Permission of Telrunya*

26 Harry Price's experiments into witchcraft were not warmly received. Here he is about to try to turn a goat into a man. The goat looks decidedly reluctant to participate. *With Permission of the German Federal Archive*

27 Joanna Southcott believed herself a vessel of God, pregnant with the new messiah. Unfortunately this proved to be a severe case of dropsy. Her cult, however, still lingers to this day.

28 When two little girls took pictures of fairies in a Yorkshire beck it caused quite a stir. Some believed the images genuine, others, including Oliver Lodge, were sceptical.

29 Spirit photography was controversial, as the medium was easy to manipulate for interesting effects. Here a young woman appears to peer out at the camera, superimposed on a man and woman. This may have been a double-exposure using a cardboard cut out. *With Permission National Media Museum*

30 This disturbing scene sums up the power of grief. A woman rests her hand on a dead loved one as a picture is taken and miraculously a ghost appears. For some this was proof of an afterlife, for others it was proof photographers were good at manipulating images. *With permission of the National Media Museum*

Above left: 31 This is one of William Hope's spirit photographs. It has the appearance of having been over-exposed and the female sitter's face is slightly distorted, indicating further tampering. *With Permission of PerfectBlue 97*

Above right: 32 A streak of light crosses between the sitters, it might have been made by a splash from the developing chemicals, or the small torch William always had to hand. Alternatively it could be a spirit... *With Permission of PerfectBlue 97*

33 In this William Hope image a mist forms over the sitters, who are from a psychical society and include Sir Arthur Conan Doyle on the far left. He was a firm believer in spirit photography. *With Permission of PerfectBlue 97*

34 Aleister hopped from one New Age cult to another, often leaving disharmony in his wake. This photograph shows Crowley while a member of the Golden Dawn (*c.* 1910) with his typical fixed stare and stoic expression.

35 Successful author Dennis Wheatley helped to promote the idea in the twenties and thirties that witchcraft and devil worship was on the rise. In actuality this was far from the case, but the media could not resist jumping on the bandwagon and printing lurid tales of scandalous practices. *With Permission of Allan Warren*

Experiments with Stella began in the spring of 1923. Using a control called 'Palma' who was supposedly a long deceased child, Stella communicated remarkable messages to her enraptured audience. Along with the usual spirit goings-on those present at Stella's performance were able to record dramatic temperature drops and at one particular séance the complete destruction of a wooden table. But it was at her fourth séance with Harry that Stella produced the evidence that would confirm to many her status as a genuine medium.

It was 12 April and in a darkened room at 16 Queensberry Place Stella slipped into a deep trance and told her audience that she could see a copy of the *Daily Mail* materialising before her. The newspaper was dated 19 May and in large capital letters she could read the words 'Andrew Salt'. She had the sensation that a boy was falling over and a man was kneeling over him and pouring white powder from a bottle or tin to give to the boy. The message was duly noted but it made little sense until the *Daily Mail* appeared on 19 May.

To the surprise of Stella's audience the paper had run a full-page advertisement on its front cover for Andrews Liver Salts. To illustrate the advert a boy was in tears having stumbled and spilled a tin of the salts while a man was nearby standing over him.

Harry quickly took the reins of this remarkable story, writing to both the paper and the salts' manufacturer about the advert. He had it confirmed that until May there had been no certainty of what the advert would be, nor had it ever been printed before. Harry submitted the evidence from the séance to the advertising manager at the *Daily Mail* who was duly impressed and convinced by Stella. With Harry's reputation, however, there is always room for doubt. How accurate was he when he discussed the exact séance during which Stella gave her dramatic pronouncement? As a paper bag seller he could have had contact with Andrews and learned of advertising plans, or he may have been aware when the company usually submitted big advertisements for publication. If he knew what the company was likely to print on the 19 May it would not have taken much to slip Stella the information. After all aside from the name 'Andrew Salt' Stella's prediction was rather hazy.

By now Harry's relationship with Stella had moved beyond the purely scientific. They were lovers and Harry was keen to have Stella tested by the *Scientific American* so he could claim the prize money. He managed to secure an invitation for her to visit the committee in America, all expenses paid, but the excitement of the adventure quickly turned sour when Harry was told he would not be allowed to take time off work to accompany her. Concerned about sending Stella alone, and probably complicit in her spirit talents (and therefore necessary to prevent exposure) he began badgering her to turn down the invitation she had already accepted. Stella had her own concerns. Though at first keen to travel, she began feeling unwell during June and July with 'stomach problems' that hinted at future troubles ahead for Harry. She turned down the invitation and never made it to America. Just as well for both of them, for had she been exposed, which was more than likely with Houdini on the case, the scandal would have been highly damaging to Harry's reputation.

Harry's relationship with Stella suddenly took a nose dive. Her letters to him became icy and strangely formal. She asked him to stop meeting her and the séances rapidly tailed off. It has been suggested that an illicit pregnancy and possible abortion was the cause of this disintegration, but no exact reason for the sudden antipathy between the pair has been left in Harry's papers.

Worse, Harry's old colleague Dingwall was raising suspicions not only about Stella, but also about Harry's involvement in her séances. He was unhappy with the inadequate scientific controls Harry had taken and made the dangerous statement; 'If genuine, how was it possible that a man of Mr Price's knowledge should not have taken the opportunity of conducting a properly controlled series of experiments instead of the kind of demonstrations that he was holding? If fraudulent, Mr Price himself must have been in the fraud.'

The Stella experiments had proved a disaster, but as usual Harry was far from discouraged. For years Harry had been pushing for some form of scholarly body to be established that would have premises in which to study psychic phenomena. He envisaged himself as its head – the only way he could possibly gain some sort of academic title for himself. In 1925, after much begging and pestering, he was informed that the London Spiritualist Alliance (LSA) had agreed to fund the project and Harry would be its Honorary Director. The National Laboratory of Psychical Research (NLPR) was born. Yet like so many of Harry's projects it would fail to flourish.

Harry was coming into more and more disrepute. There were rumours that he was faking evidence *against* mediums he had been called in to test, and in 1927 he took a gamble on his friendship with Houdini. Harry was always looking to his immediate gains and rarely gave much thought to long-term loyalty. In February 1927 he had sold an article to the spiritualist magazine *Light* about his own beliefs, with a piece about Houdini's beliefs – from Harry's perspective – tagged on as its main selling point. Understandably Houdini was not popular among spiritualists and the article, which claimed that Houdini in fact had mediumship powers which he was using to fraudulently disprove the spiritualist movement, was exactly the sort of thing *Light* would want to publish.

The claims were not new. Sir Arthur Conan Doyle regularly made them, even to Houdini's face. But if Houdini ignored Doyle's ramblings as misguided, he was deeply hurt that Harry would go behind his back in such a manner. The article was an attack on Houdini, pure and simple, and though Harry had made the effort to warn him, perhaps thinking it would salvage their friendship, it did nothing of the sort. Harry found there was money to be made in attacking his friend's scepticism, and money always came first to Harry. His relationship with Houdini was now over, while in contrast his waning acquaintance with Doyle was suddenly revitalised. Seeing Harry as a new comrade in the fight to prove the truth behind spiritualism, Doyle accepted him wholeheartedly. But this new alliance was not set to last either. In 1928 Harry repeated his Houdini attacks, but this time on Doyle. This suicidal manoeuvre was yet again motivated by a chance to put his name in the limelight and to promote himself as the great cynical debunker. His friendship with Sir Arthur Conan Doyle was also destroyed.

Joanna Southcott's Box

Spiritualism had been *the* movement of the early post-war era, but as the twenties started to fade into the thirties the world was gripped with all manner of novel ideas and revelations. Many of these were associated with forthcoming doom, as the restlessness of Europe (and Germany in particular) troubled Britain. There was a nagging fear that a new war was on the way. Hope was being sought everywhere by the desperate and if the spiritualists were becoming too openly mocked to be taken seriously, then there were other movements that offered apparent salvation. Harry was quick to recognise this mental unsettlement among the population and even quicker to exploit it.

The NLPR was just born and it needed funds and results to keep it alive. Harry decided to opt for a big publicity stunt to draw attention to his work and he had in mind a test on a strange piece of prophecy that had been circulating for some time. On 28 June 1927 Harry wrote to Rachel Fox, the president of the Panacea Society, explaining to her that in July he would hold a meeting to open a Joanna Southcott box that had come into his possession.

The Panacea Society was intrinsically linked with the Devon farmer's daughter turned mystic Joanna Southcott. Joanna was born in the latter half of the eighteenth century and after the death of her mother in 1792 was apparently seized by self-righteous fury and expounded against the ungodly. She was forty-two, a spinster in domestic service and a former Baptist. Perhaps not unnaturally Joanna felt discontent with her life and wanted something more from it, her deeply religious sentiments led her to gradually believe that she was a modern-day prophet, in fact she announced herself as the woman who was spoken of in the book of Revelations.

The 1790s was yet another turbulent time for religion. The age of reason had cast doubt on old faiths and many people felt uncertain and confused. The rise of the Industrial Revolution had changed Britain irretrievably and the horrors of the French Revolution had made traditional order and class structures suddenly seem fragile. Very much like those lost souls in post-war

Britain seeking something to cling on to, the people of eighteenth century England were looking for a religious promise that all would be ok. Joanna provided it.

From 1792 Joanna provided prophecies, often in rhyme, concerning the end of days and the coming of the Messiah. In London Joanna published pamphlets giving stark warnings of impending doom if the country ignored her visions and in 1813, aged sixty-four, she announced she was pregnant with the new messiah called Shiloh. She began work on a final book *Prophecies Announcing the Birth of the Prince of Peace* while her stomach grew in apparent pregnancy. Baby Shiloh, however, was not forthcoming. Eleven months of alleged pregnancy passed and Joanna's mental and physical condition deteriorated. Some of her followers grew disillusioned and left, but others remained staunchly at her side. Shiloh never made a public appearance, though Joanna's followers believed her when she stated the baby had been born on Christmas Day and had risen straight to heaven to be saved from the Devil. This seems a rather cowardly act from a messiah.

In reality Joanna was gravely ill. Two days after the announcement of the birth she died. Her dedicated followers held on to her body for three days confident she would rise from the grave. When Joanna failed to meet expectations, and the body was clearly putrefying, she was handed over to the Royal Physician, Dr Reece, who discovered Joanna's pregnancy had been caused by an acute case of dropsy – the retention of water causing abnormal swelling.

Joanna's death seemed to be the end of the movement at first, but that was not the case. Several dedicated followers set themselves up as 'Southcottians' to preserve Joanna's memory and also the mysterious box she had sealed up before her death. The Joanna Southcott box was said to contain prophecies of great importance and was only to be opened at a time of national crisis. With typical Joanna flare for religious ritual, she decreed that whenever it was opened it had to be in the presence of twenty-four bishops who must have spent some time previously studying Joanna's teachings.

The box was carefully preserved, passed between members of the Southcottians, who at one time numbered an estimated 100,000. An effort was made to open it during the Crimean War, but a lack of interest from the Church of England stalled the idea before it was fully formed. It seemed fortuitous as the Great War appeared to be the precise national crisis Joanna had predicted. Surely now was the time to open her box?

Unfortunately Joanna's story was almost forgotten by the Edwardian period. Her followers had faded away. As disaster loomed and countries geared up for conflict there were only four women who believed in the Joanna Southcott box and its power to end the world's troubles.

Mabel Barltrop, Helen Exeter, Rachael Fox and Kate Firth started a series of letters discussing the possibility of finding and opening Joanna's box. The women believed they were divinely inspired, Mabel in 1916 claimed to have received a message from God, which she relayed to the other women. Swiftly Mabel became known as a Scribe of the Lord and as more women joined the movement there was a growing feeling that Mabel might actually be Shiloh. By 1919 the war had passed without the women being able to convince anyone to open Joanna's box, but Mabel was being heralded as the prophesised saviour – the child Joanna had failed to give birth to more than a century before. Mabel changed her name to Octavia and, in a very traditional looking Victorian end terrace, she entertained 'The Gathering of the Believers'.

Mabel was completely convinced of her role as God's messenger. She informed her followers that she had been told she must record His Word every day without fail. For the next fifteen years she religiously sat down at 5.30 p.m., allowed herself to lapse into a trance state and wrote out His message. The message was then typed out so fellow believers could read and discuss it. Soon the psychic communications were being published monthly as The Writings of the Holy Ghost. At a time when spiritualists were regularly printing communications with dead souls, it seemed hardly extraordinary that someone would claim communication directly with the Almighty.

The Community of the Holy Ghost was formed and slowly drew new members. Mabel was surrounded by twelve female apostles, a fascinating parody of Jesus. Was this yet another means of finding equality for the sexes? Could even Jesus become a woman?

During the early 1920s the community put much of its efforts into promoting the teachings of Joanna, setting up its own printing press, obtaining the permanent loan of the cradle prepared for Shiloh (now Mabel/Octavia) and even acquiring charitable status in 1926. Mabel's little community became the Panacea Society and it was with vast interest that Mabel and her ladies learned of the arrival on the desk of Harry Price at the NLPR of a 'bulky-metal-bound walnut coffer' on 28 November 1927.

Joanna's box had vanished over the course of time. The one that was delivered to Harry was old, had clearly been stored somewhere damp and was accompanied by a letter on Carlton Hotel headed notepaper claiming the box was nothing less than the fabled sealed chest of Joanna Southcott.

The letter writer was a Mr F. (Price refused to reveal his full name for reasons of privacy) who came by the box via his servants. Mr F. had employed two servants who were the children of Rebecca Pengarth, allegedly the one-time companion of Joanna Southcott. On her deathbed Joanna had given her sealed box of prophecies to Rebecca and begged her to keep it safe, reiterating the parameters that the box should only be opened in the presence of twenty-four bishops at a time of national emergency.

Fifteen years later Rebecca married a Welshman named Morgan and had four children. Here the tale goes from being unlikely to being completely improbable. The youngest child was named John who died (according to Mr F.) in 1925 at the age of eighty-one, placing his birth in 1844. Rebecca had served as Joanna's sole companion for sixteen years from 1798, even if she was ten at the time she would have been twenty-six when Joanna died. Fifteen years later at the time of her supposed marriage to Morgan, she would have been forty-one, very late to start a family in the Victorian period and it was another fifteen years before John Morgan was born, making his mother fifty-six.

If alarm bells were not already ringing among the Panacea Society, they certainly should have been among Harry's fellow psychic investigators. Mr F. claimed in his letter (that only Harry ever saw) that John Morgan had insisted on his deathbed that his employer take the box and with his last breath gave a final warning. 'Don't forget the bishops.'

Mysterious Mr F., however, had plans to emigrate and never return to Britain. So he sent the box to Harry with the fortuitous conditions that he wanted neither publicity nor correspondence on the subject. Harry wasted no time in concluding the box was genuine, despite it being much smaller than the stated size of the original Southcott box and considerably lighter. He hastily sent out a press release announcing he was to have the box x-rayed and psychically analysed by mediums.

Considering the dubious nature of his discovery Harry's laboratory was nonetheless quickly swamped by journalists, paranormal investigators and even scientists all convinced the real Joanna Southcott box had been discovered and desperate to know what was inside.

Unsurprisingly the Church was not interested in the box or its contents. Joanna had been a nineteenth century crank and they would not endorse her by sending a contingent of bishops to be present to open the box. Harry tried to mollify them by stating he really did not believe in the box, but thought it tactful to endorse the dying wishes of an old woman.

In the end the only bishop who came to the grand opening was the elderly Dr John Hine, suffragan bishop for Grantham (a suffragan bishop is subordinate to a diocesan bishop and does not have a cathedral of his own) who came out of curiosity, and the suffragan bishop of Crediton sent his curate son, Reverend Trefusis.

If the ecclesiastical turn out was disappointing, Harry could not have asked for better atmosphere if he had stage-managed the weather personally. The day of the opening there were heavy thunderstorms, lightning over Westminster and power cuts in London. The ambience of the event was certainly eerie as a large crowd gathered to witness the opening, among the audience a large number of Joanna's new devotees.

At 9 p.m. Dr John Hine was welcomed onto the stage to be an unbiased witness and the announcer of the treasures found. The box had its wax seals broken and Hine dived in, highly amused at the spectacle, as were most of the crowd. Over the next few minutes he brought out a series of 'treasures' that had more akin to a junk shop rubbish box than any mystical, world saving hoard; a rusty horse pistol, a dice-box, a bead bag containing coins, a puzzle, a pair of earrings, a printed diary from 1715, a dusty copy of Ovid's *Metamorphoses*, two religious pamphlets, a Jubilee medal from 1791, a thin booklet called *The Remarkable Prophecies and Predictions for the Year 1796* and several other small items emerged to the great disappointment of everyone. There was nothing revelatory or world shattering in the collection, but then that was really no surprise to Harry. The box was a clever publicity stunt that raised the profile of the NLPR and gave Harry kudos among the psychic community for exposing the laughable Southcottian beliefs. Dedicated Joanna followers went off muttering it had not been the correct box anyway and the elusive Mr F. disappeared as had always been intended. When it came to drawing attention to himself Harry was no amateur.

CHAPTER SIX

The Dark Side

Spiritualism had been quietly accepted (if not entirely approved of) for much of the nineteenth century and the first portion of the twentieth. There had been odd cases of fraud being declared against a medium or spirit photographer but for the most part spiritualism had been left alone by the authorities. The 1920s changed everything.

Quaint Victorian spiritualism had turned into a money-making market for the dangerous and dubious. More and more fraud was exposed as more and more mediums started using their talents as a career path to fame and fortune, but it went largely unnoticed by the police and authorities. While in Europe mediums were coming under official fire (a German medium was arrested in Berlin in 1909 on charges of fraud – she was nabbed impersonating a ghost) in Britain there was a tendency to conclude that if people were gullible enough to be duped by a medium that was hardly the police's problem.

In 1928 everything changed. The police raided the headquarters of the London Spiritualist Alliance (who supported Harry Price's NLPR) and arrested Mrs Claire Cantlon, one of the mediums who examined the Joanna Southcott box, on charges of fortune telling. Mercy Phillimore, secretary of the LSA, was also arrested on charges of aiding and abetting Cantlon.

Twenty police officers stormed the LSA armed with truncheons; the scene was not only unprecedented, but it was one never repeated on a legitimate spiritualist society. Phillimore and Cantlon appeared before the court charged with telling people their futures, a service that was not part of the LSA's remit in spiritualism and was illegal under the Vagrancy Act of 1824.

The case however was challenging to prove. On the one hand it was argued Cantlon should be allowed leniency during tests at LSA, when she would go into a deep trance and tell people's fortunes. LSA argued Cantlon was not responsible for her actions in this state, whether they were illegal or not. The court was not prepared to state she was communicating with the dead, but they did agree Cantlon might be deemed to be unaware of the things she was saying during trances and thus not knowingly guilty of fortune telling.

If the case against Cantlon was impossible to prove, Phillimore was a more promising target. She had clearly over-stepped the limits of her duties when assisting Cantlon. Even so could she be made culpable for the unconscious actions of another? It was all very complicated (and depended, of course, on whether you believed Cantlon really went into a trance), both Sir Arthur Conan Doyle and Sir Oliver Lodge were called to the stand as eminent men in the field of spiritualism. The big question the court had to answer was whether there was a possibility of genuine mediumship. If there was then Cantlon could not be responsible for her actions as they would have been caused by her spirit guide (naturally an Indian chief) who had provided the fortunes. The police could hardly prosecute him! It was all becoming ludicrous and demonstrates why the police preferred not to involve themselves in cases of dubious spiritualism.

At the end of the case the judge declared himself open minded on the subject of spiritualism, but it was his opinion that both Mrs Cantlon and Phillimore were guilty, he added:

> I give Mrs Cantlon the benefit of the doubt in my mind, and I assume that on these three occasions [of fortune telling] she did believe she was under the control of this chief... But I would strongly advise her to get rid of a disembodied spirit who wants to know the time for lunch and tea [on the occasion of a séance going badly Mrs Cantlon had asked the time and then her spirit guide had said her powers were waning].

Both ladies were found guilty but the charges were dismissed after payment of a hefty fine.

Paranormal studies were now taking a dangerous turn and more and more people, bored with the usual séance lark, were dabbling in the so-called 'Occult'. Authors such as Dennis Wheatley were playing on people's fears about the supernatural to sell books. Other figures such as Aleister Crowley were blatantly pronouncing themselves the Devil in disguise and promoting an image of Satanism. It was actually more bluff than reality, very few people were really toying with black magic at this period, but the idea was there and it troubled a lot of souls.

Witchcraft had for two centuries been considered nonsense wrapped up in old wives' tales and rural superstitions. In 1920s Britain it suddenly seemed very real to certain sections of the population. Into this revival of age-old fears stepped Eleanore Zugun, whose story has to be one of the most tragic in the history of spiritualism.

Spiritualism has always favoured young girls, starting with the Fox sisters, but usually their talents are lauded. Not the case with poor Eleanore. Born in Talpa, Romania in 1913 Eleanore was a simple, uneducated peasant girl living in a region teeming with legends and superstition and a prevailing fear of witchcraft.

There is some discrepancy as to how exactly Eleanore's tragic step into the spirit world began, but it revolved around the finding of some money, which eleven-year-old Eleanore naturally used to buy sweets. When she was found out by her grandmother (or great grandmother in some accounts), she was told that only the Devil left out money for people to find and by using it and eating the sweets she had condemned herself to be possessed by *Dracu* (Romanian Devil).

Eleanore was already somewhat of a problem child before being told this horrific tale, so being told she was possessed by the Devil was unlikely to help. In some versions of her story it is said there had already been poltergeist activity surrounding her before she found the money, namely stone throwing. This was one of the reasons she was heading to her grandmother's house when she found the coin. Whatever the truth Eleanore's story quickly turned nasty. Stones were thrown in her presence by invisible hands, often smashing windows. A priest came to exorcise the demon from Eleanore and cast a stone carved with a cross into a nearby river. The stone re-emerged and smashed a window, thereby confirming Eleanore was in league with the Devil.

Eleanore was persecuted by her fellow villagers and even her relatives were involved in beating and hounding her. The child was condemned, deemed wilful and evil, dangerous to the village and someone they needed to be rid of. Eventually she was forced into a lunatic asylum.

Far away in Berlin, mathematician and paranormal investigator Professor Fritz Grunewald learned of Eleanore's terrible story and determined to find out more about the girl. Parts of Romania were dangerously unenlightened towards things such as mental illness, and it seemed to Grunewald prejudice and fear had condemned Eleanore. He went to Romania and persuaded Eleanore's father to remove her from the asylum and give her into his care. The Zugun family were more than glad to be rid of their burdensome child and agreed. But just as things were going right for Eleanore, Grunewald dropped down dead. She was left stranded in Romania, at the mercy of her hateful family and neighbours. Fortunately Countess Wassilko-Sereki, a keen psychic investigator, took charge of the situation and rescued Eleanore, removing her to Vienna.

Over the next year the countess documented any phenomena that happened around Eleanore, and there was certainly plenty to record. Objects frequently moved and broke, other things such as ink were spilled and clothes were ruined. Eleanore and her possessions were the target and the activities were largely self-destructive. They were soon followed by bite and scratch marks appearing all over Eleanore's body, often her face. In today's terms Eleanore was self-harming and persecuting herself. She was also completely convinced she was possessed by the Devil and was destined to be doomed. She tried to appease Draco by leaving him chocolates or small gifts. Mentally the girl was in a terrible state.

The countess was pragmatic. While she believed the phenomena genuine and caused by a psychic force, she also thought it was directed subconsciously by Eleanore. This, she claimed, was due to Eleanore suffering incest and rape during her childhood. While she never named names, it was plain the countess believed the Zugun elders were the real culprits for starting this drama.

Meanwhile Eleanore was suddenly living a life of luxury and had become the centre of media attention, not just for her ill treatment but because of the strange powers that followed her. Harry Price travelled to meet her in 1926 and found her a girl of contradictions; on first meeting her he thought her an intelligent, well-developed girl, happy to be introduced to him, but within a short while he was disagreeing with himself. She now seemed reserved and shy, rather simple in her fondness for children's toys and child-like ways. She appeared to him more like an eight-year-old than the teenager she actually was.

During the course of the short meeting a steel stiletto paperknife shot across the room, clattered into a door and tumbled to the floor, narrowly missing Harry. Startled he instantly turned around to look for the culprit but saw no one or anything that could explain the strange occurrence. Neither the countess nor Eleanore seemed unduly concerned by the malicious act and Harry was soon to discover why.

Poltergeist activity was part of daily life for the countess now Eleanore was living with her. Harry saw soft toys bouncing up and down by themselves, cushions sliding slowly off chairs, spoons falling off tables and a host of other strange sights, including the scratches and marks on Eleanore, which he was inclined to call 'stigmata' for extra emphasis. Harry searched the rooms for tricks without finding anything – though with Harry it is always wise to take any of his statements with a pinch of salt. There was only one thing for it, to bring Eleanore to London for further testing.

Alarmingly Eleanore was convinced the Devil would come with her. In a statement the countess read out to gathered pressmen in London, Eleanore said, 'The Devil has come with me to London. The Devil is very pleased to come to London, for he hopes to find plenty to do here.'

Eleanore was presented to an audience at Harry Price's NLPR that consisted of members of the Magic Circle, notable psychic investigators, a Harvard professor in psychology and the staff of a mental asylum. As a gift she was presented with a tin clockwork cat, but this appeared to irritate the Devil who hurled something at the back of Eleanore's head.

Harry just happened to be nearest to the thrown object and snatched it up. It proved to be a magnetic letter 'L' used on the noticeboard in the NLPR's reception. There was an instant rush to see the noticeboard, but none of the letters on it were missing, instead it was finally deduced the letter had come from a box of unused letters. The credulous saw this as clear poltergeist phenomena and set to work trying to comprehend why an 'L' was chosen. The more cynical remarked how convenient it was the letter had fallen near Harry. One reporter for the *Daily News* even went so far as to contradict Harry's version of events, saying the letter had dropped from the ceiling, hit Harry's shoulder and fallen to the floor without coming into contact with Eleanore. An already sceptical public found the incident rather unbelievable.

Harry drew more criticism after Eleanore's last London appearance when two of the men present separately discovered their pocket knives had a magnetic letter 'C', from the same set as the mysterious 'L', tightly wrapped around their handles. Even the SPR could not countenance this as genuine and turned suspicious eyes on Harry. The only time Eleanore was tormented by letters of the alphabet was when she was in Harry's presence.

Eleanore went on a European tour with the countess visiting various cities, particularly in Germany, and even taking part in a documentary about her possession. Her novelty value quickly diminished, along with the poltergeist activity. Free from the stress and horrors of her childhood Eleanore was regaining some sense of equilibrium, along with a better understanding of the modern world. The Devil started to seem less and less important and it was not long before he, and the poltergeist phenomena, vanished. Later psychiatrists considered this a natural conclusion to the situation after Eleanore was removed from the accusations, punishments and superstitions of her village and was allowed to develop normally. Eleanore's life finally became ordinary. She stayed with the countess (who remarked Eleanore's problems had gone away after puberty) for another year and then returned to Romania to become a hairdresser. Eleanore quietly vanished into a life devoid of possession and super-human powers.

The Ineffective Vyvyan Deacon

The overweight, dark-eyed man stepped ashore into a foggy Southampton. Dressed in a suit that showed signs of age at the cuffs and with black hair slicked back he looked mildly sinister as he gazed across the port. This was Vyvyan Deacon, fraudulent medium, patent medicine maker, charlatan and impoverished mummy's boy.

Somewhere on the same ship he had just departed was his seasick wife, the pretty and petite Eunice who had been captivated by Vyvyan when she was merely twelve and he was seventeen. Their match had been controversial, but they had been thrust together by the death of Eunice's father and resulting poverty; marriage to Vyvyan had been deemed mildly better than starving. She had followed him across Australia and New Zealand, dragging her two daughters with her. Often alone, she clung to a marriage that was both poor and unhappy.

Returning to England in 1930, Vyvyan was at once enjoying a homecoming and at the same time running away from his problems in Australia. Vyvyan was very good at problems often involving women or spiritualism or money, sometimes all three.

Vyvyan Deacon can be taken as just one example of the sort of popular medium who sprung up in the early years of the Twentieth century. There were plenty who were akin to him, with their bohemian lifestyles and constant dabbling in fraud. It was these sorts of people that Doyle and Lodge were fighting against when they promoted spiritualism, the same people critics used as examples of why the new cult was so ludicrous. Whatever its noble aspirations, spiritualism was infiltrated by a seedy sub-culture of sex, drugs and fraud, which made it near impossible for respectable men to be taken seriously when they supported the cause. Vyvyan's story was typical and a good starting point for understanding why mediums were frequently lampooned and denounced.

Vyvyan Deacon was born in Berkshire in 1895, to a mother who gave him that name because it meant 'Living One' and not (she claimed) because Oscar Wilde had a son named Vivian. She was a doting and indulgent mother who spoiled her only son and allowed him to grow up in the belief that work was optional. Vyvyan's father was absent, supposedly travelling the country on work, his mother absorbed herself in trying to keep the family afloat and telling her son about her connections to the famous writer Robert Browning. She was his cousin.

Vyvyan as a child was keen for attention and had a passion for spirituality. Once as a boy he stood up before a congregation and preached a spontaneous sermon. His mother was infinitely proud, but when she found a second husband (having claimed Vyvyan's father was dead) the relationship with her son turned sour. Vyvyan did not like sharing his mother and, always desperately seeking a father figure to replace the one he had never known, he fell in with the spiritualist crowd as a young teen.

He was 'discovered' by Charles Webster Leadbeater, who convinced him that he had clairvoyant powers. Vyvyan was not to know how dangerous a man his new mentor was. Leadbeater had at one time been a priest in the Church of England, but his growing interest in spiritualism and the occult had caused him to leave and join with the Theosophists. He rose quickly in the ranks and started taking on young boys as pupils. Vyvyan was an obvious candidate, encouraged by Leadbeater he quickly found a knack for preaching, which then developed into mediumistic talents. From Leadbeater's point of view Vyvyan was perfect; he was young, promising, naïve, good-looking and, above all, malleable.

Leadbeater was a sexual predator, in many ways similar to his friend and co-founder of the Liberal Catholic Church, James Wedgewood. Leadbeater liked the company of boys and would always take one on his tours and share a room with him. He even coached Vyvyan on how to style his hair in the way that most appealed to Leadbeater.

In 1906 the first accusations were levelled against him. The fourteen-year-old son of the Corresponding Secretary of the Esoteric Section in Chicago had recently gone on a lecture tour with Leadbeater to San Francisco. Afterwards he confessed to his parents the older man had encouraged him to masturbate in his presence. Another boy who had spent time with Leadbeater confessed the same thing. To add to the verbal accusations a typewritten letter was found from Leadbeater telling this second boy, 'Glad sensation is so pleasant. Thousand kisses darling.'

Leadbeater argued that he had only told the boys about masturbation to avoid sexual frustration that could lead them to seeking out prostitutes. To a Victorian mind masturbation was a sin, but Leadbeater argued it was a lesser sin than buying sex from a woman of the night. He also argued that the release of sexual pressure enabled the boys to focus on their spiritual studies better. However he argued it, Leadbeater knew he was doomed. He resigned from the Theosophy Society just before an investigation into his actions was carried out, claiming it was to save the society from embarrassment.

It is highly likely Vyvyan would also have been initiated into his teacher's habits of masturbation. Though he never discussed the matter and remained friendly with Leadbeater, it seems likely he was one of his victims. Another was Hubert van Hook from Chicago, who had been picked out by Leadbeater at age eleven to be his 'World Teacher'. He later told Annie Besant, the Theosophy leader, that Leadbeater had misused him as a boy. Biographers of Leadbeater have defended him as a forward thinker who was open about sexuality and wanted to remove the stigma Victorians attached to masturbation. However his influence on young boys was often over-powering and he was regularly seen marching around arm-in-arm with his favourite pupil, invariably a pretty young teen.

While with Leadbeater, Vyvyan was introduced to James Wedgewood. A homosexual with a self-confessed overwhelming sexual appetite (he once visited eighteen public toilets in a two-hour period searching for a 'friend') Wedgewood was accused in 1919 of homosexual practices with boys. Wedgewood had left the Catholic Church into which he had just been ordained because of its attitude towards Theosophy and its expulsion of another homosexual. With Leadbeater he formed the Liberal Catholic Church which incorporated Theosophy and even ideas of reincarnation with traditional

Christian concepts. Perhaps unsurprisingly with Leadbeater and Wedgewood at its head, it also attracted a number of predatory homosexuals to its order. The accusations against Wedgewood came thick and fast forcing him to resign from the Theosophy Society and to retire into private life. He was also an ill man, suffering the dementia and lunacy associated with advanced syphilis. He was addicted to cocaine, and like so many others associated with the occult at this period, Aleister Crowley being a prime example, was rapidly discovering his excesses were catching up with him.

There was no doubt among even Wedgewood's friends that he had committed the acts he was accused of, but despite this Vyvyan remained on friendly terms. Though not a homosexual himself Vyvyan viewed Wedgewood as still a 'way in' to various organisations. By 1924 Wedgewood had been able to return to the Theosophists and was even supplied with a house and a chapel to preach in. In 1930 when Vyvyan stepped onto British soil he was as likely a contact as any to aid Vyvyan's career – if such it could be called.

Vyvyan had fled to Australia in his teens, seeking a new life and a better place to practice his mediumship – Britain being a touch jaded about the whole concept. Constantly verging on the edge of extreme poverty, he found decent work impossible and by the time he was in his thirties had fallen into a pattern of sleeping late into the day and giving lectures on spiritualist ideas at night. Depending on how well these sold, he either had a little money or none at all. The whiff of fraud often floated over Vyvyan, dangerous for a man who made a chunk of his living from conducting séances. Vyvyan always claimed he did not charge for his services, though people were keen to donate money to him after a performance. Whatever the case, just before he returned to England Vyvyan became embroiled in a libel case against the Australian paper *Truth*. The paper had claimed him a fraud, but in an interesting but expensive court case Vyvyan was able to prove this a lie and won damages of £3,500 (as reported by a British paper). Despite his success Vyvyan thought it prudent to beat a hasty retreat from the country where he had fallen out with a few too many people and go to somewhere safer. England beckoned.

Vyvyan had returned home at an interesting period in British spiritualism. The number of hoaxes, frauds and dubious activities perpetuated by alleged mediums in the years just after the First World War had caused even the government to pay attention. Too many cases were being reported by the papers, too many people being fleeced. In 1931 a bill was passing through Parliament that, if it succeeded, would make mediumship illegal. Naturally the spiritualist press were outraged and horrified. Yes, there were fraudsters, but what about all the good mediums out there? Must they be condemned for the few who acted criminally?

These rumours washed over Vyvyan, as he was far too busy with his lectures and various engagements. He had managed to swing the publicity of his court case to his advantage in the British press and was forever keen to play on his connections to the dead poet Robert Browning. Browning was better remembered in Britain than in Australia and the connection fascinated eager audiences, especially when Vyvyan reported he had a message from the long dead writer. The unfortunate poet, who had thought little of spiritualism in life, was summoned in death by Vyvyan to apologise for the insulting poem he had written called 'Sludge the Medium.'

The publicity worked. In September 1931 the recently widowed Lady Conan Doyle, wrote to Vyvyan to arrange a séance. He paid several visits to the Doyles over the next few weeks, though little of what occurred during the meetings has survived. Jean Doyle was no doubt eager to get in touch with her late husband and to try out this brand new medium from Australia who was touted as something of a sensation. Vyvyan avoided scandal with the Doyles and left on good terms, but his next acquaintance in the occult world was to lead him in a far more dangerous direction.

Vyvyan was invited to the 23rd Foyles Literary Luncheon, held at Grosvenor House on 15 September 1932. It was indicative of his rise to celebrity that he was asked to come and sit with other notables of the period including aviators Jim Mollison and Amy Johnson, novelist Rose Macaulay and illustrator Arthur Rackham. But the most notable guest of the event was the speaker, Aleister Crowley.

It was hard for anyone in 1930s Britain to be oblivious of Crowley's reputation. Crowley was associated with the practice of black magic and paganism and called himself the 'Beast', or the human form of the Devil. At one time he had scandalised and frightened the public imagination with his wild excesses, dubious rituals and his one rule, 'Do what thou wilt shall be the whole of the law'. Actually by the 1930s Crowley had become something of a figure of fun. Over-weight, bankrupt and sick through drug abuse, he no longer had the same mysticism of his youth. His audience were excited, if slightly jocular about his appearance at the function, Rose Macaulay remarked that she hoped he would not 'turn himself into a goat'. But in fact the performance was rather a disappointment, as a journalist remarked, 'For a man who has been described as brilliant Mr Crowley's speech was not intelligent. It was hardly intelligible.'

There was one in the audience who enjoyed the performance. Vyvyan had read all of Crowley's works and had kept abreast of the highs and lows of his career. In return Crowley had become intrigued by this new young medium and particularly by his libel case. In late 1932 Crowley was seriously short of money, at one time he had had a sizeable inheritance, but now he lived on favours from friends. The success of Vyvyan's libel case inspired him and when he saw a sign in a bookseller's window stating his *Diary of Drug Fiend* had been removed from sale because of an attack in the sensational press, he sued for libel and was awarded £50. Spurred on by what seemed like easy money he next tried to sue the publishers of the autobiography of his friend Nina Hamnett. In the book Hamnett had suggested Crowley had practiced black magic at the 'abbey' he had founded in Cefalu, and indicated that the disappearance of a cat was further evidence of black magic rituals. Crowley sued for libel and lost, but the publicity it gained him only helped with sales. It is not clear what became of his friendship with Hamnett.

Crowley formed an unlikely friendship with Vyvyan – unlikely because Crowley was not good at friendship and the two men had both been raised and believed in very different ideas. But they got along and Crowley came to visit on Vyvyan's forty-first birthday. He got along well with Eunice, whom he thought charming. Vyvyan was enamoured with him. Always easily led since his time with Leadbeater, Vyvyan saw no harm in the old drug addict who snuffled and coughed from long-term cocaine snorting. Crowley was fascinated by Vyvyan's connections to Robert Browning, a poet he greatly admired and composed Vyvyan's astrological chart for him. Vyvyan was soon helping Crowley raise money for future publications.

But the friendship was a deadly one. Despite being a middle-aged family man Vyvyan was always beguiled by older, father figures. Crowley was twenty years his senior, a man he much admired and would follow everywhere, even into drink and drugs. On Wednesday 10 March 1937 Vyvyan went out with Crowley and did not return until six in the morning. High on a variety of substances he picked up a knife and stumbled into Eunice's bedroom, there he swayed over her and, with laboured speech, recited words of sacrifice. With a level of composure many women would have found hard to muster, Eunice reached out and put her hand on the knife before repeating the words back to him. Vyvyan wobbled in confusion and Eunice removed the knife from his hands. Her husband tumbled into bed and fell soundly asleep. In future Eunice always made sure she rose early and left the house when Vyvyan went out with Crowley.

Crowley always used his friends and Vyvyan was to be no different. The Deacons had little money, but somehow Crowley always seemed able to borrow some from Vyvyan. Trying to impress his new mentor Vyvyan introduced him to various people he knew who might be able to spare some cash, with limited success. Crowley had formed a circle of like-minded people to talk about a new book *Equinox of the Gods* which he was trying to get off the ground. They met regularly in a room above an occult bookshop, with Vyvyan always in attendance. If Crowley suggested casting a curse on a judge who had failed to support his libel case, then Vyvyan agreed. If Crowley went out on a binge, Vyvyan joined him. In among it all there was pseudo-magic rituals, talk of occult powers and women.

All this was bad for anyone's health, but Vyvyan had never been the fittest of creatures and now weighing a hefty twenty-two stone and abusing his body with drink and drugs, he was putting his life in serious harm. Vyvyan went on a fast to reduce his weight, consuming only liquids for months at a time. Not many weeks after threatening to sacrifice his wife, Vyvyan stumbled on a kerb and cracked his head open. He was taken to hospital with a fractured skull and lay unconscious for three days. When he awoke he immediately demanded his clothes and discharged himself.

Vyvyan's relationship with Crowley was growing stronger while that with his wife was rapidly weakening. Eunice kept her distance from her husband, doing her duty as a wife and nothing more. Within months of his first fall Vyvyan suffered another, this time fracturing his shoulder. The attending doctor, mistaking a break for a dislocation, yanked on his arm and the agony spun Vyvyan into unconsciousness. He again woke in hospital. When he finally returned home he was clearly far from well.

Crowley visited him, claiming friendly concern, in reality he was still intent on borrowing money from Vyvyan and came away from his sick bed with a ten-shilling note. Vyvyan failed to improve and was readmitted to hospital on 19 February. This time he was not destined to return home. He died the same night. Eunice was awoken in the dark hours before dawn to learn her husband was dead. Despite his abuse and neglect she was terribly upset, not least because she had no idea how she and her daughters would survive without Vyvyan's miniscule income.

In contrast Crowley was unmoved by the loss of his friend, though he did remark he believed the ghost of Vyvyan had appeared to him in the early hours of the morning. Perhaps he was coming to claim back the money he had loaned Crowley. So ended the career of an unlikely medium whose life and death shone a dim light on the dark side of spiritualism.

The Sinister Crowley

Crowley was born Edward Alexander on 12 October 1875 in Leamington, Warwickshire. His father was a member of the Plymouth Brethren, so stern in his religion that he deemed the less dogmatic branch of the Brethren as heretics. Anyone outside his faith was considered a hopeless sinner destined for hell. Ten years before the birth of his son, this staunch religious soul believed the world was destined to falter from the path of faith and that the Anti-Christ would rise and dominate. He could hardly know his son would take his prediction seriously enough to style himself as the Anti-Christ.

Crowley grew up as an only child, spoilt and cloistered. He was only allowed to play with other Plymouth Brethren children and was closely schooled to avoid anything unsavoury entering his education. He developed an egotistical view of his own self-worth. His father viewed himself as almost saintly and this arrogance was also apparent in his son. The combination of saintliness and his father's attitude towards non-Plymouth Brethren caused Crowley to constantly look down on those around him – no one could ever be as good as Aleister. But his ties with traditional religion were cut when his father became ill with cancer of the tongue. He was told he needed an operation but the Plymouth Brethren were opposed to such treatment and instead a committee meeting decided the unfortunate Crowley senior should take a course of electro-homeopathy. As was to be expected this failed and Crowley's father died. The young Aleister blamed the Plymouth Brethren and grew to hate his mother for her failure to stand up to them. Before long he had distanced himself from both.

Crowley drifted into a dissolute life of drink, drugs and debauchery. He was not fussed whether his sexual partners were male or female and lived for the basest passions of existence. Family money enabled him to live carefree and to dabble in whatever he pleased. He was contented to be termed an absolute sinner and saw no reason to concern himself with God. In fact he was elevating himself to stand as a rival to him.

There are few incidents in Crowley's life more shocking than his outrageous behaviour during his participation in the attempt to climb Kangchenjunga – the third highest mountain in the world – in 1905. Aside from his vicious beatings of the local coolies hired to aid them, one of which died before they had reached 21,000 feet, and despite being the expedition leader, Crowley kept abandoning his team and going on alone. Another team member, Jacot Guillarmod, had to effectively take charge and this led to arguments between the two men. Crowley later claimed this was all Guillarmod's fault as he naturally resented following an Englishman.

Crowley showed his true colours on Friday, 1 September. The expedition had halted at Camp V, and it was unspoken among them that they could not manage the last climb to the summit. As evening approached Guillarmod and two others decided to climb back down to Camp III, to spend the night in relative comfort. Crowley refused to join them. Guillarmod took three coolies with him and this was his downfall as during the descent an ill-shod coolie slipped and fell, taking the two other coolies and one of the expedition members with him. Guillarmod and the remaining man tried to hold the rope their colleagues were attached to, but the strain was too much and the snow slipped away from under their feet. Suddenly an avalanche had begun and the three coolies and the expedition member were buried under icy cold snow. Guillarmod revived his remaining colleague, who been knocked unconscious, and frantically they began digging for the others, shouting for help all the time. At Camp V Crowley and his one remaining colleague heard the cries. While the other man hurried down to help, Crowley turned over and went to sleep. He had decided Guillarmod did not deserve his help since he had tried to reach Camp III against Crowley's wishes.

There was no rescuing the fallen men. In the cold dawn light Guillarmod was still scrabbling in the snow, hoping beyond hope, when he spotted a solitary figure descending the mountain. It was Crowley; he was leaving his colleagues behind in one of the most callous acts imaginable. His former friends could only look on in disbelief as he abandoned them. Even worse when Crowley set foot on level ground he wrote damning articles about Guillarmod claiming it was his fault the accident had occurred in the first place. Crowley was smirking as he declared, if only the poor souls had listened to him…

Crowley's callousness was even more apparent when the next year he abandoned his wife in North Vietnam and returned to England. He later learned his baby daughter had died from typhoid in Rangoon and instantly blamed his unfortunate wife who he said must have been neglectful when cleaning the baby's bottle. But the death suited him, he was free of both wife and daughter and he was never happier than when alone and without responsibilities.

Aleister used his new freedom to dabble in publishing; he had a highly over-inflated sense of his own creative genius and produced sporadic collections of strange, rambling, ludicrous works. Despite this he did gain the odd fan. When he published his *Collected Works* in 1907 he set up a competition with a £100 prize for the best essay about him – Aleister never failed to be self-absorbed – and the prize was won by his solitary fan, Captain John Frederick Charles Fuller, of the 1st Oxfordshire Light Infantry. He also happened to be the sole entrant for the prize. Fuller, unsurprisingly by Crowley standards, never saw his £100. He rapidly fell out with his 'hero' and went on to worship other characters. It says much about the sort of people Aleister attracted that Fuller became a fan of the German Reich and was one of only two Englishmen who went to Germany in 1939 to celebrate the fiftieth birthday of Adolf Hitler.

Aleister managed to attract other acolytes after Fuller, most of them misguided and easily used, perfect for Crowley. The neurotic and self-loathing Victor Neuberg travelled with him in 1908 and submitted himself to whatever whims his 'master' (and lover) fancied. In Tangiers Aleister shaved Victor's head, leaving only two tufts of hair either side of his forehead. It amused Crowley because the ugly Victor now resembled a grotesque Pan. Pan had become an obsession of Aleister's (along with many other Edwardians) and he linked the god with his own brand of sexual magic. Victor was a plaything, and while he amused Aleister he was allowed into his private circle, though always as the minion; they were never equals. Aleister slept with Victor whenever it pleased him, but eventually the unfortunate boy was to be discarded, like all those Aleister used.

In the years before the First World War, Aleister became known for his anachronistic, poorly written and scandalous *Equinox* magazine; a weighty series of volumes that cost far too much for the average purchaser and remained largely unsold. The magazine infuriated a number of his ex-friends due to his revelations about various supernatural organisations, particularly the Golden Dawn which he had briefly been a member of. In *Equinox* Aleister threatened to reveal the secret Golden Dawn rites and was attacked by society members. By 1914 Aleister had established himself as an unpleasant little man obsessed with devilry and scandal. His mother was appalled with him, but that mattered little since he hated her.

In fact Aleister Crowley spent the war in America working with pro-German groups to produce propaganda against his own country. His work was so prolific it caught the attention of the Foreign Office, though they dismissed it as the hyped up burbling of a madman. Aleister was courting all the wrong people in America; he was dining with German-Americans who were looking forward to the Kaiser's triumph and drinking beer with Irish independents who were working to undermine Britain with terrorism. This was still all a game, as Aleister's new cronies could no more count on him than any of his other friends. Aleister was having fun at the expense of others, and fun for him always meant stirring up scandal. In front of his new Irish friends he ripped up a document he claimed was his passport to show his support for them. In reality it was an old, used envelope.

Aleister was now writing for the pro-German paper *The Fatherland* and produced the most appalling article concerning the execution of Red Cross nurse Edith Cavell. Cavell had been helping Allied soldiers escape from Germany and was shot by the Germans. Her story shocked British and American audiences. It seemed to sum up the monstrousness of the Germans that they would execute her. Aleister saw a grand opportunity for controversy and wrote an article *The Crime of Eidith Cavell* (he never could spell) which portrayed the poor woman as a cross between Judas and Lucrezia Borgia. She had betrayed the kindly Germans, he argued, and got what she deserved. Needless to say this outraged all but his pro-German colleagues and even reached the ears of New Scotland Yard. His mother was shocked and his aunt was visited by the police. Yet despite this, in 1919, with his sizeable inheritance all gone and his German cronies scattered to the winds with the defeat of Germany, Aleister returned to England without so much as a raised eyebrow at his (never torn up) passport.

Aleister was always more influential in his imagination that in reality. His work at *Fatherland* had done little more than stir up outrage against the Germans, and his attack on Edith Cavell had galvanised fury at her merciless treatment. The Foreign Office viewed Aleister as a nuisance, but nothing more. They were fully justified in their views as within a year of returning to England Aleister was selling his assets for ready money to fuel his hedonistic lifestyle and his new addiction to heroin and cocaine. Not that Aleister saw it as addiction, he believed that such things were all in the mind and at any moment he could simply stop. He was to be sorely mistaken as the years passed.

In 1922 Aleister wrote his book *Diary of a Drug Fiend*, the only title he is really remembered for, which is a typically self-absorbed study of his own drug-fuelled existence. Aleister's writing style had never been good, but with the influence of opiates he now churned out pages and pages of drivel. Aleister had sired another daughter by an American lover, both of whom he had abandoned in France while he travelled with a second woman looking for a site for his 'abbey'. For years now Aleister had dreamed of founding his own religion, based on his garbled sexual magic and singular law 'do what thou wilt'. Aleister would be head priest and god for the religion, looking down on all his devoted worshippers and inspiring fear and respect and, of course, sleeping with whoever took his fancy. He found a site for his abbey overlooking the town of Cefalu in Sicily.

The abbey proved to be a rundown five-room villa with no sanitation facilities. God and acolytes camped out in the rooms with barely a stick of furniture and little but the droning of the stoned Aleister to look forward to. Only the most devoted remained long as anyone who stayed for more than a day in Aleister's company usually found themselves being dosed with the same stuff he was taking. He was liberal in that sense, though he completely failed to realise the dangerous nature of his generosity. It all came to a head with the death of Frederick Charles Loveday.

The *Sunday Express* had been busy reporting on the dubious goings-on at the abbey, referring to black masses, orgies and animal sacrifices, when the death of Loveday gave them a renewed focus. They told stunned readers, 'Children under ten, whom the Beast keeps at his 'abbey', are made to witness sexual debauches unbelievably revolting. Filthy incense is burned and cakes made of goats' blood and honey are consumed in the window-less room where the Beast conducts his rites. The rest of the time he lies in a room hung with obscene pictures collected all over the world, saturating himself with drugs.'

Much of the revelations were provided by Loveday's distraught wife Betty. Betty had gone with her husband to the abbey and had been appalled by the villa. It was filthy, children and dogs roamed about the courtyard, and there was no running water or flushing toilet. Nobody ever cleaned – that was anathema to the Bohemian lifestyle they had gone there to enjoy. Drug and alcohol abuse was prominent and Loveday fell into the abuse wholeheartedly, much to his wife's disgust and horror. Loveday fell sick soon after, to an infection of the liver and spleen, which Betty blamed on the messy sacrifice of a cat her husband had attended. It was only later the doctor realised Loveday was actually suffering acute gastroenteritis, no doubt caused by the appalling lack of hygiene at the abbey. Loveday quickly deteriorated and on 16 February 1923 Betty returned from Cefalu to find her husband dead.

Betty almost collapsed in grief-induced hysteria and fled back to London, as did many of the residents of the abbey. Only Aleister and his two female lovers were left, along with the daughters of both women and the British press had a field day. Crowley was a monster in their eyes, a supporter of the Germans, a Devil in disguise and they filled column inches with stories of the horrific things he had done. Aleister, remarkably, could not understand their fury. Though he had deliberately stirred up trouble, he was like any naughty boy who fails to realise the true consequences of their irresponsible actions. In his own mind, Aleister was a genius and the press seemed oddly incapable of understanding that. He was known in Britain as the 'Wickedest Man in the World', and like it or not, Aleister was a hated figure in his homeland.

The experience was crushing. Collins refused to publish *Diary of a Drug Fiend*, Aleister was kicked out of Italy and returned home once more, penniless, addicted and fast approaching his fiftieth year. Even so, he might have gained some attention from the usual crowds who loved notoriety and association with such an 'anti-establishment' figure. Unfortunately the old man that greeted them from self-imposed exile was not the prince of darkness they had hoped for. Aleister was old, sickly and spaced out most of the time. There had been little concern for personal hygiene in Cefalu and he was a disgusting, shambolic figure. Penniless and powerless, the wickedest man was rather disappointing. He quickly became a figure of fun, rather than a figure of hate.

Aleister's women had long abandoned him. He briefly remarried, but his second wife went the same as the first and turned to drink before vanishing. By 1946 Aleister was ill and alone. He was living in a boarding house in Hastings when he was contacted by John Symonds, the man who would become Aleister's first biographer. Presumably Symonds did not know Aleister long enough to be disenchanted by him like so many other acolytes. He was smitten by the man.

Aleister died in his bed at Hastings on 1 December 1947. He was so alone in the world that he appointed the man he had known for barely a year, John Symonds, to be the executor of his will. Symonds was not there when he died. His sole companion was a nurse who reported he died unhappily, tears streaking his face. As death called for him he mumbled his last words; 'Sometimes I hate myself.'

The Beast Meets the Devil

It was a dark night in the early thirties when Dennis Wheatley, eccentric writer and wine connoisseur, escorted the budding politician Tom Driberg home, after some unpleasant business involving concerns Driberg might be jumped.

The charming, if insincere, Driberg was a head taller than Wheatley and a complicated mismatch of charisma, rudeness and, to quote one psychiatrist who met him, 'evil'. Driberg was gay and frequented public lavatories; his manservant was in fact an ex-lavatory attendant. In later years he would befriend the Kray twins, who would supply him with youths to satisfy his lusts. Driberg was the sort of character Wheatley seemed to fall in with, but his real attraction was his association with the Beast himself, Aleister Crowley.

Driberg met Crowley after writing him a fan letter. He would become just one of many adoring acolytes who came and went through Aleister's life, but as the years went by Driberg's interest in the old eccentric waned. Aleister was constantly asking him for money or meals and Driberg gradually began to ignore him. He had almost washed his hands of the old man when he stumbled into Wheatley's company. Wheatley had a fascination for magic, usually in a very practical sense. He was an indefatigable writer, supporting himself and his wife through various articles and novels. He was always after new material to keep his stories fresh, in particular for the *Duke de Richleau* series, which was to feature various encounters with supernatural or paranormal activities. In 1934, the same year he met Aleister Crowley, he published *The Devil Rides Out* an adventure thriller where the main characters must rescue a friend from the clutches of a devil-worshipping cult. A meeting with Aleister would not only prove interesting, but could spurn some new ideas.

The meeting was to prove a disappointment. Aleister was at the end of his strange career. He reeked of ether, which he drank in copious amounts partly to aid sleep. He was dishevelled and queer looking, one contemporary described his face as that of a 'horrible baby'. Wheatley came away from their lunch meeting with the firm decision to never see Aleister again, but a string of letters from the Beast followed. Wheatley avoided committing himself to any further lunches with excuses about the amount of work he had to do. If he did not like the man himself, Wheatley did enjoy telling stories about him as part of the self-publicity of his own work. Almost accidentally Wheatley had discovered that the general public was fascinated with the occult during the inter-war years, and he would tap that fascination for all it was worth.

Wheatley was neither the demonic successor of Crowley, nor a gullible spiritualist like Sir Arthur Conan Doyle; in fact he was terrified by the mere thought of spiritualism. He had a firm idea that the dead existed in some form of after-life and had no desire to seek them out. In contrast he found black magic and Satanism laughable. Wheatley had served in the First World War until he was gassed at Passchendaele and invalided out. It had been time enough in the trenches to develop a distinct sense of other-worldliness concerning the vast war-torn and desolate landscape. On entering an area recently captured from the Germans he was struck by the sensation of a hate-filled presence looming over the soldiers. Wheatley was attuned to experiences such as this and it was natural enough when he began to write that he would draw on the darkness he had once experienced.

The Devil Rides Out established Wheatley as a supernatural thriller writer. Published at Hallowe'en 1934 its overt Satanism is set against a backdrop of fears of a future war with Germany. The leader of the Satanists is clearly Aleister Crowley. Fighting against Nazism and dark forces Wheatley's characters tapped into a very real fear of the time; that a return to war was inevitable.

Throughout the thirties Wheatley's name became firmly established with the occult. Though he wrote several books that had nothing to do with black magic, it was *The Devil Rides Out* that stuck in people's memories. Critics were off-hand about his work, but while Wheatley was not the finest of writers, he did have a certain charm that turned his books into bestsellers. Others were more dubious – was Wheatley promoting devil worship and the practice of black magic? More than once Wheatley was asked to comment on the rising fashion for dabbling in the occult, a fashion mostly in the imagination of newspapermen and Wheatley. Never one for missing a publicity opportunity Wheatley made ludicrous comments about the reality of black magic practices and witchcraft, careful to point out his own books made it plain that devil worship was evil and despicable.

Between Wheatley and the press the general public developed the view that all about them were Satanists and modern-day witches. The next-door neighbours might be cavorting naked behind closed curtains to summon demons and sacrificing the odd chicken and cat. The media had created a panic about something that did not exist. There is very little evidence to suggest black magic was being widely practiced in the 1930s. Later, in the 1960s, when a revival of Crowley and Wheatley occurred, there was a turn to devilish practices, but not three decades before. Yet the public were prepared to believe it, as society had changed so dramatically from the Edwardian age. The Church was no longer an overriding factor in peoples' lives, alternate religions and strange trends had emerged instead. The press prominently covered stories on haunted houses, fairies and other strange creatures. What had started rather sweetly in the early 1920s with hopeful images of dancing sprites and deceased relatives had taken a dark and sinister turn.

It all seemed to be coming to a head when Wheatley was asked for his opinion on a murder that had taken place in Warwickshire in 1945. An elderly labourer, Charles Walton, had had his throat cut and had been pinned down with a pitchfork. Police opinion was that his employer was to blame, but that did not stop a local folklorist putting forward ideas of ritual sacrifice. Wheatley was asked what he thought and said it was very likely, given the circumstances. It was all nonsense, but at the time people were prepared to accept it.

Wheatley, Crowley and Deacon all exploited associations with dark magic. For Wheatley it was very tongue-in-cheek, for the other two it was a lifestyle, but spiritualism had turned dark, in many ways a logical progression. That was little consolation to the great men who had tried to bring comfort to a grieving world through communication with the dead. Sir Arthur Conan Doyle escaped the worst, dying in 1930, but Sir Oliver Lodge lived another decade and saw how mediumship and the supernatural had been twisted in on itself.

CHAPTER SEVEN

Proof in a Picture

Spiritualism, even for a man of science like Lodge, suffered the disastrous flaw of being impossible to prove. What proof, other than anecdotal, could be gained from speaking with the dead? There was nothing to measure, nothing to study. Experiments had to be based on unquantifiable experiences, not the sort of standard a scientist was used to. Worse, rarely were results repeatable. In essence, much like a faith in God, it was very much down to personal beliefs.

This appeared to change with the advent of photography. Almost as soon as the camera was invented some ingenious soul started to take pictures of spirits to prove an afterlife. It caused a huge furore; in 1869 the spirit photographer William Mumler found himself in a New York courtroom accused of trickery and fraud when taking supposed photographs of people's long dead loved ones. Mumler was charging ten dollars for a dozen photographs, when the going rate was three dollars for a dozen (in today's terms Mumler was roughly charging $170). Mumler got off, despite expert testimony proving how easy it was to fake a photograph. The problem the judge had was that too many people were determined to believe the photographs genuine.

The issue did not go away over the next fifty years. Spirit photographers were setting themselves up across Britain, charging a fee to bring the dead back to life. Today the images they produced look clumsy and artificial, but the sitters were living in an age before television or even radio. Special effects were reserved for the theatre or films and the general innocence of people concerning photography left them wide open to fraud.

We might think photograph manipulation a device of the late twentieth century, but Victorian and Edwardian photographers worked with paintbrushes to achieve the same results we today equate to digital manipulation. It was incredibly easy to create an image on the glass plates of the early cameras; it might be caused by a double exposure, or using two plates, one with an extra image glued to it. A figure could be added during the production of a negative, or simply pasted onto an ordinary photograph and a second photograph taken. Looking at old spirit photographs it is clear that many were created from cut out images superimposed onto a glass plate, either at the time of the photograph being taken or at a later date. Exposed spirit photographers often had stacks of cardboard cutouts of random people ready to be used, in some cases certain ones were so popular they appeared in multiple photographs for different sitters.

M. J. Vearncombe of Bridgewater saw the potential for spirit photography in 1920. Already working as a photographer, he claimed that if he was sent personal belongings of someone who had passed he would be able to produce spirit extras in a photograph. The concept, which had been popular in spirit photography circles for a while, was that personal belongings absorbed the magnetic force of their owners and this could be tapped into by gifted mediums.

Vearncombe's earliest attempts impressed his clients. Sent the flying logbook of Lieutenant J. M. J. S. (his full name was withheld) sealed in a packet, Vearncombe was able to produce a picture with three ghostly faces hovering near the logbook. Two of the faces appeared to be male and one was wearing a flying cap, while the third seemed to be female. In 1921 Vearncombe became more daring by including live sitters in his photographs with the personal object of the deceased. One client, the strait-laced looking Mrs L. M. Humphry, posed for a photograph with the letter of a departed loved one. Two 'extras' appeared in the finished picture, one apparently a young boy, the other a man whose lower face was obscured. Psychic investigator Henry Blackwell also visited Vearncombe and had a photograph taken with three unidentified faces emerging from the dark background. It didn't seem to trouble him that they were upside down (a common issue in spirit photography) as though the 'extras' plate had been placed in the camera the wrong way up.

Vearncombe was doing well with his spectral pictures and started to request that clients send him packets of sealed plates which he would carry on his person, so that via him the spirits might impress themselves on the plates. After a set period of time they were sent back to the client supposedly unopened. When developed they would reveal ghostly faces.

The Occult Committee of the Magic Circle, a group of stage magicians who specialised in exposing the tricks of fake mediums, smelt a rat. They sent their own packet of plates, with the top left-hand corners of the glass marked with red varnish, impossible to see in a darkroom. When the plates were returned, now bearing ghostly images, all of them had been reversed in the packet. Vearncombe maintained that they had not been tampered with. The SPR had a similar experience when their packet of plates was returned. Miss Ina Jephson, who was in charge of the experiment, wrote to Eric Dingwall 'I had hoped that the conventions of swindling and of psychic photography combined might have led Vearncombe to take a little more trouble – such laziness is really rather enraging.'

More troubling for the believer was the number of repeats found on photographs. Why did the same face appear on a dozen photographs for different and unconnected sitters? The answer to this troubling dilemma slowly emerged via none other than the spirit photographers themselves. They explained that images on the plates were not always true representations of a person, rather they were faces that had been moulded from the ether by spirits using what was called 'spirit memory'. The faces were difficult and draining to create, so once made spirits often reused them. This explained why they did not necessarily look like the deceased. Sometimes they even appeared to resemble famous people from newspapers and magazines, and this was because the spirits had been focusing on these images while creating the faces. Aiding the spirit photographers in the continuation of this fraud were desperate spiritualists who could not bear the idea that these photographs were fakes and helped to propagate and promote the spirit photographers' excuses as genuine psychic theories.

The Dear Old Lady – Ada Deane

Sir Oliver Lodge was not immune to the lure of spirit photography. He believed Raymond had already given him proof of the continuation of the soul after death in the form of a photograph and was intrigued by the possibility of capturing snapshots of spirits. Prior to the war his friend and colleague Professor Charles Richet was invited to Algiers to investigate a nineteen-year-old girl named Marthé Beraud, the daughter of an army officer, with psychic powers. Marthé was able during her séances to summon the full-bodied apparition of a long dead Indian Brahmin named Bien Boa. Concealed in a curtained cabinet – the necessary trappings of an early medium – Marthé would conjure the spirit of a man who had died 300 years ago and he would emerge into the darkened room wearing a helmet, long, flowing white gown and a beard. Richet took a photograph of Bien Boa in one of his materialisations. With closer inspection Bien Boa looks decidedly flesh and blood, a real person dressed in white sheets, and with a resemblance to the medium herself beneath the clearly false beard. Early spiritualists and psychic investigators were not dissuaded by solid ghosts as they believed it perfectly natural for a spirit to render itself 'in the flesh'. Richet sent his Bien Boa pictures to Lodge who was deeply impressed and thought them the best psychic photographs he had ever seen.

Marthé changed her name to Eva C., moved to Paris and spent much of the war being investigated by various people, including Schrenck-Notzing. She was photographed multiple times producing ectoplasm or spirits, and in each case the modern observer will notice a decided cloth-like texture to the ectoplasm and a suspiciously cardboard quality to the spirits. There is a good irony to Eva's photographs which claim to be true images of psychic phenomena. Because she performed often stark naked her photographs had to be edited before they could be published and her breasts were carefully painted out. So despite claims Eva had not faked anything her photographs have been distinctly tampered with – even if it was for censorship purposes – it goes to show how easy it was to alter a photograph even 100 years ago.

Lodge continued to be fascinated by spirit photography, he had heard of a spirit photographer called Ada Deane who was an amateur with a camera and had seemingly begun her career by accident. Lodge invited her to his home where she stayed for three nights taking numerous pictures of the family. Extras appeared in the processed photographs as Lodge had expected. He was deeply impressed by Deane, like so many of her admirers he found her a quiet, almost shy, lady, simple in her habits and without guile or cunning. He said he would pay her a large fee if she would stay on his estate for several months to be examined further. Deane declined as she had three children to take care of.

Lodge would hear no criticism of Deane, particularly as Raymond had been good enough to confirm her skills through two separate mediums. Through Mrs Leonard in London, a well-known medium, and through an amateur medium Raymond told how he had watched the experiments and even could name the extras who had appeared on the photographs. Lodge told the forever sceptical Eric Dingwall that it could not possibly have been a hoax as it would have to be assumed that Deane was in a conspiracy with the two mediums, one of which was so new on the scene she could not possibly have been in contact with the others.

Ada Deane had a tendency to endear herself to people who viewed her as a sweet, little old lady. At fifty-eight she was hardly that old (in comparison to some of her clients) but she looked aged and worn. Appearing in one self-portrait as a small, Miss Marple-like figure, with her thin hair scraped back and her face heavily lined, a pair of round, metal-framed glasses perched on the bridge of her nose, she looks more like a batty aunt than a cunning fraudster.

Deane's life had been far from easy. Abandoned by her husband with three young children to raise, she had had to work as a servant and charwoman. The stresses and strains of this period, the hard work, exhaustion and financial worries, had taken their toll on her and left her looking much older than her actual years. Once her children had grown up, Deane found herself with the free time and money to dabble in a hobby. She took up pedigree dog breeding and photography, buying an old quarter-plate camera for 9*d*. It should be noted when she visited Lodge and made an excuse about having to take care of her children to refuse his offer to stay longer, her children were already grown-up.

Deane would later claim she had had psychic experiences since she was a child; playing with a spirit girl in the attic, being teased by a spirit boy at night and at one time saying she was witnessed floating down a flight of stairs by a group of nuns. However, ordinary life got in the way of her psychic powers and it was not until 1920 that she started to renew her interest, joining the spiritualist movement and eventually dabbling in spirit photography. Her first image of a ghost was probably a fluke caused by a previously exposed plate or a quirk of the camera. She photographed a friend and a stranger's head appeared over the face of the sitter. This minor technical accident spurred Deane into exploring her 'powers', assisted greatly by a London medium telling her she would become a spirit photographer. Deane sat with the medium for six months developing her skills before producing her first psychic photograph in 1920. We will never know exactly what went on during those six months, but later evidence would prove that Deane was not the humble, guileless creature so many believed.

Before long Deane was the new sensation and her work was prolific; she held over two thousand sittings making her the busiest medium and photographer in Britain. Psychic investigator Fred Barlow invited Deane to his home with her daughter Violet. Like Lodge he was fascinated by the possibility of spirit photography and was captivated by the mild-mannered little woman he welcomed into his home. Deane had dressed up for the occasion and her pretty daughter Violet (also now experiencing psychic powers) was keen to explore the new world her mother had opened up for them.

Barlow was convinced Deane was genuine. He had given her some plates before she visited which she was to carry about on her person and imprint with friendly spirits. On developing them Barlow saw numerous unknown faces gazing out at him. He was even more convinced when he took a picture of Ada and Violet Deane (with himself and his wife) just before the ladies were due to leave. He used his own camera and glass plate, but when developed two figures appeared to be floating over the mediums. Deane identified these as Stella and Bessie, spirit controls that had attached themselves to Ada and her daughter. Barlow's photograph shows chiffon draped figures, the head of one looking like a drawing from a Victorian scrapbook, but this did not perturb Barlow at all.

Barlow was further convinced a year later when Ada and Violet visited for their August holidays. Barlow had lost his father not long before and believed he had made contact with him at a family séance. When Deane visited she took a photograph of his cousin and in the corner, shrouded in a cloud-like substance, appeared Barlow's father. The whole family were convinced the extra looked just like Barlow senior before he died. Comparing Deane's photograph with a photograph taken during the lifetime of Barlow's father, there is a fleeting resemblance, but the extra's face is considerably thinner and elongated. Deane's image is also so fuzzy that a little imagination can turn it into virtually anyone. A short time later Barlow visited William Hope, the other famous spirit photographer, and obtained another picture with the same spirit extra. This image is so blurred and indistinguishable that it takes a really determined believer to conclude that it is a true representation of Barlow's father.

Deane had made her name, but along with the glory and income this fame brought, came the scepticism and the detractors. Deane was wily enough to fool her clients, but in many ways she was still a naïve old lady. *John Bull* (the newspaper which had so determinedly call soldiers saints during the war) decided to test Deane. They sent two anonymous investigators who brought their own plates to the sitting. Unsurprisingly the plates, never touched by Deane, developed quite ordinarily with no ghostly interlopers. Deane, in a moment of obvious foolishness (though admittedly she thought these were ordinary clients and she didn't want to disappoint) offered the investigators plates she had previously magnetised. Almost beside themselves with delight the investigators raced to the nearest photographic manufacturer in Ilford and showed them the plates. They explained the plates had already been exposed to light in a plate-holder, somewhere on them would be Deane's spirit fakes. *John Bull* wasted no time running the headline:

AMAZING SPIRIT CAMERA FRAUDS, PYSCHIC EXPERIMENTERS CAUGHT RED-HANDED IN TRANSPARENT DECEPTION AND TRICKERY

Eric Dingwall also tried to expose Deane. He sent an anonymous investigator to a sitting, but the final photographs were inconclusive. Dingwall personally went to try and catch out Ada Deane. He sent his packet of plates as requested to be 'pre-magnetised' and took elaborate measures to enable him to detect any tampering; sable hairs were lightly glued in the folds, invisible ink used to dye the ends of the cotton and pin-holes pricked through so they perfectly aligned. He arrived at Deane's studio to find the package untouched. Dingwall was asked to load the plates into the holder, but he was convinced they were switched when Deane carried the plate to her capacious handbag and reached in (with the plate) to retrieve her hymnbook.

Where Dingwall failed the Occult Committee succeeded. The packet of plates they had sent in had clearly been tampered with and they concluded Deane was a fraud. Sir Arthur Conan Doyle quickly jumped to her defence.

> The person attacked is a somewhat pathetic and forlorn figure among all these clever tricksters. She is a little elderly charwoman, a humble white

mouse of a person, with her sad face, her frayed gloves, and her little handbag which excites the worst suspicions in the minds of her critics.

Also firmly on Deane's side was the Spiritualist F. W. Fitzsimons who paid her several visits. He found her an unassuming woman, slightly naïve in her understandings of the workings of the world and hopelessly disorganised (she regularly double-booked herself and had two different sitters coming for the same appointment time). In his mind he could not see how such an honest, uncomplicated creature could possess the skills to perform the cunning sleight-of-hand others were accusing her of. When he first met her he found her dressed in overalls washing a litter of pedigree pups and they fell into a discussion about dogs. There was nothing about her manner or conversation that gave him the slightest hint she might be deceitful.

On another occasion Fitzsimons found he was double-booked with a mournful looking clergyman. The man was clutching a psychic photograph taken by William Hope and showed it to Fitzsimons, before explaining his presence at Deane's house:

My wife and I had been married twenty years, and we were childless. She was all I lived for. Recently she died, and my religion has given me no comfort or solace. I was in despair, and grew resentful against God. A friend told me about faces of deceased people appearing on photographs. I had four exposures made. Two were blanks, one had the psychic face of someone I did not recognise and the other held that of my wife, and here it is.

The clergyman was deeply torn between wanting to believe what was in the photograph and doubting the truth of it all. He was like so many who came to psychic photographers, desperate for some clue, some sign that life continued after death.

F. W. Warrick was the wealthy chairman of a wholesale druggist firm when he met Deane and decided to pose for her. Utterly convinced of her powers he arranged experiments to test her skills and over the next few years produced thousands of photographs, mostly inconclusive, taken under strict conditions. Warrick noted all this to Eric Dingwall who was not impressed. The more stringent Warrick's controls, the less likely it was that Deane would produce a psychic photograph. Instead of noting this as a strong indicator of fraud, Warrick switched his attention to the streaks of light, smudges and chemical blots that regularly appeared on the photographs. Ignoring the fact these could be the accidental contributions of an unskilled photographer developing her images, he saw them as indications of Deane's innate powers. By now Deane was also performing traditional séances and her various spirit guides would remark to Warrick that the restrictions he was putting on Deane were off-putting to the 'invisible operators' who helped her create photographs. Warrick believed this whole-heartedly. Dingwall was ambivalent and he had plenty of cause for suspicion. Deane's brother was a professional photographer and had taught his sister how to use a camera and develop pictures. The brother, in Dingwall's opinion, had helped his sister to develop her 'gift' by showing how to add extras to a photographic plate. The result was a nice little earner for Deane, enough to save her from having to work for others and to live in a degree of comfort enjoying her dogs.

Some of her photographs look obvious frauds today. In a couple of pictures taken of herself and her daughter showing their spirit guides, the extras in the images look distinctly like illustrations cut from a magazine. There is no depth to the faces and the flowing cloth that is draped over them only highlights the flatness of the spirits. In Deane's picture of her spirit guides, a pre-Raphaelite style girl superimposes herself completely over the medium, her long flowing tresses are not completely covered by reams of chiffon that are designed to sculpt her body shape. The outline of her hair is distinctly hard and solid, the sort of line caused by cutting out an image.

Even Warrick had to admit these photographs were suspicious, yet he still would not accept that Deane had committed a conscious act of fraud. Instead he believed the spirits were either creating the fakes themselves or inducing Deane to make them while in a trance state out of pure mischievousness.

Deane was now duly notorious and in 1921 came into contact with Estelle Stead, the daughter of the famous Victorian psychic investigator W. T. Stead. Stead was said to be clairvoyant but his powers had failed him when he booked passage on the *Titanic* and subsequently drowned in 1913. His daughter was of the firm opinion her father had returned through séances and even wrote a book allegedly dictated by her father from the other side about the experiences of the passengers of the *Titanic*. It was published under the title *The Blue Island*.

Stead told his daughter during séances that there were a number of Tommies and Hearts of Oak men (sailors) killed during the war who were now prepared to be photographed. He told Estelle that if she got Deane to photograph the platform used during the two-minute silence of the Armistice Day ceremony, the spirits would try their hardest to appear. Deane accepted the challenge and in November 1921 she was in London with her camera at the ready. She exposed the picture during the two-minute silence and the result was a strange cloud of heads superimposed over the bowed heads of the living attendants of the ceremony. Several of the heads wore hats of either military or navy style and were clearly representing men lost in battle. Above them all, looking mildly menacing was the face of an America Indian chieftain. Indian guides were the norm for mediums at that period and Deane had her own personal one called Brown Wolf. He had apparently gathered the group of disembodied heads together and helped to project them onto Deane's glass photographic plate.

The image took the spiritualist movement by storm, just three years after the end of the war there was enough raw emotion circulating to make many jump at the photograph and to believe it real. The following year Deane took two pictures, one just before the two-minute silence at Whitehall and one during the silence. The first image shows a faint circle of light hovering over a group of spiritualists who had come for the occasion of Deane's photograph and were devoting themselves to prayer to help the waiting spirits. The second, exposed for the full two minutes, shows the same crowd with a hazy, swirling circle of faces drifting over them. The faces were extremely faint, some barely discernible, but in the left corner there were enough distinct images for people to claim to recognise loved ones. Sir Arthur Conan Doyle thought the image incredible and took it with him when he went on his 1923 tour of America. When shown to audiences they gasped and sobbed.

November 1923 saw Deane take two more photographs during the ceremony and yet again faces appeared (this time upside down). These were shared among the spiritualist community and immediately people recognised loved ones and those already passed on would pop up in séances to point out they were in the photographs too.

When November 1924 rolled around Estelle Stead and her spiritualist friends were expecting big things. In the weeks running up to the event there were many messages through mediums about who would appear in the picture. In the spirit world, it appeared, there was a great deal of excitement and rivalry as to who would get their face exposed on Mrs Deane's photographic plate. There was even talk of spiritual training being undertaken on the Other Side for the event.

On the day Deane took two photographs that when developed showed a huge crowd of faces. Spiritualists everywhere were excited, but the secular world was also starting to take an interest in the little old lady who photographed dead soldiers on Armistice Day. The *Daily Sketch* managed to get the rights to reproduce the photograph and published it under the title 'Who are they?' Two days later they came back with the answer:

HOW THE DAILY SKETCH EXPOSED 'SPIRIT PHOTOGRAPHY'
'GHOSTS' VERY MUCH ALIVE. FACES OF POPULAR SPORTING
IDENTITIES IDENTIFIED IN ARMISTICE DAY PHOTOGRAPH

The paper had analysed the picture and discovered that no less than thirteen of the faces were those of famous, and very much alive, sportsmen. They reproduced the photograph next to images of the thirteen men, numbering the faces to enable readers to compare them for themselves. Most damning was the very recognisable face No. 5 of Battling Siki, a black boxer from Senegal, peering from the centre of the cloud.

Deane's supporters protested her innocence. Would anyone be foolish enough to compose a fraudulent picture using such recognisable faces? But for many it did seem all too plausible. Deane had been under-pressure to produce a good image and had not considered anyone would bother to compare her photograph to images of the real people she had used. Even more damning was the extraordinarily long exposure times Deane used for her photographs. A staff photographer for the *Daily Sketch* demonstrated that one method of superimposing an existing image over a blank plate also required a lengthy exposure time, and for many readers of the paper it seemed impossible to accept Deane as genuine.

One reader was appalled 'that individuals, especially women, should resort to these spirit photographs, thereby ridiculing these heroes of war, and perhaps causing sorrow and distress in many homes…'

Publically Deane had been exposed, but in private circles she was still respected and visited. She carried on her spirit photography for another decade, including Armistice Day pictures. In 1931, the year after Sir Arthur Conan Doyle's death, she produced a photograph of his face among the faces of soldiers captured during the two-minute silence. Deane always denied she had tricked her clients, she remarked that she deeply regretted discovering her 'gift' for it had added little to her life except worry and misery. We must take that with a pinch of salt. The photography earned her an income and saved her from going out to work, and while she might have been disparaged in the papers, she never gave up her craft.

The Man of Hope

William Hope, another psychic photographer, had a similar rise and fall as Deane. Trained as a carpenter, Hope was dabbling with a camera on a Sunday afternoon in 1905 when a face appeared on a photograph which a friend recognised as that of his deceased sister – or at least that was the story Hope told years later when explaining the emergence of his gift.

Hope came into contact with Mrs Buxton, the wife of the organist for the Crewe Spiritual Hall, and together they formed a circle of spiritualists (the Crewe Circle) to explore Hope's photography. Mrs Buxton was an amateur medium and sitting in the dilapidated greenhouse behind Hope's home she helped to bring forth spirits for him to photograph.

In 1908 Archdeacon Thomas Colley came for a sitting with the circle and was fascinated by the appearance of his mother on the finished picture. Unfortunately his mother had never been photographed in life and it was therefore difficult for anyone, other than the Archdeacon, to give a positive identification. Colley advertised in a local paper for people who knew his mother to come forward and examine the picture. Eighteen people came and identified her. So amazed was Colley, that he produced a flyer about Hope's talents and he presented the Crewe circle with a better camera. Hope later on liked to inform sitters of the spot where the Archdeacon knelt and thanked God for what he had seen.

The Crewe Circle would have remained a local novelty without the Great War which sparked a fascination in the supernatural and a desperate desire among many to contact lost loved ones. After the war Hope's work was examined by the Society for the Study of Supernormal Pictures (SSSP), which had formed in 1918 to examine the rising tide of psychic photography emerging in grieving, post-war, Britain. Hope took a picture of the society members in 1921, and the reclining image of a deceased man appeared on the final print. He was recognised as the late father of one of the members. Impressed, the SSSP starting promoting and endorsing Hope's work and drew attention to him from the wider world.

Hope charged sitters the modest sum of 4*s*, 6*d* for a dozen prints, basing his fee on his earnings as a carpenter. Slowly his fame grew and he was able to give up his old work and enjoy travelling among well-to-do spiritualist circles. The British College of Psychic Science (BCPS) invited him to London and he started to work through them. The BCPS charged two guineas for a sitting with Hope, though he refused to give up the old camera Colley had given him. Despite promoting him in this way, the BCPS preferred to hedge its bets on psychic photography and had sitters sign a document before leaving that they would not bring any legal action against them. They also insisted negatives were retained at the studio.

Hope had a keen supporter in Sir Arthur Conan Doyle, vice-president of the SSSP. Doyle believed he had obtained a picture of his lost son Kingsley in a photograph Hope had taken, and reproduced it in the *Sunday Pictorial*. Other spiritualists were equally convinced and not only posed for Hope in life, but kindly returned as spirit extras in death. Dr Gustave Geley, an international psychic investigator, planned to call on Hope and test his skills with his companion and translator Stanley de Brath. Unfortunately he was killed in a plane crash in Warsaw just before he was due to come to England and meet Hope. De Brath went alone and was astonished when a picture of him was taken and Geley appeared in the background. Nine days later another photograph of de Brath was taken and again Geley emerged hovering over his friend's head.

Hope had certain styles of spirit extra he could conjure, the first was a head globed in a circle of light (this was how Geley had appeared). The second was similar to Deane's work, with a face appearing swathed in luminous material.

Experts in photography and magic tricks were quick to denounce these images. The first could be created by a positive image of a face being taped over the tip of a small flashlight and, with the light turned on, being briefly exposed to the glass plate in the camera. The flashlight could be safely hidden in a sleeve. The second was even simpler; the cut out would be pre-exposed onto the plate before a photograph was taken.

Throughout his career Hope was exposed and forced to admit his skulduggery. In 1915 he had to confess in the *Psychic Gazette* that the famous image of Archdeacon Colley's mother was in fact taken from a portrait of a completely different woman, the grandmother of someone he knew. In 1920 Hope was ridiculed in a pamphlet by Edward Bush, who had tricked the photographer by sending an image of his still very much alive son-in-law, claiming it was a person who had passed that he wanted to get in touch with. In due course he was presented with a photograph containing the image of his son-in-law, quite obviously copied from the photograph he had sent. It was Bush who explained the flashlight technique for adding images to a glass plate in a camera.

Doyle was still a loyal supporter of Hope, but his friend Houdini was less convinced. After hearing about Hope, Houdini decided to investigate him. He rang for an appointment and was told Hope was fully booked for the next month. Suspecting his reputation had gone before him, Houdini asked a fellow magician to request an appointment – remarkably Hope's diary was suddenly free and a sitting was arranged. During the meeting Hope was spotted switching plates and when the photograph was developed the image emerged faster than might have been expected, as if the plate was already partly exposed. Houdini's comrade had also brought his own camera and glass plate, which he asked Hope to try. Hope agreed, but instead of using the camera's shutter he insisted on regulating the exposure by cupping a hand over the lens. When the photograph was developed a vivid spot of 'light' appeared over the magician's face. Mrs Buxton enthusiastically called this a 'spirit light'. When it was reported back to Houdini, it was decided to be more likely a spot of a phosphorescent substance on Hope's hand, hence why he had controlled the exposure so oddly.

Hope was even more dramatically exposed by the SPR and Harry Price with carefully marked plates that demonstrated he had switched them during the sitting. Hope's many supporters, Doyle included, jumped to his defence and attacked the subterfuge used by the SPR to obtain a sitting and questioning their methods. Despite these disasters Hope still enjoyed a healthy client base, much like Deane, and continued to work until his death in 1933. During this time he was able to take a photograph of Doyle as a spirit extra following the great man's death in 1930, another thing he shared in common with Ada Deane.

After his death Hope was attacked by none other than the man who had been an ardent defender of his skills for fifteen years. Fred Barlow had a fascination for psychic phenomena and had originally fully believed in Hope, but as the years passed he drifted into the company of Eric Dingwall and slowly became more and more sceptical of the talents of his old friend. Perhaps it was a remnant of loyalty that had kept him quiet until Hope's death, or was it because he preferred to publish his experiences without fear of retaliation? In any case Barlow issued a series of articles condemning Hope, remarking that during the 1920s a friend had discovered a flashlight in Hope's bag with a cut-out face stuck on and ready for use; just as Edward Bush had described. There was the usual back and forth of arguments, but in the end even Mrs McKenzie, owner of the BCPS had to admit she had once found a similar flashlight in a bag Hope usually kept locked. She had said nothing because she still believed that on occasion Hope produced genuine phenomena. Yet again Hope's hard-core believers could not give him up and a subscription was raised by spiritualists for a memorial brass to be placed in his honour in a church in Yorkshire.

CHAPTER EIGHT

An Age to Believe?

It was natural, with the rise in disbelief or alternative religion, that the media would tap into the prevailing tide of change concerning spirituality. It is always debatable whether mass media leads a cultural change or merely showcases it. With the First World War it was probably the latter. As the movie industry slowly returned to normal after the conflict, especially in France, there was a growing trend to expand the silent film into something more than just entertainment and something that would cause an audience to think. How better to do that then to explore the growing spiritual confusion in Europe?

Early silent movies were very short, often no more than a few minutes, and filmmakers liked to focus on everyday events that would amuse their audience who were still revelling in the novelty of moving pictures. It wasn't long, however, before moviemakers started to experiment and create longer films that told a story. Georges Melies was an early pioneer, having begun his career on the stage. He had a passion for magic tricks and was fascinated by the possibility of special effects on film. He created over 500 films between 1896 and 1913, many of which were designed to display a certain special effect and had no plot. Others, such as *Joan of Arc*, were short stories within which Melies could dabble with film illusions.

Like so many early movie-makers Melies stuck to retelling traditional stories, though in 1902 he made the bizarre *The Devil and the Statue*, with Melies playing the lead role of Satan, who grows to gigantic proportions and terrorises the Shakespeare character Juliet, before the Virgin Mary appears and cuts him down to size. Story-wise there was little plot, but that was not Melies' purpose. He wanted to demonstrate another technique he had been dabbling with, using camera movement to change the size of an actor.

Melies most celebrated movie was made in the same year. In *A Trip to the Moon* a group of astronomers decide to send a bullet-shaped capsule to the moon, where they duly encounter hostile aliens and the lunar goddess. The fourteen-minute film includes the iconic scene of the space shuttle crashing into the Man in the Moon's face. As spectacular as the film was it was still a very basic action story, something Melies specialised in. But as the first decade of the twentieth century drew to a close audiences were wanting more than short adventures. They wanted character interactions, sub-plots, tangled love triangles and something to think about. Melies was bankrupt by 1913 and the war finished his movie career. During the conflict his main studio was taken over to be used as a hospital for wounded soldiers and the army confiscated many films and melted them down to retrieve the celluloid and silver. Melies creations' went to make boot heels for the army.

The war had an impact on many filmmakers. From a practical sense it disrupted studios, stealing young actors to fight at the front. There was also a social outrage that frivolous things such as films should continue to be created while the world was in chaos and men from many nations dying. From an artistic point of view, the content of films was changed dramatically by the horrors of war. Plot lines became darker and endings were less certain to be happy. American movie-maker D. W. Griffiths' *Birth of a Nation* makes most right-thinking people cringe today. It was produced in 1915 when the war had been going on for a year and in its warped sense of patriotism and 'good against evil' plot, it can almost be viewed as a propaganda piece to remind Americans that not standing up and fighting can end in trouble on your doorstep. Unfortunately to emphasise its point it used the Ku Klux Klan as the 'good guys' rescuing white women from the brutal attentions of black men. Misguided as the film was, it shows how the idea of what a film should mean was changing.

Griffiths was heavily criticised at the time for his film. He went on to produce *Intolerance* in 1916, partly in response to the verbal assaults he had received for *Birth of a Nation*. *Intolerance* is truly an epic for the silent era running at a length of three and a half hours and following four separate storylines. In this case Griffiths turned to his Bible for possible subject matter and intersected Christ's mission and death with the fall of the Babylonian empire in 539BC, the St Bartholomew's day massacre in France 1572 and a contemporary story of crime and redemption. The film was a flop, some critics believed this due to its message of peace and forgiveness that was anathema to an audience gearing up for entering the war. The modern story thread of *Intolerance* threw a barb at the perceived hypocritical morals of the middle and upper classes. The mill owner in the film decides to help his sister's charities by cutting the pay of his workers and passing the savings on to her. The irony, of course, is that he ends up forcing the workers into the very poverty his sister is trying to counter. A young woman sees her husband sent to prison, framed by the same mill owner and her child is nearly taken away by his sister's moral charities. Griffiths was really taking a stab at the attitudes of the age and, in a side slash, at the religious fervour behind them.

Spiritualism featured in a number of silent films, sometimes being portrayed as genuine, at other times being lampooned. In *Darkened Rooms* an American talkie from 1929, the actress Evelyn Brent poses as a fraudulent medium working alongside a genuine clairvoyant. Though the main plot of the film is about the clash between the faked and the real, that quickly becomes secondary to the various ways the medium is caught out. *Darkened Rooms* used the real methods of psychic sceptics such as Houdini to give authenticity to its story. In contrast the 1920 film *Earthbound* portrayed a murdered man's spirit trying to positively influence the lives of those he has wronged, so he can be saved and reach heaven. In a séance-type scene he eventually appears to his wife to make amends for his sins. In *The Bishop of the Ozarks* 1923, spiritualism becomes sinister when Dr Earl Godfrey tries to seduce a woman by mental telepathy and mediumship. The magazine *Moving Picture World* remarked when reviewing *The Bishops of the Ozarks*, 'Mysticism has been resorted to in several instances. There is a spiritual séance, a persistent strain of mental telepathy and a definite instance in which the occult powers of evil are demonstrated.'

Post-war filmmaking had two roles, first to produce movies that would provide escapism for the audience (this included retellings of classic stories and light-hearted comedies) and secondly trying to shock the audience and bring fresh ideas to the screen. In post-war Germany there was a move towards Expressionist film, which included the remaking of *Dracula* for the big screen as *Nosferatu: A Symphony of Horror* (1922). Though based on the book (and suffering from copyright infringements) *Nosferatu* was lauded for its use of light and shadows and silhouettes to expand the media and induce terror in the audience.

Far more disturbing and shown in the same year was, *Haxan: Witchcraft through the Ages*, a film that claimed to be a documentary on the history of black magic and argued that witches were suffering a psychological hysteria. A mixture of fact and fiction, the film was shocking for its portrayal of torture, nudity and sexual perversion. Similar to other individuals of the time who wrote about the occult (notably Dennis Wheatley) the film's director had his idea for *Haxan* after finding a copy of the *Malleus Maleficarum*, a medieval book on the prosecution of witches, in a Berlin bookshop. And just like Wheatley, though his film aimed to demystify the occult and remove its seriousness, its shocking images instead forced the idea of black magic into the audiences' minds. In Wheatley's case he had tried to demonstrate how wrong and evil black magic could be, but glamourized it so much that he achieved the opposite effect. Naturally *Haxan* was heavily censored in countries such as America, but it demonstrated the way people's minds were working. Black magic, witchcraft and Satanism had suddenly become a worrisome topic after several centuries of being deemed nonsense.

Similar ideas were fermenting in Scandinavia. Having remained neutral during the war, the various Scandinavian countries – notably Denmark and Sweden – had less problems rejuvenating their film industry compared to war-torn countries. They became leading lights in post-war Europe and they also found influence in the growing diversity of afterlife beliefs. *The Phantom Carriage* was released on New Year's Day 1921 and concerns a tale of redemption and the supernatural. Set on New Year's Eve, dying Salvation Army girl Edit has one last wish – to see again the alcoholic David Holm. Edit had set her heart on helping the hopeless Holm, who has ruined his life and his marriage. Edit persuaded Holm to come to a Salvation Army meeting to try and draw him back to God, but Holm refused to believe. Instead he continued his path of drinking, eventually becoming dangerous and violent towards his wife and children.

As Edit lies dying asking for Holm, he is sitting in a graveyard (already a prominent feature in horror stories) with two friends, drinking the last hours of the old year away. The talk turns to Georges, a friend who passed on the previous New Year's Eve. Holm recalls a legend that the last person to die in the year is commandeered by Death to act as his coachman and collect all the souls who die over the next twelve months. As Georges was the last he must now be Death's coachman. As they are talking, a friend of Edit finds Holm and begs him to speak with the girl before she dies. Holm simply refuses and begins arguing with his friends over the matter. A brawl breaks out and Holm is accidentally killed just as the local clocks strike twelve.

In a classic movie effect Holm's soul rises from his dead body as Death's carriage appears and, who should be driving, but Georges. Georges reminds his old friend of his life before drink and all the good things he has cast aside. He takes him to Edit who, close to death herself, can see the spectral Holm. For a few moments they are alone and Edit reveals how guilty she feels for bringing Holm and his wife back together earlier. She believes her interference pushed him further into drink. Holm promises her it was not her fault and as he kisses her hand Edit dies at peace with herself. Georges next takes Holm to his family, where he sees his wife, driven to poverty and despair, conclude that her only option is to kill her children and herself. Holm suddenly realises the influence his actions have had on so many others and begs Georges and God to let him help his wife. With a little bit of New Year's Eve magic Holm is allowed to return to the land of the living and the movie ends with him embracing his wife. We are left to presume he reforms and takes better care of his family.

Aside from clear parallels with Dickens' *A Christmas Carol*, the movie is starkly influenced by the despair that seemed to be overwhelming Europe since the war. Holm could be viewed akin to many returning servicemen who found their old lives incompatible with what they had experienced and witnessed at the front. Many turned to drink, abandoned families, or simply wallowed in depression. Families were torn apart and driven into poverty, and the movie emphasises that there is only one true hope, the salvation of God. It is interesting that the movie focuses on a Salvation Army follower, as opposed to a priest, to bring across this message. The Salvation Army was relatively new and some had thought it a dubious sect, but it had shown its worth during the war. It is also interesting to note that the message comes from a woman and not a man. In a society where typically God's message came through Church*men* it is interesting that a woman was chosen to save Holm. Was it because she was deemed of a softer nature and more likely to be listened to by the cynical Holm and the movie audience? Or because it was the womenfolk who were left to pick up the pieces after the war?

Even more tragic and disturbing is the French film *J'accuse*, first released in 1919 in France, but not reaching England until 1920 and the US until 1921. The film was a stark reminder of the horrors of war and the effects it had on ordinary people. Director Abel Gance was heavily influenced by his time at the front working for the French Army's cinematography section and the film would later include actual footage of real battles that Gance had filmed. He was discharged from the army due to ill health and turned his attention to creating a film that would capture his bitterness and sorrow at the loss of so many friends in the war.

J'accuse uses a backdrop of a love triangle to bring across the tragedy of war. François Laurin, a jealous and violent man, is married to Edith who is carrying on an affair with poet Jean Diaz. When war breaks out François and Jean both enlist and Edith is sent to Lorraine to live with François' parents. While there she is captured and raped by German soldiers.

François and Jean find themselves serving in the same battalion and the camaraderie of combat sees them forming a close friendship despite François' suspicions that the poet has been making love to his wife. Both men survive until 1918, when Jean is invalided out due to ill health. He returns home to find Edith, who has been released by the Germans, with a young half-German daughter. François is due home soon and both fear what he will make of the child, so they try and hide her. When François arrives this only fuels his suspicions and he fights with Jean. The truth at last emerges and both men agree to go back to the front and avenge Edith's honour in battle against the Germans.

It is at this point Gance's film takes on a supernatural element based on the many legends of spectral armies and figures appearing on the battlefield. The French forces are led into a great battle by a mythical figure, representing French freedom and patriotism. François is wounded and dies, Jean is severely shell-shocked and is sent home once more, where he rapidly goes insane.

Jean becomes tormented by a vision of dead soldiers rising from their battlefield graves and marching home together in a huge army. He rushes to

Edith's village and gathers everyone, demanding if they are truly worthy of the sacrifice their men have made. To the horror of the villagers ghostly soldiers begin to appear, standing on the thresholds of their old homes. The vast crowd of dead men parade before the living before vanishing back to their unmarked graves.

Jean runs home and finds a book of his poetry which he rips up in disgust. He pauses at a poem called *Ode to the Sun*, sparked into an insane outrage he rants against the very sun itself, which he believes has been complicit in the crime of war. As the room fades out Jean falls back and dies.

The film was remarked upon for its clear portrayal of the director's bitterness and heartache. There is little in the nature of redemption or forgiveness. God is not present in Gance's bleak world, instead Jean rails against the much older pagan god, the sun. The rising of the dead to return home was horrifying for several reasons, not least for the sheer number of them and the knowledge that so many would never return. The 'returning dead' sequence was filmed in 1918 using 2,000 soldiers on leave. The horror for so many was seeing dead men on the screen pretending to be ghosts.

> The conditions in which we filmed were profoundly moving... These men had come straight from the front – from Verdun – and they were due back eight days later. They played the dead knowing that in all probability they'd be dead themselves before long. Within a few weeks of their return, eighty per cent had been killed.

J'accuse was considered a pacifist, or perhaps more appropriately, an anti-war film. Gance claimed he had no political motivations behind the film, he was just angry and he was accusing everyone, from the universe down, for standing back and letting the war happen. For this reason the film was not initially accepted in the US and Gance found it necessary to get the American director Griffiths on his side before *J'accuse* could be widely released. The rising of the dead is still the most emotive part of the story, a stark reminder that war costs lives which tapped into the anguish of millions. It was not the only time an image of the fallen returning was used to play on the public's emotions, as in the case of the famously fraudulent Remembrance Day spirit photograph, but at least in Gance's case it was an honest attempt to capture in simple terms the huge loss the world had suffered.

Life on Mars

As people found their faith in religion shattered, along with their faith in humankind, there was a growing trend for looking beyond the confines of earth and out further afield. While some in the 1920s were looking backwards, to simpler times and pagan beliefs that seemed more innocent and carefree than the current world they were living in, others were becoming convinced there was life on Mars. This was hardly surprising considering the curiosity shown to the planets beyond earth and the possibilities they held. Mars has always been the centre of attention when it comes to extra-terrestrial life. Visible from earth to the naked eye, until the 1960s it was thought it could have the potential to support life, with what appeared to be oceans covering parts of its surface. Only when *Mariner 4* flew by in 1965 did these theories start to be disproved.

In the post-war era of the 1920s and 1930s Mars could be looked at and imagined to be a place teeming with life; not only that, but it was deemed by a disillusioned world to be far more advanced and sophisticated, with intelligent Martians who could teach humans a thing or two about life and behaving themselves. H. G. Wells' vision of invading Martians in *War of the Worlds* (1898) was replaced by the idea of Martian kings and queens, elaborate cities and cultural superiority. This was a world where war was seen as pointless and unnecessary, where peace and unity reigned. To the survivors of the First World War, Mars became a focus of hope and harmony.

In *A Message from Mars* (1921) this idea of the majestic, noble Martian was played upon. The lead character Horace Parker is a wealthy young man with little interest in anything outside his own world. He has invested money in a device that can communicate with Mars on the condition that he is credited (erroneously) with its invention. He is so wrapped up in his project that he refuses to go with his fiancée Minnie to a party. Left alone he falls asleep and a figure appears before him. The bizarrely clad stranger claims to be a messenger from Mars who has come to earth to transform the most selfish man on the planet, Horace. Horace is shown the dark side of the world he is living in, again in a sequence akin to Scrooge's transformation in *A Christmas Carol*. He ends up at the home of a soldier and his family, who he has previously refused to help. Shaken by the Martian messenger's words he finds himself awake in the same house, which is now ablaze. He rescues the family and from that moment becomes a changed man. He invites the less fortunate to his home and redeems himself in the eyes of Minnie.

A Message from Mars was highly contemporary on its release, as there had been a growing trend in both the UK and US to try and contact Mars. Psychic detective Harry Price was also in on the game and created his own Mars communication device and certain mediums and former spiritualists turned their attention from the dead to the ruling elite of Mars. One British gentleman claimed he could turn himself into a human conduit for communication. He wrapped himself in copper wire, sat in a tin bath full of chemicals and used a stick to propel himself about the room until he found just the right spot for good reception, then he would begin to relay messages from Martian princesses and noblemen.

The most famous psychic to communicate with Mars could be argued to be Helene Smith (1861-1929) who lived in France. She had actually begun her communications as early as the 1890s, but these were considered to be infantile imaginings by the people who examined her at the time. Three decades later, when Helene was an old woman, a new excitement in communicating with aliens became more widespread and in certain circles her work was taken more seriously. Helene used automatic writing to talk to the Martians and wrote out messages in their own language, which she then translated into French. As more stories emerged about life on the red planet some were entranced by the idea, others considered it nonsensical, particularly when conflicting tales of conditions on Mars were circulated. The fascination with space, however, would not go away.

In 1924 Russian director Yakov Protazanov created a dystopian alien world in *Aelita: The Queen of Mars*. In Protazanov's vision of Mars it is the human hero who is out to save the dysfunctional aliens by inducing a revolution, just as had happened in Russia. He is helped by the beautiful queen Aelita who has watched earth through a telescope and has fallen in love with the human hero. While the story might be pure Soviet propaganda, what captured the minds of the western world were the extraordinary sets Protazanov created for his Martian scenes and the strange and unearthly costumes. It also showed a turning point in the 'noble alien' genre. No longer were Martians messengers of peace and goodwill, they were as disillusioned and politically corrupt as mankind, in fact *they* now needed to be save by *us*.

If Mars was not going to save the world at least films about space could be viewed as pure escapism, a modern retelling of the classic adventure story of a journey into the unknown. The pinnacle of this trend was the flawed masterpiece of German expressionist Fritz Lang, *Metropolis* (1927). The iconic image from the film is the feminine robot that can be seen on the movie posters. Creepy, yet attractive, the machine is meant to be a recreation of the character Joh's dead wife. Conjuring up the notion of the dangers of wishing the dead back to life, Joh is consumed by his desire to reinvent his wife Hel, to the detriment of his workers. *Metropolis* is dominated by the skyscrapers where the elite live and work while the ordinary men toil in underground caverns, exposed to danger at every turn and driven to exhaustion.

In many ways *Metropolis* expresses the growing discontent in Germany towards the rich and influential minority who dominated the lives of the poor majority. A similar disaffection had occurred in England, though to a lesser extreme, when the ordinary soldier in the trenches realised how insignificant he was in the eyes of the commanding officers. In Britain this began the overhaul of the class system and the way the army was run. In Germany the misery of the class system had a more fundamental and dramatic influence – it paved the way for Nazism.

If space was the final frontier, it was also a good indicator of the mindset of the population and the changing political climate of post-war Europe. Space introduced ideas of vastness and of looking beyond the sphere of man. Technological advances made space travel seem suddenly feasible, but more importantly people could look out into an untarnished universe and wonder about possibilities. For some, it seemed the only hope humanity had left, was to find a new world and to start again.

CHAPTER NINE

Fairies, Pixies and Ghoulies, Oh My!

Every war in history has created legends, but the Great War took things to an entirely different level. So many people were affected by death. The massive, unnatural trench systems forged ideas of other-worldliness, isolation and eeriness. At any moment death could come from a well-timed sniper's bullet. This constant unease and exhaustion conjured up strange ideas. Stories of dead soldiers' spirits returning to the trenches were commonplace, as were premonitions of disaster. Superstitions were rife, each man making his own pact with God or fate to survive.

Into this heady mix of imagination and spiritual bargaining came the news that Kitchener, the great figurehead of the war, had vanished without trace. Shock was rapidly replaced with fear – wasn't Kitchener going to help Britain win the war? Fear turned into a dangerous combination of speculation and rumour. Was he really dead? And if he was, what did that mean for Britain?

Kitchener is best remembered as the stern face pointing a finger at potential soldiers from a recruitment poster. It is easy to forget that during the early part of the war he was actually a key figure in the politics of the conflict as Secretary of State for War. Kitchener attracted extreme loyalty and hate and was unpopular for predicting at the start of the war that it would be a long, drawn-out conflict, sapping the strength of Britain and mining the country's manpower down to the last million. He was proved right, but he had spoken up at a time when optimism buoyed opinion rather than realism. On the other hand, Kitchener's triumph, according to Cabinet Secretary Maurice Hankey, was how he transformed a country that had previously favoured seapower, into having a sizeable, fully equipped army that could be sent into France.

Sir John French, Commander-in-Chief of the British Expeditionary Force loathed Kitchener, and said he had 'gone mad'. It very rapidly became common knowledge at GHQ that there was strong hostility between the two men. Kitchener never adapted to being a politician rather than a military commander, and his palpable dislike of discussing military matters with members of the cabinet had a negative effect on his own reputation. During

1915 the man who had at first been seen as the public face of the war, was becoming a nuisance, at times even an embarrassment.

Kitchener was not a politician and the strain his new role placed upon him aged and wearied him. By early 1916 the new Commander-in-Chief of the BEF (Kitchener having ousted French), Douglas Haig reported that Kitchener was, 'pinched, tired and much aged' when he met him and considered his mind to not be not as sharp as it had once been. Kitchener's thoughts were turning more and more to what would happen after the war. He wanted a peace of reconciliation, not the vindictive peace the politicians were vying for. It is interesting to wonder, if he had survived the war, whether he would have made a difference to the Treaty of Versailles which was in part responsible for the rise to power of a certain Adolf Hitler?

In any case, the Cabinet wanted him out of the way and in 1916 he was sent on a mission to Russia to negotiate with the Tsar over military matters and the support Britain could expect from the country.

Kitchener stepped aboard the armoured cruiser HMS *Hampshire* in June 1916. He was supposed to have been accompanied by the Minister of Munitions David Lloyd George (later Prime Minister), but Lloyd George had cancelled at the last moment. Kitchener was not expecting to enjoy his voyage as he suffered from seasickness and the weather forecast was not promising for a calm sea. There had been attempts to delay the voyage, but Kitchener would not have it, so he stepped aboard *Hampshire* and set sail for his fate.

On the evening of the same day HMS *Hampshire* is believed to have hit a mine launched by German submarine *U-75*. A passage through the German minefield surrounding northern Britain had recently been swept for the *Hampshire*, but the Germans had caught wind of this action and acted quickly to re-mine the cleared route. There are other theories blaming sabotage. There was a man allegedly on board who planned to kill Kitchener, but it appears that he left the ship before it hit the fateful mine.

In reality the rough weather, the decision to use an unusual route (thus raising German suspicion) and the bungling of the Naval authorities when it came to rescuing the *Hampshire* survivors all led to the disaster. Only a handful of men out of a crew of over 650 survived. One reported seeing Kitchener standing on deck as the *Hampshire* sank, refusing to get into a lifeboat. His opinion was that Kitchener went down with the ship.

But Kitchener had been an immensely popular character with the British public. He had his detractors, but many considered him the face of the war, the icon of British victory, and the man that would lead them through. His loss scared many people, but it was not long before stories of Kitchener's survival emerged. A woman on Orkney, off the shores of which the *Hampshire* had sunk, claimed to have seen a man who resembled Kitchener walking the cliffs and living in a cave.

Kitchener sightings were reported all over the place, but as the months passed it seemed unlikely the man was still alive. Instead, his ghost was spotted in the front line trenches, leading troops into the fray. Naturally, due to their own bungling, the Admiralty was reluctant to release full details of what had really happened to the *Hampshire*, so the ground was ripe for conspiracy theories. The Russian communists did it. The Irish Republicans did it. The Jews did it. Even Winston Churchill was held up as a suspect, though he successfully sued for criminal libel. After the war ended the Kitchener mystery still captivated a number of people. His body was never recovered and this carried the hope that he might just be alive – perhaps a prisoner in Germany or Russia? Or had he lost his memory and was wandering somewhere as a stranger?

It seemed as though the mystery would finally be laid to rest in 1926, ten years after Kitchener's disappearance, when a man named Frank Power claimed a Norwegian fisherman had found the military commander's body. Anyone might have wondered how a body could be identified after ten years at sea, but there were enough people willing to believe in Power's story that he went to the lengths of bringing a coffin back from Norway and preparing it for burial in St Paul's. At this point someone thought it a smart idea to check the contents of the coffin, which proved to be nothing more than lumps of tar for weight.

The Kitchener mystery, like the Angels of Mons has become one of the most enduring stories of the First World War. Though the truth of the sinking of the *Hampshire* has long been revealed there are still those who believe in a conspiracy behind the death. No one wanted to believe Kitchener, the icon of patriotism and victory, could perish due to human error. But whatever they wanted, the simple truth was that Kitchener was gone and a new mystery had been added to the annals of history.

The Cottingley Fairies

They greatest fairy story of the modern period all began when two lonely cousins came together in the last years of the First World War. Frances Griffiths had arrived back in Britain from South Africa with her mother – her father was serving at the front. For the first nine years of her life Frances had led a privileged existence in sunny Africa and now she was in England, living with her cousin and aunt and uncle in a small cottage in Yorkshire. It was cold, damp and rainy. Frances had been ripped from her idyllic life and her only consolation was the bubbling beck at the bottom of the cottage garden. Tucked among trees, with various streamlets and waterfalls feeding into it, it was a mystical place to escape to, but Frances was prone to falling in and would regularly return home with sodden shoes and stockings. Her outraged mother asked what on earth she was doing down there, and Frances just burst out, 'I go to see the fairies! That's why – to see the fairies!'

The statement drew an unpleasant silence from both Frances' mother and her aunt and it looked likely Frances would be in deeper trouble when her cousin came to her aid. Elsie, sixteen and close friends with her cousin, stepped beside Frances and said, 'I've seen them too.'

The two girls were scoffed at. Away from the adults Frances wept bitter tears at being disbelieved and Elsie tried to comfort her. She even suggested trying to take a picture of these creatures.

Elsie's father happened to be an amateur photographer. One Saturday in July 1917 Elsie asked if she might borrow his new Midg camera so she could take a picture of Frances down at the beck. He was naturally reluctant. His daughter had never handled a camera and they were fragile things with glass plates. Elsie persuaded him to allow her to try, so he demonstrated how the Midg operated, installed a single glass plate and watched the two cousins vanish down the garden.

They were back within half an hour, eager for their photograph to be developed. Arthur, like most photographers of the period, had his own dark room tucked into a tiny cupboard under the cellar stairs. Elsie squeezed in beside her father, while Frances waited outside, leaning on the door to hear what was happening. As the various chemicals swirled over the developing paper strange shapes began to emerge. Frances stared out of the picture, her chin propped on her hands, while about her several lithe figures danced. Elsie was ecstatic. 'We caught the fairies!'

Arthur was less impressed. Well aware of his daughter's skills as an artist and her love for drawing fairies, he instantly suspected the fairies were cut outs. Had he looked in the book Frances had brought with her from South Africa, *The Princess Mary Gift Book*, his suspicions would have been confirmed as it contained identical drawings of dancing fairies.

The original photograph was over-exposed and fuzzy and the detail on the fairies difficult to make out. Later when the same picture appeared in the *Strand* in a retouched form the fairies looked even more like two-dimensional figures. If Arthur was uncertain, his wife and sister-in-law were the exact opposite. Both women had been drawn to the teachings of Theosophy and they could not comfortably dismiss the strange creatures their daughters had captured. Elsie borrowed the camera again and returned to the beck, this time Frances took a picture of her cousin holding her hand out to a prancing gnome. Elsie's hand appears elongated on the photograph, caused by camera slant when the inexperienced Frances took the snap. When Arthur saw the photograph he was furious with the girls and refused to lend them his camera anymore. Despite this, the two shots were reproduced several times and distributed among family and friends.

It is almost impossible to modern minds to understand how people could be so inspired and fooled by the fuzzy pictures taken by two little girls. The gulf the Great War had left in people's spiritual beliefs played a pivotal role. Frances' mother Annie had gone bald through worry over her husband in the army, and Elsie's mother Polly had teetered on the verge of atheism, before finding Theosophy. Both were very desperate in 1917 to find some ray of hope in the darkness, some proof that the spiritual world and God still existed.

It is also important to remember that both Annie and Polly were from a background of modest education and cultural awareness. Polly's husband was fairly new to photography and she had no knowledge of its inner workings. Photography, in itself, was still a novelty to many. Only in recent times had the more humble sections of society found any opportunity to have pictures taken, and naturally they were unaware of how easily photographs could be faked. If you could capture the spirits of the dead on a glass plate why not fairies? In many rural regions there was still a firm, unquestioning notion of little people existing somewhere in the wild places. Older people still left out plates of milk to appease them, and imagined that things going missing were the works of invisible hands. In this atmosphere, photographs of fairies seemed quite logical.

Any doubts Polly and Annie had about their children's photographs were soon quashed when the renowned writer Sir Arthur Conan Doyle became involved in 1920. He had seen copies of the pictures and was intrigued, though he retained a cautious sense of doubt about their authenticity. Why, for instance, if the fairies were so willing to be photographed, were there only two pictures?

Tentative attempts to disprove the photographs were made. The girls' bedroom was searched for scraps of paper or earlier drawings and the beck was examined for signs of tampering. Elsie would have been wise enough to mask any fraud by destroying paper cuttings or early drawings and would have certainly covered any traces at the beck. The time between the photographs being taken and the searches being made would have allowed the girls to dispose of any evidence. Tiny paper fairies would quickly disappear in a fire.

Doyle showed copies of the photographs to Sir Oliver Lodge. By now they were close allies in the promotion of spiritualism, but Lodge was not convinced by fairies and dismissed the images, sensing fraud. Doyle agreed with him, but something was drawing him in, not least his memories of his uncle who was fascinated by, and believed in, fairies. Doyle decided the best way to solve the issue was to have Elsie and Frances take more pictures down at the beck.

On a drizzly August afternoon, conveniently at a time when Polly had gone out, Elsie and Frances ventured down to the beck with a camera they had been loaned by Theosophist and convinced fairy-hunter Edward Gardner. He had been working as go-between for the girls and Doyle, and was happy to provide the equipment which would prove the existence of these creatures. Down by the beck Elsie took the first new fairy photograph, featuring Frances turning her head to look at a leaping fairy. Perhaps aware of earlier criticism that she had not been looking at the fairies, this time she was pointedly gazing on the leaping creature, which had even caused her to lean back slightly. But there was a rather obvious flaw with the image. Frances' head and hair are caught moving, so they are blurred slightly, the fairy, leaping, should also have been blurred due to movement. Instead it is perfectly clear and sharply in focus.

The next picture was taken by Frances and shows Elsie looking at a stationary fairy who is offering her a small bunch of harebells. The harebells were a bad idea to put against the paper fairy, as they tended to highlight the 2D nature of the drawing.

The final picture sparked the most controversy, not least because neither girl could agree on who took it. It supposedly shows a fairy sunbath being created. A gauzy film hangs between strands of grass as a fairy moves away to one side and another almost disappears into the background. The heads of the grass are blown over and blurred as they move in the wind but the fairies, as usual, are static.

At last Doyle was convinced – here were real fairies doing fairy things! He started comparing the images to all he knew about fairy folklore, drawing out more proof from this that they were real. The sunbath was a revelation, but that in itself could indicate authenticity – wouldn't a genuine hoaxer ensure all his images corresponded with existing knowledge on fairies? Doyle wrote a piece for *The Strand* about the phenomena, publishing the photographs alongside. The backlash was almost instant. The *Manchester City News* wrote:

> It seems to us at this point that we must either believe in the almost incredible mystery of the fairy, or in the almost incredible wonder of faked photographs. Which is it to be?

Poet Maurice Hewlett remarked: 'It is easier to believe in faked photographs than fairies.' Major Hall-Edwards, radium expert and medical man, was even more shocked by people believing in these images. He told the *Birmingham Post* that not only were the pictures faked but that it was dangerous to encourage children's beliefs in such absurd ideas. This, he declared, would result 'in later life in manifestations of nervous disorders and mental disturbances.' The magazine *Truth* made perhaps the fairest comment.

> For the true explanation of the fairy photographs what is wanted is not a knowledge of occult phenomena but a knowledge of children.

In 1921 a new expedition was mounted, this time with Gardner and a medium Geoffrey Hodson in tow. There were no photographs of fairies on this venture, perhaps not surprising since the girls were under almost constant watch. Hodson, however, believed he saw fairies everywhere around the beck and described them later to Doyle. The girls later admitted they found this quite amusing and pretended to see fairies just to attract another ecstatic cry of, 'I see them!' from an excitable Hodson.

After the failure of the 1921 expedition the interest in fairies swiftly evaporated. Doyle had other work to attend to with his lecture tours though he would still be mocked regularly for his belief in the Cottingley Fairies. Elsie and Frances grew up, married and started their own families. Hodson disappeared into his own world, populated by sprites and angels, and Gardner dabbled on and off with his book on the case until it was finally published in 1945. The case caused minor interest in certain circles, but never the public debate it had sparked in 1920/21.

In 1981 Frances revealed the truth – she and her cousin had faked the fairies, all except the last one – Frances insisted that was genuine. Frances, therefore, did not deny fairies; she just denied taking pictures of them.

The Cottingley case has to be one of the most curious of the post-war era. In a time when people were struggling to justify the idea of an eternal God and an afterlife, some were prepared to believe in an alternative of pixies and fairies. That they appeared at all indicates the strange mingling of old and new that was happening in Britain. Victorian attitudes were colliding against modern ideas, old barriers were being broken down, but some were afraid to let go of the ways they had always known and understood.

Borley and the Manx Weasel

Borley Rectory was built in 1862 by the Reverend Henry Ellis Bull. It has been often described as a dark and damp place, largely due to blocky extensions being added to accommodate Bull's huge family. In fact remaining pictures show it as a typical Victorian rectory. Set among well-grown trees, the red-bricked house had large bay windows at the back and an ironwork veranda, from which family members could look across the large lawn.

Bull lived there for thirty years without incident, though elderly residents later told investigators of the haunting that the family had always been plagued by ghostly footsteps about the house. This seems unlikely. Bull died in 1892 and there was no whisper of a ghost until eight years later in 1900, when Ethel Bull, one of Henry's seven daughters, claimed to see a ghostly nun cross the garden. It was around 9 p.m. on 28 July and Ethel was walking in the garden with two of her sisters after returning from a party. Ethel told her story for BBC radio thirty years later:

> *[My sisters] wondered why I didn't take any notice and they looked down at me and I said, 'Look there's a nun walking there!' I was terrified and so were they when they saw her – and it sent cold shivers down our backs and we simply flew into the house. Then we saw my eldest sister, who was staying with us.*
>
> *'She said 'Oh I'm not going to be frightened', so she came down, and when she saw the nun she made to go across the potato bed to meet the nun, and the nun turned and came as it were to meet her, she was seized with panic and simply flew up to the house.*
> [BBC interview broadcast 29 June 1947]

As fascinating as Ethel's story was it was not recorded until nearly thirty years after the event when Borley had become big news. Was Ethel elaborating a more minor incident, or inventing it altogether? One has to wonder if in the dark of the evening the sisters had mistaken an ordinary person taking a shortcut across their garden for something spectral.

Ethel was encouraged in her fantasies about forbidden love and spectral nuns (a popular choice for a spinster who herself had missed out on romance) by her elder brother Henry (commonly known as Harry to avoid confusion with his father). Harry Bull took over the Borley living when his father died and, aside from a short period between 1911 and 1920 when he married and moved to Borley Place, he lived at Borley Rectory until his death. Harry Bull was typical of his age, the Victorian parson with a fascination for ancient history and local legends. Under his watchful gaze it seems the ghosts of Borley emerged. Aside from the nun, there was now a spectral coach drawn by two bay horses, said to have been seen sweeping through the garden hedge and pulling up outside the rectory before vanishing. Needless to say, the coachman who drove this ghostly carriage was headless.

How much was invented for Harry's benefit by keen sisters and servants and how much he elaborated on himself we cannot say. Harry was not unduly fazed by the ghosts and until his death in 1928 they were just local rumour.

Borley Rectory was now over sixty years old, in poor repair and badly in need of modernisation. The roof leaked and rainwater had made several bedrooms unusable. There was no internal plumbing and water had to be drawn from a well in the courtyard outside. In short the house was in desperate need of extensive refurbishment, but that cost money which a struggling Church could not afford. Twelve clergymen turned down the living at Borley after seeing the ruin they would have to live in. Finally it was offered to Guy Eric Smith and his wife Mabel, who were out in India and did not have the opportunity to inspect the property before they arrived. Needless to say Mabel was appalled at the damp, crumbling house she was expected to live in.

Guy Smith complained, without success. After several failed attempts to get themselves moved there was only one option, to look for another curacy, but first he would have to offer a sound reason for leaving Borley.

Suspicious minds now begin to wonder about the motivation behind a letter Smith wrote to the *Daily Mirror*, asking if they could give him the address of the SPR as strange occurrences at the rectory needed investigation. At the time the *Mirror* was suffering a drop in sales and the then editor, Alexander Campbell, sensed a good story to boost circulation in the Smith letter. He dispatched Home News reporter V. C. Wall to nab the story and quickly phoned the NLPR to ask if they could send an investigator. Harry Price was also looking for a new case, something that would again raise the profile of the NLPR and bring in much needed funds. The laboratory was never self-sufficient and always haemorrhaging money, so Harry needed regular high-profile stories to get new wellwishers and benefactors to keep his pet project alive.

Three different sets of people now came together at Borley, all with different reasons for proving the reality of the ghosts. Immediately the odds of an unbiased investigation were limited.

Wall was the only one to remain inwardly sceptical. He saw and heard nothing during his time at the rectory, aside from a brief glimpse of what he believed was the nun. In fact it was the Smiths' maid who had pulled her apron over her head to scare him. Throughout the Borley hauntings there was a tangible element of servant-interference in the sightings of ghosts.

Wall might not have witnessed much but the story he conjured from the bare facts he was given certainly convinced the *Daily Mirror* audience that Borley was seriously haunted. The Bull sisters were still alive and acquainted with the Smiths and had told them all about the legends. A cynical person might assume this was where Guy Smith got his idea for reporting the haunting of Borley to give himself and his wife a good excuse to leave.

Daily Mirror readers gasped when they learned of the events at Borley. Cold rooms, unpleasant smells, knocks, raps, bells ringing, mysterious lights in unoccupied rooms, miserable groans and the strange sightings of witnesses (now only too eager to come forward) captured the imagination of a public looking for evidence of life after death. Wall knew how to weave a story and he added to the Smiths' experiences with the legend of the ghost nun. For the first time her story appeared in print, an elaboration of the Bull sisters' own imaginative invention of her history. Wall described how an old monastery had once been on the site of Borley Rectory and a young monk had carried on a secret relationship with a nun from a nearby convent. When the unfortunate couple were discovered, the monk was executed and the nun bricked up alive in the convent. The nun's spirit had somehow remained (though her lover had apparently found salvation) and now wandered the grounds of Borley looking for her beloved monk.

Wall was not concerned that there was absolutely no evidence of a monastery or convent in the area, as early as 1938 it was proved there was no historical record for such a place. Instead he was more interested in the story Mabel Smith told him of finding a brown paper package in a cupboard when she first arrived and opening it to discover a young woman's skull. How Mabel knew the skull was female, young or otherwise, and what became of it was never explained.

Harry arrived with his new assistant Lucy Kay just as the story broke. Like the others he had a vested interested in maintaining and propagating the story, so it was happily convenient that upon his arrival the haunting suddenly elevated itself to a new level. The shadowy figures, noises and smells now were replaced by thrown objects – including pebbles, stones, coins, keys and a vase. Spirit messages were tapped out on the frame of a mirror and the mild raps and knocks now became heavy bangs and clattering noises. Mabel Smith later remarked that she came to suspect Harry of producing this new and extensive repertoire of ghostly happenings.

However in 1929 the Smiths had their own agenda and the new phenomena was only adding to their case for moving. The evening of Harry's arrival they invited over the Bull sisters and a séance was conducted, during which messages were tapped out and a cake of soap was thrown so hard at a metal jug it left a dent. Mabel saw bluish sparks in the room which she had never witnessed before and never saw again.

Harry was his usual non-committal self about the spirit activities. 'Whatever was producing the taps could not spell…' he remarked, complaining that no useful message had come through. Lucy Kay on the other hand wrote a completely different account, stating it was the late rector who was trying to communicate, begging for help as he felt his will was being misinterpreted. Whether or not the rector was making contact, he would get no help from Harry.

By the time Harry had left and Wall had forwarded his last article on the haunting, the Smiths were coming to regret the publicity their case was getting. Hoards of curious onlookers appeared in the rectory gardens, coach trips were being run from Long Melford to see the 'haunted house' and day-trippers trampled the flowerbeds and invaded the family's privacy. Beer bottles were thrown at windows and in the end the police had to be called in. Fortunately for the Smiths the inconvenience proved fleeting as, within weeks, the diocese agreed to move them.

Harry paid a visit to the newly empty rectory accompanied by Lucy and Lord Charles Hope, a well-known psychic investigator. The poltergeist that only appeared for Harry now returned and threw pebbles at them, showered them with ten keys taken from various doors in the house and rang the house bells, the strings of which had been cut. Among the keys Harry discovered a Romish medallion which Guy Smith, when later asked, could not identify. This was taken as evidence of the nun, or perhaps her monk, though it was known Harry had a collection of such antiquarian objects.

Lord Charles Hope was unimpressed, he had a sneaking suspicion Harry was behind the phenomena, as did Charles Sutton from the *Daily Mail* who went with Harry on a subsequent visit. He wrote how Harry had made a point of looking up and showing Sutton a window allegedly smashed by the poltergeist on his last visit. '

Within two or three seconds of Price pointing out to me the glassless frame of this window, its neighbour suddenly smashed and another cascade of glass tumbled down. Just before this, I realised Price had taken a step behind me. I heard a swishing sound as if a missile had been thrown and then the window broke. I was a little suspicious how this had happened.
[Unbroadcast interview for the BBC 10 September 1956]

Sutton walked into the house with Lucy and Harry following. At each room Harry locked the door behind them, but not before there was a bang as if something had been thrown. On the first floor they stood in a bedroom and looked out over the lawn, Sutton dimly aware he was expected to witness the nun, but seeing only the typical shadows of a summer night. At one moment a faint moaning could be heard, which Sutton realised in disgust was Harry's attempt at ventriloquism. Finally they walked downstairs, again Sutton in the lead, when a half-brick bounced down the staircase beside him. Sutton spun and grabbed Harry by the arms; in his pockets he found several pebbles and stones.

'What are you going to do?' Harry asked helplessly.

''Phone in my story.' Sutton snapped and marched off to nearby Long Melford to do just that.

Harry was close to exposure and there was nothing he could do about it. He had been rumbled and the fraud would ruin both the NLPR and his credibility. As it happened Harry was once again given a lucky break. The night lawyer at the *Mail* believed Sutton's story (elaborated on by his editor) could expose the paper to legal action by Harry and so it was never published. Harry feigned illness from a heart attack to excuse himself from further investigations of Borley, at least in the immediate future. Lord Charles Hope arranged another visit for the 28 July, the date the nun walked the garden according to Ethel Bull. He invited Harry but the offer was turned down, Harry didn't want to connect himself with the case now Sutton was suspicious. Hope went to Borley without Harry and saw nothing all night.

Borley Rectory had developed a life of its own. The papers printed increasingly fantastical accounts of the legend of the nun and the poltergeist activity, adding the two reverend Bulls to the list of suspects for the haunting. The story had become fixed in the public imagination, along with all the make-believe that went with it.

Marianne Foyster was the next performer in the Borley story and yet again she had good reasons for wanting to prove the Borley ghosts were real. She moved into the rectory with her husband Reverend Lionel Foyster, a cousin of the Bulls, and her adopted daughter Adelaide in 1930. Marianne's mental state has been much debated and it is clear she could be both hysterical and something of an attention seeker. She was also carrying on an affair with the Foysters' lodger and later claimed to have caused 'ghostly' phenomena to cover up her liaison. The quiet rectory erupted with poltergeist phenomena, objects were thrown and the nun's persona seemed to have changed from a pitiful mourner to a violent, evil entity. Adelaide was locked in a room that had no key, and small fires were started. Marianne claimed to have been thrown from her bed and writing appeared on the walls. Most of this was gibberish, but there was a repeated refrain for help, prayers and mass, as if a spirit was asking to be laid to rest. In fact Lionel tried two exorcisms without success.

Harry risked a return to Borley in 1931 to examine the new phenomena at the invitation of the Bull sisters. He made an instant impression on Marianne who felt he was creepy. In return he said he was unconvinced that the hauntings were caused by anything supernatural. He disliked Marianne and believed her to be the cause. Some of the evidence of the 'ghost' does have more of the ring of domestic disharmony than anything else. For instance Marianne had allegedly received a black eye from the poltergeist, or was it rather from a jealous husband?

Other investigators came to the rectory and all retired with the opinion that Marianne was the source, possibly unconscious, for the phenomena. The house fell quiet again in 1935 when the Foysters moved away.

While Marianne was inventing ghosts, Harry was busy with other problems. The NLPR was in serious trouble and would shortly have to be dissolved. He was still at loggerheads with Sir Oliver Lodge, who he criticised for his work in psychic investigation, and had almost ruined his career by attempting to perform a black magic ceremony in Germany. Harry arranged for a ritual to be performed in the name of science, where a male goat would be turned into a handsome man. Perhaps not unexpectedly the spectacle included a scantily clad virgin and a magic unguent which Harry had the pleasure of smearing on her chest. The rational press were appalled that this ludicrous act could be called scientific and Harry came close to stretching the credulity of his followers and sponsors. Unsurprisingly the goat failed to turn into a man and

Harry announced with a smile that yet again science had proved the irrational nature of old superstitions.

Harry's attention was now drawn to a strange story from the Isle of Man. Miss Florence Milburn wrote to him describing a weasel-like creature that had attached itself to local farmer James Irving. The animal could apparently talk in several languages, liked to sing the Manx National Anthem, was telepathic, had acute hearing and liked to take the bus to go around the island and do its shopping. Even Harry found this initial story far-fetched and sent a spiritualist friend, Captain M. H. Macdonald to follow up the case.

Macdonald was smitten with the Irvings and their strange story. James Irving was a former piano salesman from Canada who had become embroiled in a failed English engineering business. He had gone to the Isle of Man in 1916 allegedly to escape the war in Europe, but there was also a hint he was escaping his debt problems. Unfortunately financial disaster haunted Irving and, now with a family to support, he was badly hit by the economic crisis caused by the Wall Street crash of 1929. Business was bad. The family isolated itself and survived on very little money in a remote farmhouse.

Gef burst into their lives at this dark moment. Fourteen-year-old Voirrey Irving, the only child still at home, was the first to meet him and there is a great deal to suggest she invented Gef as a form of amusement and companionship in her very lonely life. Voirrey explained to Macdonald that Gef was not a weasel but a mongoose, and an 'extra clever' one at that. He had been born in Delhi, India in 1852, but gave little explanation for his arrival on the Isle of Man. Gef had a den on top of a cupboard in the Irving house and spent his time killing the rats that infested the property and bringing the Irvings fresh rabbit. There was also a dark side to his antics, as at one time Gef had turned violent and threatened to kill the whole family.

Macdonald never asked himself how the remote, anti-social Irvings and the secretive Gef had come to the attention of Miss Florence Milburn, living in another part of the island. Could it just be coincidence that the secret came out at the same time the Irvings were in a financial hole and could do with the sort of money a good newspaper story might provide?

Spending two days and one night with the Irvings, Macdonald tried to pin down the illusive Gef. He heard him talking often, in a high-pitched, oddly feminine voice. Gef told him he was rather pleased with his singing skills, perhaps he should have also mentioned how pleased he was with Voirrey's ventriloquist skills. Macdonald never saw Gef, but he asked that the mongoose provide some hairs from his tail which he could take back to London and have analysed. Gef duly obliged. When the tail hairs were studied by a zoologist they were confirmed as being that of a dog.

Macdonald was taken by the Irvings and Gef but Harry was not. He disregarded the case and it took three years of constant letters from the Irvings to Harry before he gave the story his full attention. The Irvings were clearly keen to exhibit Gef and have him known to the world, and they told Harry of Gef's latest antics. He could now sing 'Home on the Range', use sign language, and speak a small amount of German, French, Italian and Afrikaans. He was also taking an interest in current affairs by reading the newspaper.

Harry dispatched Macdonald again in the spring of 1935. Still he did not see the little mongoose, let alone witness his skills at sign language. However he did hear Gef speak, repeatedly stating he did not want to see Harry Price, in fact he hated him and wanted assurances from the Irvings, particularly Voirrey, that Price would not come.

The mongoose's hatred was finally enough to spur Harry into action and he decided it was time to visit the Irvings himself. Gef then pulled a disappearing act. He vanished for five weeks and James Irving had to tell Harry that he wasn't sure if the little creature was dead or simply hiding. Harry and a fellow investigator spent several hours on the farm; they pottered about the grounds, exploring bushes and trees, lifting up stones and prodding around in the barns but Gef was nowhere. Finally they retired to the gloomy farmhouse the Irvings called home. Dark, wood-panelled and depressing in appearance Harry was glad to leave the house and make arrangements to go home.

Gef reappeared shortly after Harry was safely off the island. Amused with himself and far from contrite, he told the Irvings he had been wandering the island listening to gossip and eating cream buns. He conceded it had been unkind to vanish on Price and agreed to press his paws into some plasticine Harry had left to prove he existed. Harry had also given Voirrey a camera to take photographs of Gef and the results soon arrived on his desk. He was disappointed at the fuzzy images, one clearly being a small rock and the other some shape it was impossible to distinguish, but certainly not a living animal. Gef's paw-prints were even less inspiring when they arrived. Again they were examined by a zoologist who said one resembled no animal footprint known to him except perhaps a raccoon. The second paw-print was exceptionally large and could not possibly have been made by the same creature as the disparity between the size of the front and hind paws would be impossible. He was adamant that they were not made by a mongoose.

Harry was inclined to be generous towards Gef and made excuses that he was playing tricks on the investigators. Yet even Harry couldn't make up his mind. At one moment he was declaring Gef a 'picturesque swindle' the next he was publishing a book on him. *The Haunting of Cashen's Gap* appeared in 1936, advertised as one of the best books of the year despite being mainly a rehash of other people's work.

Poor James Irving had once again missed the boat. Forever incompetent in business he had been pipped to the post in marketing Gef by Harry. He wrote to Price, just as he was concluding his own book on Gef, saying he thought the mongoose would like to write a book about himself and that money from the sales would help the family out of their dire financial circumstance. Finally the Irvings had laid their cards on the table but it was too late and Harry turned him down. No one would believe the story he told the struggling farmer – besides his own book was soon to be out and he didn't need any competition.

Hope seemed to come in the form of an American film director who offered James Irving $50,000 for the full rights to Gef's story. Unfortunately Gef refused to turn up for the screen test and the deal fell through. The Irvings struggled on somehow. When James died in 1945, his wife was forced to sell the farmhouse at a loss and move in with Voirrey. In 1946 the new owner claimed he had shot Gef and displayed a black and white creature. A statement from Voirrey, however, assured the world it was not Gef. She maintained to the end she had not made him up.

Harry's attentions were once more back on Borley. He was negotiating with the Nazi government about shifting his failing lab to Germany, this is the dark side of Harry. To impress on his Nazi contacts his skills at tracking down hauntings he restored the ghost to Borley (now empty) and went with a team to perform vigils at the site. Yet again his fellow investigators suspected Harry of fraud. This was the last hurrah for Borley; in 1939 its new owner Captain W. H. Gregson claimed he was unpacking boxes in the house when an oil lamp overturned in the hall. Borley went up in flames. Some felt this was the final act of the ghost, who Harry said had issued a warning in 1936 that it would burn down the house. The woman who lived in Borley Lodge said she had seen the nun in an upper window as the house burned, but wanted to earn a guinea for the tale. The insurance company were more practical; they determined the fire was fraudulent, started deliberately by Gregson.

Harry tried one last time to revive the story in 1943 when he excavated the remains of the rectory cellar and found human bones. It was yet another failure as local opinion maintained that the remains were really pig bones planted by Harry. It was all over by that point. Borley had turned out to be the least haunted house in Britain, though from the perspective of publicity it could claim to be one of the most successful ghost stories. Harry's days as a ghost hunter were soon to be over too. In 1948 he sat down in a chair at his home and died from a heart attack. Dennis Wheatley, that other famous occult figure of the twenties and thirties remarked on his passing that he deserved a knighthood. High praise for a man who spent most of his career faking ghosts and making them real!

CHAPTER TEN

Mysteries of War

Somehow it seems almost natural that the First World War should be steeped in ghostly tales, legends and mysteries when even its origin was dreamt about by Archduke Franz Ferdinand's old tutor. On 28 June 1914 the Archduke was assassinated in Sarajevo, an action that is deemed one of the major catalysts for the First World War. Yet it was also on that very morning that some believe Bishop Joseph Lanyi had an opportunity to save the world from the greatest tragedy of the twentieth century.

Lanyi woke from a nightmare on the morning of the 28 June. His dream had been about the death of the Archduke and it haunted him so much that he immediately wrote down what he had seen. The full story is best presented in his own words.

I dreamed that I had gone to my desk early in the morning to look through the post that had come in. On top of all the other letters there lay one with a black border, a black seal and the arms of the Archduke. I immediately recognised the latter's writing, and saw at the head of the notepaper in blue colouring a picture like those on picture postcards which showed me a street and a narrow side-street. Their Highnesses sat in a car, opposite them sat a general, and an officer next to the chauffeur. On both sides of the street, there was a large crowd. Two young lads sprang forward and shot at their Highnesses. The text of the letter was as follows: 'Dear Dr. Lanyi, Your Excellency, I wish to inform you that my wife and I were the victims of a political assassination. We recommend ourselves to your prayers. Cordial greetings from your Archduke Franz, Sarajevo, June 28th, 3.15am.' Trembling and in tears I sprang out of bed and I looked at the clock which showed 3.15. I immediately hurried to my desk and wrote down what I had read and seen in my dream. In doing so, I even retained the form of certain letters just as the Archduke had written them. My servant entered my study at a quarter to six that morning and saw me sitting there pale and saying my rosary. He asked whether I was ill. I said: 'Call my mother and the guest at once. I will

say Mass immediately for their Highnesses, for I have had a terrible dream.'
My mother and the guest came at a quarter to seven. I told my mother the
dream in the presence of the guest and of my servant. Then I went into the
house chapel. The day passed in fear and apprehension. At half-past three, a
telegram brought us news of the murder.

Taken at face value the bishop's dream was surprisingly accurate. The
Archduke had been in his car during the time of the assassination, though it
was only one man who shot him and the officer sitting next to the chauffeur
in the dream (in life Lieutenant Colonel Franz von Harrach) was actually
stood on the running board. The Archduke's assassination had been planned
for some time, and the original setup had not involved shooting him, rather
several young men had been recruited to stand with the crowd along the route
the Archduke would drive down. Each man had a grenade and was supposed
to throw it into the car, and if one missed it was down to the next in line to
try and be more accurate. The grenade attack had failed for various reasons
including one assassin's sudden fear he might hurt an innocent and general
incompetence among the group. It was a chance coincidence and a wrong
turn (caused by Harrach) that resulted in Gravilo Princip, one of the failed
bombers, being able to take a pot shot at the Archduke.

When Lanyi's dream was made public there were as many who thought
it laughable as there were who wondered why he had not tried to warn
the Archduke. Some suggested the dream had not been written down as
immediately as Lanyi claimed and had in fact been influenced by actual events.
However, there seems plenty of evidence to suggest Lanyi was preparing for
the death of the Archduke before the assassination. So did Lanyi really have
the power of premonition as some contemporaries thought?

There are two key possibilities to explain the dream. First, as an important
and controversial political figure the Archduke was always at risk of an
attempt on his life. Also his trip to Bosnia was known to be dangerous, his
eldest son later stated this was the reason Countess Sophie insisted on going
with her husband as she was worried for his safety. There were those in Bosnia
who perceived the Archduke as a threat as he favoured the creation of a Slavic
kingdom as a barrier against Serbian annexation. With such turbulence it
would be natural for a friend of the Archduke to worry about his safety and
for this to transfer into a dream.

The other possibility is more sinister. Could Lanyi have had some inkling
of what was going to happen in Sarajevo? It is unlikely, but if some rumour
had found its way to him it might have slipped into his subconscious. The
Black Hand, a band of Serbian terrorists, was behind the attempt and there
is no link between Lanyi and them. Still, if he really did dream of the fate of
his friend, why did Lanyi not act? Whatever the reason, Lanyi is occasionally

branded as a fool for not acting on his premonition. In any case, the war began with a superstitious controversy and throughout its four years, it would be surrounded by legends and ghostly phenomenon in a way no other war, before or since, has quite been.

The Mystery of HMS *Natal*

The horrendous tragedy of the sinking of HMS *Natal* happened at Christmas 1915. The *Natal* was a Duke of Edinburgh class armoured cruiser built in 1904. She had acted as an escort for the Royal yacht in 1911/1912 when the newly crowned George V went on a trip to India. *Natal* had proved a safe haven for her crewmen in the first year of the war; though a member of the 2nd Cruiser Squadron she had yet to participate in a single battle. Her most exciting adventure had been the transporting of the body of US Ambassador Whitelaw Reed from Britain to New York in 1912. Her crew had affectionately nicknamed her 'Sea Hearse', a pun that would cruelly become reality on a dark night in December.

HMS *Natal* was lying at anchor in Cromarty Firth, Scotland on 30 December 1915. Many of the officers had been granted leave to visit with family over the Christmas period, but those that remained were invited to attend a film party hosted by Captain Eric Back. Among them were the wives and children of the officers and nurses from a nearby hospital ship. Aside from the remaining crew, seven women, three children and one male civilian were aboard that afternoon.

Meanwhile small boats were departing from *Natal* to take sailors ashore for a few days' leave. At 3.20 p.m. as the December evening was turning to darkness and the cold was piercing even the thick clothes of the sailors, there was a terrific explosion. From one of the small boats a rating turned. In horror he saw the stern of HMS *Natal* engulfed in a sheet of flames reaching up into the sky. Helpless the sailors watched as the rear decks and gun-casements disintegrated from the heat and flames and the whole ship heeled over to port. It seemed impossible that anyone could survive such an inferno.

One man was still alive however. Debonair Lieutenant Denis Quentin Fildes had been standing on the quarterdeck when the explosion happened. He was flung from his feet and landed dazed on the deck. As he looked down, half-stunned, trying to work out what had just occurred, he realised in horror that the pitch between the teak deck boards was bubbling and boiling out of the very seams as fire raged below him. Fildes was badly burned, and only had minutes to regain his senses before *Natal* heaved violently and another explosion ripped her open. Stumbling about seriously injured, Fildes did not even have time to try and evacuate survivors before he was cast into the sea as *Natal* sank beneath the water, taking with her at least 350 people

What had happened to *Natal*? Instant suspicions fell on an enemy submarine torpedoing the ship while she lay in the peaceful waters of Cromarty Firth. This was troubling as the Firth was considered well protected against submarine intruders. A diving team was sent down to investigate the wreck and came back with an even more sinister report – *Natal* had blown up from the inside.

The Admiralty were keen to play down the unpleasant insinuations this news caused, they were already hiding the fact that women and children had been aboard at the time of the incident and had perished. Public outrage did not need to be roused further as there were already rumours of German sabotage. A commission of inquiry was called and Lieutenant Fildes was well enough to give testimony. He remembered hearing a strange crackling noise in one of the ventilation shafts leading to the magazine not long before the explosion. He had sent down a rating to investigate, but nothing had been found. Could Fildes have heard the beginnings of a fire? The commission examined what little evidence there was and concluded the *Natal* had sunk due to an accident with her magazine. Her aft magazine contained cordite, a material notoriously unstable and easily ignited. It was postulated that a stray spark or the cordite deteriorating (very possible in a ship that had never entered battle to use the explosive) might have begun the tragic explosion.

Some of the cordite aboard *Natal* had been there for twenty months, and in usual situations cordite was regularly taken ashore and tested to see if it was deteriorating and thus becoming a potential explosive hazard. Though some checks had been done, these were far fewer than was prudent. There seemed every likelihood that cordite was the culprit for the explosions that sunk *Natal*, however the cause of the ignition was another question.

Cordite was known to be hazardous. A stray spark or heating of the explosive could cause it to combust, which was why workers in ships' magazines donned felt slippers and cordite storage areas were kept deliberately cool. The Admiralty could give no explanation as to how the cordite caught light and that left room for rumour.

There were other circumstances that made people uneasy. Was a secret German sabotage plot behind the tragedy? German agents had become very cunning about sneaking small incendiary devices into ships docking at New York, resulting in terrible fires. Two years after *Natal*'s sinking another tragedy occurred in very similar circumstances. HMS *Vanguard* suffered an internal explosion and was destroyed and again old cordite was suggested as the cause. However, a few hours before the explosion two civilian ordinance fitters from Chatham had been aboard *Vanguard*, one of them was a chargeman. When he was called before the commission investigating the case he was evasive and left his interviewers with the distinct impression he knew more than he was prepared to say. That same chargeman had been aboard HMS *Natal* performing the same duties as on the *Vanguard*, on 30 December

1915 and left just hours before her explosion. Was it just coincidence? Or was the strange crackling Fildes heard evidence of an incendiary device left by a German sympathiser?

The *Vanguard* inquiry became more controversial when a German Bible and several German letters were recovered from the wreckage. There was even talk that a man had been secretly executed for the sabotage, but the official reports stated an internal cordite explosion was responsible. There was one glitch the Admiralty could not clear up; there was no known cause for the explosion, just as in the case of *Natal*. Both the tragedies remain enduring mysteries of the First World War and are just a sample of the stories and myths that kept the British population awake and uneasy in their beds at night.

The U-Boat Captain

It was not just the British who suffered from unexplained catastrophes; the Germans had their fair share too. Many legends were forming around the new submarines the Germans were using, not least because they could easily become metal coffins to their crew. The idea of a U-boat curse emerged early on in the war.

The German *U-65* submarine was considered one of these 'cursed ships'. Built in 1916 *U-65* was surrounded by death, her first victim had been a dockworker at Bruges who was hit and killed by a girder being lowered into place in her hull. On her first trial run at sea her engine-room filled with toxic fumes and three men suffocated. Sailors are naturally superstitious, the sea has a tendency to make a man that way, with its unpredictable nature and the way it can suddenly eat a ship whole. Knowing the nature of their sailors the German Admiralty was very careful to keep the deaths quiet and for a short time it worked.

U-65 went to sea for more trials with a pack of sister ships. There were already rumours aboard that the submarine had an odd influence over her crew, which were not helped when *U-65* prepared for her first dive. A sailor was sent forward for a routine inspection of the external hatches before the manoeuvre. He never came back; without seeming explanation he appeared to step overboard and was washed away. The crew was decidedly jumpy as the captain closed the hatches and ordered the dive. *U-65* went down to 30ft, where the order was given to level off. Unfortunately the crew now found their vessel unresponsive. *U-65* continued to sink until her nose bumped the seabed and there she stuck, completely immovable. For twelve hours *U-65* remained underwater, her crew slowly suffocating and the engines leaking diesel fumes. Almost as inexplicably as she sank she suddenly started to rise and the crew had a lucky escape when she broke water. It later emerged a fracture in a ballast tank had caused the problem.

U-65 returned to Bruges for an overhaul and to be armed. During the process a torpedo warhead exploded, killing several including Second Lieutenant Richter. By now the submarine had a serious reputation for trouble among her crew. While being towed into dry-dock a sailor became hysterical when he saw the dead Lieutenant Richter standing on the ship's prow with his arms crossed. A short time later another sailor saw the same ghost and promptly deserted.

Despite her reputation *U-65* was sent to sea for her first mission in the Dover Straits. During her tour of duty the persistent Lieutenant Richter make regular appearances. The duty officer was found almost paralytic with fear on the bridge, having seen the dead officer walk onto the bridge and then fade from sight. Otherwise the tour was uneventful until *U-65* was returning to base under aerial attack and a lucky bomb killed her captain as he walked down the gangway.

The crew's morale had been so seriously dented by the ghost of Richter and the submarine had developed such a reputation for being cursed that the German Admiralty decided it needed to do some damage control and sent in a priest to exorcise the sub. The initial optimism this caused was quickly crushed on *U-65*'s next tour when a gunner went mad, the chief engineer broke his leg and a crewman committed suicide.

In July 1918 *U-65* made her last voyage. She was spotted apparently drifting by American submarine *L-2* which went on the attack, but before they could fire a shot there was a sudden explosion and *U-65* sank. For a time the sound of her small propellers and an underwater signalling device could be heard, before all went silent. *U-65* took herself and her crew of thirty-seven to a watery grave.

For many years it was believed *U-65* sank off the Irish coast, but in 2004 *U-65*'s wreck was found off Padstow in Cornwall. Examination of the wreck showed no signs of weapon damage and it still remains unclear why she sank, though experts favour shock damage from a depth charge. Her aft hatches were found open, suggesting the crew had made a desperate bid to escape. Yet the question remains, if *L-2* thought it had sunk *U-65* off the south coast of Ireland, a belief the German Naval records agreed with, then how is it *U-65* was actually sunk off Cornwall, and what mysterious sub vanished without a trace off Ireland?

The Angel of Mons

The Battle of Mons began on 23 August 1914 as the first rays of dawn broke across the French landscape. It was the first major action the British Expeditionary Force (BEF) had been involved in, even if it was considered a subsidiary action of the Battle of the Frontiers with the British attempting to hold a defensive line at strategic points along the French borders. Around 80,000 British troops formed up at Mons, facing a German force that was said to outnumber them three to one. There had been odd skirmishes before 23 August, but it was on that morning the battle truly began.

Surprisingly the initial German attack was repulsed with heavy enemy losses. The Royal Fusiliers were defending the Nimy and Ghlin bridges with machine guns and when the Germans marched forwards in close formation they were able to cut huge swathes of them down quickly. Realising their error the Germans switched to an open formation, making it harder for the defenders to hit many men in rapid succession. It was still a bloodbath, but the Germans were aiming for the weak point in the British line, a salient formed by the curve of the river. With overwhelming numbers and determination it became apparent by the afternoon of the 23 August that the British could not hold it. They had incurred heavy losses and now began a strategic retreat, hoping to fall back to a new defensive line, but with the French also retreating and the heavy German onslaught they were pushed further and further away from the borders, fighting all the way. For nearly a fortnight the British were forced into orderly retreat. Pursued all the time by the enemy, huge numbers of men were killed, whole units disappeared and the chaos inflicted on the BEF could only be offset by the heavy toll they inflicted on the attacking Germans as they withdrew.

It was in the middle of this retreat that the strangest story of the war emerged. Welsh journalist, Arthur Machen, wrote a short story for the *Evening News* about a remarkable apparition of angels appearing in the lines of the retreating British troops and defending them from an onslaught of German soldiers. Machen wrote the piece as if it was a report from the front, hardly expecting anyone would take it as genuine. To his astonishment people took his story for truth; new reports began to come in, giving details of the angels' appearance. The daughter of a clergyman at Clifton, Bristol published the statement of a British officer anonymously in the Parish Magazine. The officer had sworn to her that while his company was in retreat a German cavalry unit had come across them. Knowing their only hope was to make a last stand, the officer tried to reach higher ground where his troops might at least have a chance of fighting and surviving. Unfortunately the German cavalry reached the ground first. Expecting to be massacred the British turned to make a good show of it, only to be amazed to see a troop of angels standing between them and the Germans. The German horses were so startled and spooked by the angelic force they stampeded in all directions and the officer was able to get his men to safety.

A similar story came from army chaplain Revd C. M. Chavasse, brother to the Bishop of Rochester. He had heard an account from a Brigadier-General and two of his officers of angels appearing and protecting the troops. Another Lieutenant-Colonel reported his battalion had been escorted during the retreat for at least twenty minutes by a spectral body of cavalry. Intriguingly stories even came from the German side. One account claimed German soldiers had refused to charge a broken point in the British line because of a large number of troops present there, even though Allied records show no British troops were in the area. The account seems slightly implausible considering the consequences for refusing an order.

Machen was appalled at all these accounts. He came forward, admitting his story was just a work of fiction, and was promptly shot down in flames. Various critics came forward adamant they had met men who had witnessed the angels, a number of them were from the Church, so had a vested interest in believing God was on the side of the British. However it remains plain that people were prepared to believe in the angels, and so popular became the idea that there was even a waltz written around the story.

What did people see at Mons? Firstly, there appear to be no first-hand accounts of the angels, all the stories come from sources who heard it from someone else, and that 'someone' chose to remain anonymous. Like all good urban legends it is always a 'friend of a friend' who has witnessed the event in question. Another interesting factor is that all the witnesses were officers of significant rank – in class conscious Britain the word of an officer was to be taken as impeccably trustworthy. Some may have been deluded, but others genuinely believed in the angels and saw them as a sign that Britain was in the right and being guided by God. In the early days of the war this was very important to the general public and to the Church who were pushing the war along as an action against evil. Later opinions would turn against such naïve thinking, but for the time being the angels fed into this idea.

They also gave people hope; God was watching over loved ones and protecting them against hideous odds. It is not unreasonable to suppose that some, seeing how outnumbered the British were, believed the only way they managed to hold on and successfully retreat was with divine intervention. The other factor of the angels' story was that it came at a time when faith in the traditional church was still relatively high. Fundamentally, the story shows the power the Church held at the beginning of the war and how rapidly and dramatically this was lost as the slaughter dragged on. The power of the Angels of Mons legend comes from its association with the divine right of Britain to fight and conquer the Germans, as such God was seen as not just a supporter but an active participant in the conflict. In some regards the legend was a perfect publicity opportunity for the Church, which was actively encouraging people to fight and to volunteer for the military. Machen could never live down his story, and there are still those out there who would argue he was lying when he declared his angels a complete work of fiction.

The Ghost of Montrose

On the Bleak East Coast of Scotland near the mouth of the river South Esk the authorities of 1913 decided to build an airfield for their newest form of warfare – the aeroplane.

The aeroplane was useful both for reconnaissance and for attack, there were glitches that needed to be ironed out of course, not least how photographs could be taken from a moving plane or how it could be successfully armed, but war tends to spur on developments and soon the newly formed Royal Flying Corps was proving its worth.

Flying over the Western Front was almost as hazardous as walking across it. The Germans had planes too, not to mention ground-based guns that they were upgrading to be suitable for shooting planes out of the sky. Then there was the constant danger of a fault occurring in a plane, or bad weather knocking it out of the air. Pilots died, perhaps not in the huge numbers of the infantry, but still they perished and each man that didn't come back needed to be replaced. So Montrose was set up as one of the earliest flying schools.

Learning to fly, especially in those early planes, was only a little less dangerous than flying over battlefields. Accidents happened, novice pilots made errors or did not know how to deal with the unexpected and planes crashed. Such was the origin of the Montrose ghost story that started to circulate in 1916.

Rumour had it a young student pilot had been deemed ready for his first solo flight by his instructor, much to his consternation. The student felt very under-confident in his skills and tried to put off his first solo, to no avail. He was sent up in a Maurice Farman trainer, a cumbersome looking biplane, all struts and canvas. Initially the flight was good, but the student pilot's apprehensions appeared to get the better of him as he made a turn at 300ft; he was flying too slow for the manoeuvre and as the wing tipped the plane stalled and fell from the sky. The pilot was killed, his instructor was horrified, but that was the nature of learning to fly and he would not be the last casualty to die before he reached the front.

The instructor was said to have awoken that night in his room and seen the dead student in a blood stained leather jacket standing beside his bed looking at him sadly. When the instructor screamed the ghost vanished. The next day the Commanding Officer found an agitated flight instructor in his office requesting a transfer to another unit. Presuming he was still shaken by the death of his student he agreed and the instructor's room was given to another officer.

Three nights later the officer refused to stay in the room. He had awoken to seen a mournful, blood stained boy standing at his bedside. Another officer was given the room and he too lasted only a matter of days. Pilots are notoriously superstitious and the room was deemed cursed. It was locked and supposedly never used again.

The student pilot was not the first soul to return to Montrose after death, and the second aeronautical ghost has a name, Lieutenant Desmond Arthur. Arthur's story is sometimes muddled and combined with that of the student pilot and for obvious reasons as their legends were virtually identical.

On 27 May 1913, a year before the war broke out, Arthur was practising in a Be2 when his plane crashed. Arthur lived long enough to tell his rescuers that the plane had been sabotaged, but the official view was that Arthur had been performing unauthorised acrobatics and had lost control. The story was spread publically and soon rumours were rife that Arthur's ghost was haunting the airfield and confronting his colleagues insisting they clear his name. There was a fresh enquiry, which found that the Be2 had crashed due to faulty maintenance – the sabotage Arthur had claimed – and the ghost vanished. The dead student pilot on the other hand kept appearing for another half century and it was common practice to officially warn new arrivals of the ghost.

Another 1916 ghost story has the ring of plausibility. We also have a named witness to the ghost – Lieutenant David Simpkins who was stationed in 1916 at a base in Scampton, Lincoln. It was one of the better units to be with as they had been issued with Sopwith Camels, one of the best planes available to First World War pilots and of course helped to fly by the Lodge Spark Plug. Simpkins colleague was Lieutenant Peter Salter, a good-natured soul who was renowned about the base for his noisiness in the simplest of tasks; he crashed through doors, banged his way about the building and, in short, was always easy to hear coming.

On 7 December 1916 Salter glanced out of the base window and declared to Simpkins that he was going out for a practice flight on the firing range. Simpkins was settled by the stove and hardly paid attention as his friend left. Before many minutes had passed Salter crashed back through the door in his usual style, distracting Simpkins from a book, 'I'm not going on the range. I've got to take an aircraft to Tadcaster. I'll be back in time for tea. Cheerio!'

He blustered out of the room again, but no sooner had he gone he was hammering on the window and indicating to Simpkins that he had left his maps on the office table. Simpkins passed them to him and was mildly relieved when Salter finally departed as he could return to his quiet morning.

At 3.45 p.m., as the dark winter night was fast drawing in, Simpkins was surprised to find Salter at the office door. Not only was he back much sooner than could be possible but he had entered the room quietly, which was remarkable enough to be noted in Simpkins' mind. Simpkins smiled at his friend, 'Hello. That didn't take you long. Good trip?'

The oddly quiet Salter nodded and then said, 'cheerio' before abruptly leaving again. Simpkins had to wonder what had put out his friend so badly that he had lost his usual robust and clumsy manner. He doubted the trip had been as easy as Salter had made out. Still, he was bound to be back to normal in the morning.

Barely fifteen minutes after the quiet arrival of Salter, Lieutenant Garner-Smith came into Simpkins' office. 'I hope Peter gets back soon, we're going into Lincoln this evening.' Winter on the airfield was rather dull.

'He is back.' Replied Simpkins, thinking a trip to Lincoln would be just what Salter needed to stir him out of his odd mood, 'He may be in the locker-room or having tea.' Garner-Smith went off to find the elusive Salter.

Later that evening Simpkins decided to make a trip into Lincoln himself and made his way to the Albion hotel where several officers from Scampton were settled in the lounge. He had only just arrived when he heard snippets of a conversation and the words 'crash' and 'Tadcaster'. Simpkins wandered over to a table where several officers were sitting. 'Excuse me chaps, couldn't help overhearing. Has there been a crash?'

An officer looked up at him; 'Afraid so, the word came through just before we left the station. Peter Salter's dead – crashed on the way to Tadcaster. They found him in the wreckage. Apparently his wrist watch was smashed and it had stopped at twenty-five past three.'

Twenty minutes later an unusually quiet Salter had said, 'cheerio' to Simpkins for the last time.

Simpkins' ghost story is just one of the many strange incidents that emerged post-war. Over the pages of this book it has, hopefully, been shown how the Great War was a catalyst; it broke down old beliefs and supplanted them with new ones, many of which in themselves were not set to last. It destroyed the long held bonds between the Church and politics. It opened the doors for freedom of religion, however bizarre that religion might be, and it altered the minds of many. The religious turmoil left behind by the conflict is often overlooked, or ignored, mainly because the human cost overshadows, quite rightly, any philosophical debate. But it *was* significant because it heralded our modern age when people can believe in the powers of crystals, white magic and fairies without being persecuted.

The war had an astonishing impact on the power of the Church, one that it may even be argued is only just being overcome, but it also marred and twisted the memories of those who had served. It has cast up false facts, perpetuated in history books, such as that Church of England chaplains never went into frontline trenches, a complete fallacy that can still be found in high-quality history books. Religion, faith, belief, the Great War affected them all and without recognising that, we fail to recognise the fundamental way that war changed British society. No longer do men go into battle with the Church declaring it is their divine right to triumph, no longer is faith so blind to the sufferings of the enemy, no longer is God used (at least in the British military) as a tool for stirring up fighting spirit and finding recruits. The war changed us in many ways, not least in the way we think about religion and belief.

Appendix 1

And the Lord replied, 'I myself will go with you and give you success' Exodus, xxxiii, 14

'Let not you heart be troubled. You are trusting God, now trust in me. There are many homes up there where my Father lives, and I am going to prepare them for your coming. When everything is ready then I will come and get you, so that you can always be with me where I am.' John, xiv

'I told you all this so that you will have peace of heart and mind. Here on earth you will have many trials and sorrows; but take courage, I have overcome the world.' John, xvi, 33

Once you were under God's curse, doomed forever for your sins. You went along with the crowd and were just like all the others, full of sin, obeying Satan, the mighty prince of the power of the air, who is at work right now in the hearts of those who are against the Lord. All of us used to be just as they are, our lives expressing the evil within us, doing every wicked things that our passions or our evil thoughts might lead us into. We started out bad, being born with evil natures, and were under God's anger like everyone else. But God is so rich in mercy; he loved us so much that even though we were spiritually dead and doomed by our sins, he gave us back our lives again when he raised Christ from the dead...' Ephesians, ii

O Lord, please hear my prayer! Heed the prayers of those of us who delight to honour you. Nehemiah, I, 11

Who then can ever keep Christ's love from us? When we have trouble or calamity, when we are hunted down or destroyed, is it because he doesn't love us anymore? And if we are hungry, penniless or in danger or threatened with death, has God deserted us? No, for the Scriptures tell us that for his sake we must be ready to face death at every moment of the day – we are like sheep awaiting slaughter. Romans, viii, 35

'Come to me and I will give you rest – all of you who work so hard beneath a heavy yoke.' Matthew, xi, 28

Our help is from the Lord who made heaven and earth. Psalms, cxxiv, 8

For you are God, my only place of refuge. Why have you tossed me aside? Why must I mourn at the oppression of my enemies? Psalms, xliii, 2

The eternal God if your refuge, and underneath are the everlasting arms. He thrusts out your enemies before you; It is he who cries, 'Destroy them!' Deuteronomy xxxiii, 27

Rejoice, you nations , with his people, for he will avenge the blood of his servants; he will take vengeance on his enemies and make atonement for his land and people. Deuteronomy, xxxii, 43 [Raymond's ordering]

I, even I, am he who comforts you and gives you all this joy. So what right have you to fear mere mortal men, who wither like the grass and disappear? Isaiah, li, 12

You shall not leave in haste, running for your lives; for the Lord will go ahead of you, and he, the God of Israel, will protect you from behind. Isaiah, lii, 12

See, God has come to save me! I will trust and not be afraid, for the Lord is my strength and song; he is my salvation. Isaiah, xii, 2

Come, let's talk this over! Says the Lord; no matter how deep the stain of your sins, I can take it out and make you as clean as freshly fallen snow. Isaiah, I, 18

But they that wait upon the Lord shall renew their strength. They shall mount up with wings like eagles; they shall run and not be weary; they shall walk and not faint. Isaiah, xl, 31

And now – all glory to him who alone is God, who saves us though Jesus Christ our Lord; Jude, 24

For we were slaves, but in your love and mercy you did not abandon us to slavery; Ezra, ix, 9

'These are the ones coming out of the great tribulations,' he said; 'they washed their robes and made them white by the blood of the lamb.' Revelations, vii, 14

'He will wipe away all tears from their eyes, and there shall be no more death, or sorrow, or crying, or pain. All of that has gone for ever.' Revelations, xxi, 4

Bibliography

Baker, Phil, *The Devil is a Gentleman: The Life and Times of Dennis Wheatley,* Dedalus 2009

Barrett, Duncan (Ed), *The Reluctant Tommy: Ronald Skirth's Extraordinary Memoir of the First World War,* Macmillan 2010

Blunden, Edmund, *Undertones of War,* Collins 1965

Brandon, Ruth, *The Spiritualists: The Passion for the Occult in the Nineteenth and Twentieth Centuries,* Weidenfeld & Nicolson Ltd 1983

Browing, Vivienne, *The Uncommon Medium,* Skoob Books 1993

Brownlow, Kevin, *The Parade's Gone By...* Columbus Books 1968

Bunyan, John, *Pilgrim's Progress,* London 1678

Chapman, Paul, *Cameos of the Western Front: A Haven in Hell,* Leo Cooper 2000

Cooper, Joe, *The Case of the Cottingley Fairies,* Robert Hale Ltd 1990

Currie, Jack, *Echoes in the Air: A chronicle of aeronautical ghost stories,* Crecy Publishing Ltd 1998

Goffin, J. R. (Ed), *The Carlton Colville Chronicles of Canon Reginald Augustus Bignold,* Norwich Union Insurance Group 1982

Groom, W.H.A, *Poor Bloody Infantry: A Memoir of the First World War,* William Kimber & Co. Ltd 1976

Dixon, John, *Magnificent but not War: The Second Battle of Ypres 1915* Leo Cooper 2003

Donald, Graeme, *Mussolini's Barber and other stories of the unknown players who made history happen,* Osprey 2010

Edmonds, Charles, *A Subaltern's War,* Peter Davies Ltd 1929

Graves, Robert *Goodbye to all that,* Cassell 1929

Higham, Charles, *The Adventures of Conan Doyle: The Life of the Creator of Sherlock Holmes,* Hamish Hamilton 1976

Hutchinson, Roger, *Aleister Crowley: The Beast Demystified,* Mainstream Publishing 2006

Jolly, Martyn, *Faces of the Living Dead: The Belief in Spirit Photography*, The British Library 2006

Jolly, W. P. *Sir Oliver Lodge,* Constable 1974

Kobel, Peter, *Silent Movies: The Birth of Film and the Triumph of Movie Culture,* Little, Brown and Company 2007

Ed. Lellenberg, Jon, Stashower, Daniel & Foley, Charles, *A Life in Letters: Arthur Conan Doyle*, Harper Perennial 2008

Lodge, Sir Oliver J. *Raymond or Life and Death,* Methuen 1916

McCormick, Donald, *The Mystery of Lord Kitchener's Death,* W & J Mackay & Co. 1959

Morris, Richard, *Harry Price: The Psychic Detective,* Sutton 2006

Muller, Jurgen, *Movies of the 20s,* Taschen 2008

Ed. Nason, Anne, *For Love and Courage: The letters of Lieutenant Colonel E. W. Hermon; from the Western Front 1914-1917,* Preface 2008

Oppenheim, Janet, *The Other World: Spiritualism and Psychical Research in England 1850 – 1914*, Cambridge University Press 1985

Palmer, Svetlana & Wallis, Sarah, *A War in Words*, Simon and Schuster 2003

Prior, Robin & Wilson, Trevor, *The First World War,* Cassell 1999

Remarque, Erich Maria, *All Quiet on the Western Front,* Germany 1929

Unknown Soldier, *A Month at the Front: The Diary of an Unknown Soldier*, Bodleian Library 2006

Wilkinson, Alan, *The Church of England and the First World War*, SCM Press Ltd 1978